PENGUIN B

Inventing New

Claudia Bell was born in the Wa... war baby-boom generation. She grew up totally immersed in the rural 'great way of life' myths of the 1950s, eventually writing her PhD thesis on this topic.

For some years Claudia worked as a freelance social researcher, lecturer and writer, then as an organiser and lecturer in adult education. She is now a lecturer in sociology at the University of Auckland. Claudia has three adult children, all currently living overseas.

Inventing New Zealand

Everyday Myths of Pakeha Identity

Claudia Bell

PENGUIN BOOKS

PENGUIN

Penguin Books (NZ) Ltd, 182-190 Wairau Road, Auckland 10,
New Zealand
Penguin Books Ltd, 27 Wrights Lane, London W8 5TZ, England
Penguin USA, 375 Hudson Street, New York, NY 10014, United States
Penguin Books Australia Ltd, 487 Maroondah Highway, Ringwood,
Australia 3134
Penguin Books Canada Ltd, 10 Alcorn Avenue, Toronto, Ontario,
Canada M4V 3B2

Penguin Books Ltd, Registered Offices: Harmondsworth, Middlesex,
England

First published by Penguin Books (NZ) Ltd, 1996

1 3 5 7 9 10 8 6 4 2

Copyright © Claudia Bell, 1996

The right of Claudia Bell to be identified as the author of this work in terms
of section 96 of the New Zealand Copyright Act 1994 is hereby asserted.

All rights reserved. Without limiting the rights under copyright reserved
above, no part of this publication may be reproduced, stored in or introduced into a retrieval system, or transmitted, in any form or by any means
(electronic, mechanical, photocopying, recording or otherwise), without
the prior written permission of both the copyright owner and the above
publisher of this book.

Editorial services by Michael Gifkins and Associates
Designed by Pages Literary Pursuits
Printed by Australian Print Group

Acknowledgements

Special thanks to John Lyall, who fairly good-naturedly went with me to almost every site discussed in this book, including Big Fresh Supermarket (often!), the Expo Pavilion (twice!), numerous museums, outdoor tourist attractions and bush campsites, and to nearly every town in New Zealand. His comments and observations have always been valued. John's extensive photographic documentation of New Zealand in the 1990s has been a further important contribution to my work on this project.

Grateful thanks also to Nigel Clark, who accompanied me to various museums, to Katikati, to the America's Cup Welcome Home parade, and to theme-parks, shopping malls and live museums in Queensland. He has also lent me lots of books and articles, and cheerfully discussed this material with me over several years.

My sociology students in 1995 are also warmly acknowledged, for their lively engagement with me in debate of topics discussed in this text.

Contents

Acknowledgements	*v*
Preface	*1*
1. *Where am I?* Invention and myth-making	*3*
2. *Clean, green and beautiful* — the nature myth	*28*
3. *'My grandmother had one of those!'* At the museum	*55*
4. *One million dollars worth of hokey-pokey ice-cream* Expo 88	*83*
5. *Have you seen the giant roadside shearer at Te Kuiti?*	*103*
6. *All we need to know, because TV tells us so*	*128*
7. *Nostalgia and kiwiana*	*163*
8. *But we are all New Zealanders!*	*183*
Endnotes	*197*
Bibliography	*202*
Index	*204*

Preface

This is a book about a national preoccupation. New Zealand is a country that constantly tells itself who it is. Every single day there are messages and statements to affirm that this is a great country. Well done!

The 1980s and 1990s have, however, been an often difficult time of self-examination for both Pakeha and Maori New Zealanders. The Maori cultural renaissance has led Pakeha to respond by taking a closer look at who we are. Some of our chest-thumping is starting to sound a bit hollow.

Are all kiwi kids Weetbix kids? Why do we call ourselves kiwis, anyway? Who claims identity for us, and why?

This book investigates the agencies and processes we rely on to know just who we are. It asks on our behalf the questions we may not have ever had to answer for ourselves.

1
Where am I?
Invention and myth-making

When I was a child sometimes we kids wrote our full addresses as 'New Zealand, Southern Hemisphere, Earth, Solar System, Milky Way, Universe'. In those days, not confused by politics and international communications networks, we had a very clear idea of where we were placed in the global scheme of things.

New Zealand was easy to find on any map: just look for a pair of small dots at the bottom of the world. Occasionally we'd come across a map of the world that had left New Zealand off. This made us a bit indignant; but it was also amusing. Imagine: there were people out there in the rest of the world who didn't even know where we were! We laughed at their pathetic ignorance.

Eventually we learned that New Zealand as a geographic reality lies from latitude 34° S to 47° S and from longitude 166° E to 179° E in the southern hemisphere. The group of islands is surrounded by three oceans: the south Pacific Ocean to the north and east, the Tasman Sea to the west, and the great Southern Ocean to the south of Stewart Island.

Early invention

Abel Tasman came across this land mass in 1642. He named it Staten Landt because it was thought to be linked to South America, which had been named Staten Landt by another explorer. When this geographic guesswork was proved wrong, this country was renamed in Latin, Zeelandia Nova, from the Dutch, Nieeuw Zeeland. Although the land Aotearoa was already occupied by the Maori population who had arrived here centuries earlier, Tasman is documented as having first 'discovered' it. He literally put it on the European map. In naming it, he began the long process of invention.

Captain Cook arrived here in 1769. Meticulously, he charted the coastline, 'discovered' the flora, fauna and native people, and gave European names to numerous geographic features. In the 1800s 'New Zealand' was further 'invented' by British settler agencies. To get people to come and live here, to settle it as a new outpost for the British Empire, potential settlers had to be wooed and convinced that the arduous journey would indeed take them to a paradise.

A propaganda campaign was mounted, with each provincial settler association vying with the rest to offer an attractive destination and a glorious future to those who came to their part of the country. For instance, one prospectus claimed that:

> Taranaki offers the greatest advantage to the petty capitalist or small farmer immigrant. Land inferior in quality to none in the colony, and superior to most is obtainable at a reasonable rate and within reasonable distance of a town. . . . True, most of it is covered with forest, but this is rather an advantage than a drawback to the industrious small farmer settling down on his 50 acre section with the determination to make a home in the bush.[1]

The process of invention was under way. Numerous promotional publications depicted idyllic visions of New Zealand.[2] Arcadian versions of the country were used to boost immigration and capital investment, in order that it would thrive and grow. The Arcadia of New Zealand was not a passive one, where one simply plucked from nature's abundance and enjoyed her beneficent fruits. This was an Arcadia in which nature provided the fertile earth and the good climate; but one in which settlers could have an active role, bettering themselves beyond their dreams through physical application. Historian Miles Fairburn explains that in the New Zealand version of Arcadia was 'the Victorian imperative of material progress, the belief that material betterment stimulates moral growth which in its turn produces more material growth and so on in an everlasting upward spiral'.[3]

The colony

By the middle of the nineteenth century, New Zealand had become a colony. Its inventors had more than their own adventurous interests at heart. This new outpost of the British Empire would provide a home for surplus British population, and in time should produce goods useful to British markets, from British money invested here.

The early settlers went about the business of building something new, in a new environment: the conquest of land, and its appropriation from the Maori population, was justified by the need for 'development'.

While Maori struggled against the economic and cultural impact of the new settlers, the state adopted race relations policies which were really administrative policies for the appropriation of Maori resources.

Pakehas' growing relationship with the land quickly became a component of national identity constructs. Settlers did not have the kinship networks and family relationships, or long-term family associations with place, that they had in Britain, or that the Maori had here. Identification with the environment gradually became defined not by one's connections or family location in Britain, but by owning land here. This early influence of the environment on 'national character' has been claimed by historians as having an enduring affect on national imagery for New Zealand.[4]

In the earliest days of colonisation it was difficult for settlers to quickly develop some sense of collective identity. The population was dispersed around the coast and up rivers, with very limited communications systems. Indeed, it was not until 1868 that New Zealand had a single standard time for the whole country. There was not enough capital generated in New Zealand to develop a national infrastructure. Money was borrowed from Britain and this investment capital meant New Zealand was still dependent. Success in the export of agricultural products back to Britain, especially with the first shipment of frozen meat in 1862, further consolidated links. New Zealand became known as Britain's farm.

As the Pakeha population grew and new settlements sprouted up, the state engendered loyalty in its citizens by encouraging a sense of something in common, a national identity. 'A nation' needed an integrated population. Gradually the state became a large employer of the colonial population, further cementing its position as a primary influence on national identity. As New Zealanders broke free of old bonds and constructed new ones, aspirations for a new nation meant a new sense of identity and 'difference'. With growing affluence, social and labour reforms took place, which underlined the difference between 'there' and 'here'. In the 1860s and 1870s workers here had a far higher income and standard of living than in Australia, Britain or the United States.[5] Women's Suffrage in 1893 meant New Zealand could proudly claim to be the first country is the world to allow women to vote. These achievements were great advertisements for New Zealand, and objective references for self-congratulation.

British heritage

The new residents had a clear national identity where they had come from. They arrived here, still referring to their place of origin as 'home'. They had brought with them many components of British identity: their allegiance to the British crown, language, customs, social rituals, food traditions, and so on. The new colony they were creating drew heavily from the ideas of culture that the British settlers had brought with them. Indeed, many found it impossible to settle permanently in barbaric New Zealand, so made the long journey back across the world.

For those who stayed, as they became more attached to the new place (first through survival; then economically; and, gradually, emotionally and spiritually) they needed to fill the gaps in their sense of identity, as this place became their home. For the succeeding generations 'home' was New Zealand, because they had no other; but many still referred to Britain as 'home' because of values and attitudes passed on by parents.

Some commentators have suggested that affiliation to 'home' (Britain) persisted to the point of slowing New Zealand's claims for distinctive identity. One writer claims that 'lingering British allegiance stunted the growth of full-fledged New Zealand nationalism; indigenous national symbols have been slow to take over from symbols of the British Empire'.[6]

The hunt at the end of the nineteenth century for a suitable official symbol for New Zealand illustrates this observer's comment. Museologist Richard Wolfe explains that when European settlers needed appropriate symbols to express their new identity, they looked to symbols of 'home' that might be adapted to the new environment. Britain's three great symbols at that time were John Bull, the lion, and Britannia.

Britannia had been around since Roman times; a classical figure with trident and shield. A version of Britannia was developed for New Zealand, and Zealandia was born. She made it onto a postage stamp in 1901–9, was popular on trademarks, and was familiar for years on the copper penny. In 1911, when New Zealand evolved from colony to dominion, a coat of arms was required. Zealandia found a place here, holding the flag, opposite a Maori chief. The shield between them has images of the Southern Cross, sailing ships and references to the agriculture and mining industries. In 1956 this design was modified, but a contemporary version of Zealandia is still included.[7] While other symbols have become far more popular to represent New Zealand, Britannia's daughter Zealandia seems to have found a permanent home. And the Union Jack still waves, as it always has, from the corner of the New Zealand flag.

For generations the school curriculum disseminated imperialist ideology. Indeed, strong memories I have of primary school in the 1950s include dusty classrooms with the famous scroll wall map on which all countries of the empire were coloured red. The teacher would indicate the 'red' countries with a wooden pointer, and we'd have to recite their names. We didn't need to know the names of any others, apparently. And in history lessons we learned a list of British kings and queens, who all had the same names. In fact, 'history' seemed to *mean* kings and queens, as monarchy was the assumed 'natural' historic state.

I don't remember ever having a school lesson on Te Rauparaha, Prophet Rua, Hone Heke, or on Kate Sheppard. These gaps had to be filled many years later, long after school days were over. Meanwhile, we children (mostly Pakeha, with a few Maori and one or two Dutch) sat up straight at those wooden school desks and simply believed everything we were told.

New heritages

While New Zealand is a nation of immigrants, across the span of history immigration has further complicated clear definitions of national identity. Much of New Zealand's history has included resistance to newcomers, for instance the resistance to the Chinese miners and merchants in the 1860s and more recently the 1990s 'Asian Invasion', which is seen as a problem by residents of some city suburbs. An influx of people from various Pacific Islands expanded the labour force during the 1950s manufacturing boom. Some Pacific Islands are represented by greater population numbers here than in their islands of origin; for instance Niue and the Cook Islands. For those immigrants not automatically entitled to residency here, a formal system of gaining citizenship officially resolves the possibility of exclusion. Through this system they too can be absorbed into the dominant structure. If one is not assimilated then one remains outside the dominant culture, and is not part of its identity.

Efforts in the 1980s to claim a 'Pacific Identity' for New Zealand, outlined in Labour's document in 1990, 'Towards a Pacific Island Community', received little enthusiasm. The current trade-motivated cry is that we are 'part of Asia'. For most of the population, this appears very hard to swallow. However, it does illustrate the point that the process of selecting identification is politically and economically driven, and involves a programme of persuasion.

What is a nation?

There is no natural evolutionary theory of 'nation' that is elevated in each successive version.[8] The building of a nation is nothing to do with nature at all, but with the politics that enables one culture to obliterate or assimilate another, through such processes as colonisation, genocide and immigration policies. We can add to this list the forms of 'social engineering' that take place within a nation, the political processes that bring about divisions in society between ethnic groups, classes and gender, and economic divisions: the divisions that split groups.

The connection between 'nature' and nationality — that we are *naturally* New Zealanders through being born here — is facilitated in the socialisation mechanisms that 'guide' us as citizens. Through such constantly present devices as language, education and media, the population absorbs values and assumptions of identity which are unconsciously taken on board. These transmissions are absorbed without clear recognition or resistance. National identity values are therefore read as 'natural'. This poses an implicit connection between nation and nature, enabling policy-makers to present ideas as 'common sense', an intrinsic part of the natural features of the nation. For instance, before women had the right to vote, it was believed to be 'only natural' that they be excluded, as they were considered ill-equipped to have a say in public affairs. We can see that 'national identity' is plainly a politically motivated invention, fostering a fake unity expressed in terms like, 'in the nation's interests'.

The invention of the modern nation obliterates or renders powerless pre-existing cultures, such as Maori. Different groups are supposed to make up the nation; indeed, 'nation' is a way of ascribing group membership to a diverse population. If some groups are peripheral or marginal, this is not acknowledged in the term 'nation'.

A dilemma in the idea of nation is the assumption that those comprising 'nation' are a united entity, with similar beliefs and views, and with heritage, language, history and culture in common. In fact all that might be held in common is territory, and government.

If we understand that national identity is fostered for political ends, then inevitably different groups are going to jostle for dominance. As one group supersedes another, the version of nation is slightly altered. The version offered as a public representation depends on whose interests this presentation serves. In this way, those currently with the most power can recreate 'nation' in their own interests, and have the rest believe in it as 'commonsense' reality.

Prominent theorist of 'nation', Benedict Anderson, presents an analysis of nations as 'imagined communities'. By this he means that while most fellow-nationals will never meet or know about one another, 'yet in the minds of each lives the image of their communion'. The consciousness of place as nation requires this level of imagination: a sense of people occupying space, who all affiliate to the same state. The definition of nation requires the construction and representation of this image. Official versions of nation are determined by the state.[9]

An illustration of this is the founding myth of New Zealand. The Treaty of Waitangi was signed in 1840 between the Maori and the imperial representatives of the colonists. This act was subsequently mythologised as the founding of a harmonious, bicultural New Zealand, despite obvious contrary evidence. Internationally, this has given New Zealand the image of a place of good race relations, a peaceful country. The bloody land wars between Maori and European that took place after the Treaty signing are seldom mentioned in recitations of history. While the past comprises injustice, war and bloodshed, the history that a population chooses to remember is that which supports the peaceful myth that prevails for Pakeha New Zealanders.

This is an example of New Zealand as 'imagined', and of history as a reconstruction to support beliefs and values in the present. National identity is comprised only of what is in the best interests of certain social groups, and consists of mainly positive messages. It does not take into account that people are different, from different backgrounds, and with different experiences.

Popular imagery

In 1993, identity researcher Matthew Hirschberg tested a group of students' received notions of identity through a word association test. The subjects stated their ideas about what they thought constitutes national identity in New Zealand. They also showed that they were aware there was a difference between the idealised images of New Zealand they felt dominated national identity imagery, and their daily experience of living in a New Zealand city.

For instance, one said:

> When I think of the words 'New Zealand' I still think of the stereotypical real tourist image, and wide open spaces and happy people. The things that happen to me everyday, the places I go, I don't tend to think [of those] as being New Zealand.

Another wrote:

> I tend to think of the whole country except Auckland as New Zealand. Auckland is too cosmopolitan to really fit in.

In this remarkable revelation, we see that received imagery of what 'New Zealand' is, is accepted as more meaningful and true than what is lived on a daily basis.[10]

A similar test on some of my own students showed the same sort of findings. One wrote:

> I am from the country and I understand that is the 'real New Zealand'. Most of the population lives in cities, but cities and suburbs are not promoted as true New Zealand.

The notes of another were familiar:

> We keep seeing New Zealand as the perfect place. When I was overseas I found myself saying the things I had heard, about it being very green, and clean, and friendly. I don't really believe those things but they are a handy way of telling people what they want to hear, and what we think we should say.

A third scribbled:

> There seem to be two New Zealands: the one we show off about, and the one that we actually live in. The perfect New Zealand is beautiful, has no social problems, and everyone plays sport and goes to the beach. We know it is not like that, but it makes us feel good, so we go along with it.[11]

While acknowledging the extreme limitations of the samples, what these two little tests both show is that the subjects were aware that national identity is a construction of what *should* be. The students recognised mythologies when they saw them, but liked to believe in them, because they are so attractive. The images are so pervasive that it takes some consideration *not* to believe in them.

In an earlier study of US students, Hirschberg reported very contrasting findings. In that study, 66% responded to the word 'USA' with 'freedom'; 66% mentioned 'democracy'; over 50% the United States flag (described by the writer as 'an official political icon of substantial condensational potency'); 33% mentioned the president; and 35% used the word 'powerful'. From this study he concluded that 'while New Zealand national self-image focuses on landscape and lifestyle, the American national self-image is strongly rooted in politics and ideology. New Zealanders' conceptions of their country concentrate on the experientially based but idealised and emotionally laden notion of a safe, secure home, nestled in an unspoiled natural paradise. Americans' notions of their nation focus on ideologically based, idealised and emotionally charged conceptions of freedom and democracy . . . like New Zealanders, Americans are proud of their nation, but the central reasons are different.' His study clearly shows that the younger generation of New Zealanders has grown up with one set of messages, the Americans with another. Through these comparisons we can see that a large part of the understanding of our own national identity is something we are taught; that it is ideologically driven; and that it stays with us.

The teaching of 'civics' in American schools obviously makes a profound impact on that population's concept of their own country.[12] And in a culture that generates most of the international media events for the English-speaking world and is the cultural aggressor for most of that world, American self-identity is virtually never challenged. In contrast, in New Zealand we have to construct on a daily basis a self-identity that is quite fragile and fights to compete against a daily bombardment from America, British and Australian news and popular culture. This is the context in which New Zealand identity has to be forged.

In the 1950s and 1960s terms like 'clean and green' were never heard. The favoured ideological myth was that of egalitarianism. We understood that this was an inherent part of our culture. Its basis had been in colonial times, when, compared with conditions at 'home', a working person here could do as well as his or her betters in Britain. The early achievement of a high standard of living in this country served to support this myth.

Over many generations this popular myth effectively hid inequities. An illusion of equality, and an official belief system that supported it (democracy), persuaded the population that there was one common goal: support for one's nation.

The egalitarian myth has been tackled by various writers, including David Bedggood[13] and Bob Considine. Considine, for instance, insists that this is 'the most fundamental and persistent historical myth about our society, deeply embedded in the Pakeha psyche'.[14] The 'ordinary bloke' so often referred to by late Prime Minister, Rob Muldoon, was symbolic of the mythical equality it suits politicians to claim (whilst excluding themselves). The concept 'ordinary bloke' paternalistically omits women; and excludes anyone 'extraordinary', such as politicians and business people. But now that myth has faded.

These days New Zealanders openly recognise and admit that there are advantaged groups in society. Any idea of egalitarianism (apart from in the right of every individual to vote) has long been eroded. The interests of the least advantaged are generally labelled 'social problems' (for instance the disproportionate numbers of Maori and Pacific Islanders represented by unemployment figures and in the prison statistics; and the figures for both groups in lower levels of health and education).

The strongest place in public representations of New Zealand way of life is claimed by the events, celebrations, lifestyle and material consumption of the more advantaged group. Just as the economic and political interests of the most powerful in the Pakeha group are manipulated into prominence and maintained there, so does this same group have most access to constructing national imagery. This is available because of the social status and political power of Pakeha: symbols of Pakeha culture are the dominant icons for national identity. The loudest voice proclaiming identity is the one that persuades the nation. Television has the loudest voice of all.

The America's Cup

A brilliant illustration of this was the America's Cup welcome-home parade up Queen Street, Auckland, in May, 1995, sponsored by TV One.

The America's Cup was shown on every news broadcast, so this event looked like a very important part of national culture. This occurred through negotiation by several agencies: the sponsors, the event organisers, the decision-makers in the media (from the same social group as the yachtsmen), politicians (who made what mileage they could out of the event by being 'good sports' and stating 'how good this is for the country'), and the audience, who gradually 'learned' to be interested.

In the satellite age, television sport is an arena in which individual national identities retain important commercial and ideological functions. Winning the cup was claimed by television as being a win for the nation as a whole: 'we' salute 'our' heroes; 'we' won the cup! — an especially delicious win, given the far greater resource power of the opposition.

The cup challenge was a key event in 1995 to illustrate the expression of national identity. It might seem a bit unlikely to match an expensive sport like yachting to the tradition of achievement of ordinary New Zealanders. The nature of the race — offshore, far away, out of sight — is such that without television it was not and could not be a spectator sport. Ordinary New Zealanders could not go along for a few hours and watch and cheer. An event thousands of kilometres away raced by an exclusive group of white male professionals with access to a vast amount of money was seen as a major milestone in national history. Converted from offshore race to media spectacle, it allowed 'everyone' in the nation to participate.

The America's Cup win conveniently distracted us from more contentious events occurring at the same time, that 'we' would not want to be taken as 'representative' of 'us'. Race relations issues were also in the news that week, with Maori activist Mike Smith taking a chainsaw to the iconic pine tree on One Tree Hill, the Motua Gardens demonstration in Wanganui, and two Members of Parliament playing racist games on a day-time radio talk show. Politicians and media people do not want these latter occurrences to be seen as 'representative' events. The 'Welcome Home' America's Cup parades could be described as therapeutic symbolic displays of nationalism. Appropriately fostered, patriotic feelings cut across class groups, and affect women and men, adults and children, alike. With all eyes on the event, a nation could feel united.

The welcome-home parades held in major cities did a lot of things at once. They served the purposes of the sponsors, while publicly celebrating continuity with a claimed tradition of sports heroism in the international arena.

Parades across the nation gave citizens beyond Auckland a fair share in the celebration: this was not just an Auckland event (as the return home of the Whitbread yachts had been, the year previously). New Zealanders from all over the country could stake a claim in this success, and feel united in one great celebration. The parades overtly celebrated kiwi men, and kiwi manhood. While yachting is not a new arena for New Zealand sport, this race pushed images of traditional kiwi masculinity into a new high-tech computer age of male power. And it demonstrated a chirpy national impudence: 'we' dared to take on the might of America! The America's Cup possibly added another emblem to the national icon collection: red socks.

Those red socks: the orchestrated 'spontaneity' is a further demonstration of how identity and its symbols are selected for us. Through such a simple, accessible symbol (anyone might own a pair of red socks!) this campaign openly fostered unity and celebration. The agenda appeared to be to give 'everyone' the opportunity to participate: to over-ride any acknowledgement that we are celebrating the affluent class. Through wearing red socks, one showed one was celebrating values in common. National pride could be actively and visibly expressed.

What a day! Queen Street was festooned with ticker-tape; and at the same time, myths of a stable and united nation were acted out for the world, and for us. Favourite mythologies of national character were reinforced: of strength, of gutsy determination, of the heroic man against the elements — while everyone cheered! It could not have happened without television. The event demonstrates the sheer power of television, through which the entire population could be encouraged to link as one. Television could spread the ceremony beyond those physically present. We could not be present at the race; but we were all welcome — urged! — to attend.

A telling moment in the television evening news was footage of schoolgirls pouring out of the gates of Auckland Girls' Grammar School. The girls were heading up the road to the welcome-home parade. The male voice-over asked, 'So why is a multicultural girls' school closing down to celebrate a victory by sixteen white male yachties?' The school principal replied, 'Ours is a very diverse school, with people who are New Zealanders, and people who have chosen to make New Zealand their home. We thought it was an opportunity to bring the country together, to celebrate a victory, that of the little people, doing it for the big people.' She had received the ideological messages loud and clear, and passed them on to her girls.

Many of all those thousands of people attending the parade held no particular interest in yachting at all. To participate was to be part of current history; to be at the place where it was happening, while it was happening. This was a chance to join in a ritual that looked like fun, that was free, accessible, requiring no qualification to be present, and officially sanctioned by their being allowed to take time off work or school to attend. This was a rare event in that it claimed to be 'for everyone'. It supported easily understood and acceptable values: Pride in Winning. On television news commentaries the parade was referred to as a 'party'.

The televisual America's Cup event is perhaps the supreme example in recent times of the media's conscious, blatant appeal to chauvinistic sympathies, and its aggressive nationalism. Through such an event the sense of communal links between individuals is heightened, and our collective identification with 'the nation' reiterated. Political and other tensions dissolve as television helps build up the idea of a unity through this shared cultural experience. The America's Cup, held out of sight a long way away, is transformed by television from a sporting event to part of a far wider ideological process. We are encouraged to believe we are seeing drama and history in the making, with sport as symbolic representation of New Zealand culture. In this mass celebration, we are essentially celebrating ourselves.

Television, radio, newspapers: they were all full of the national glory this win had brought. The Chief Executive of the Auckland Chamber of Commerce made this statement: 'If ever we wanted an example of what New Zealanders can do when they set themselves an objective, and work together as a team, we have it in this victory — a victory which should give us all some vision, inspiration and hope for our people and our nation.'[15] Even before the final races were won, there was widespread eager speculation of what the win would bring with it. Great fortunes were anticipated from the future challenge. There would be many promotional opportunities — for 'us'.

Were there any dissenters? A few killjoys wrote letters to the paper, saying that the parade, like yachting itself, was racist and elitist; that the America's Cup was essentially a Pakeha myth-making event for the benefit of large corporations. Such critics were attacked on the basis of 'sour grapes'. Someone pointed out that the *Herald* newspaper coverage of the welcome home — a whole separate cover page enfolding the usual daily paper, the third such souvenir of the 1995 America's Cup[16] — showed all these euphoric bourgeois Pakeha people celebrating; and that the only pictures of Maori or Pacific Islanders were of street cleaners, sweeping up the ticker-tape. Anyone this critical was quickly labelled 'unpatriotic' or 'whingeing'.

Through television, sport becomes part of popular culture. It fosters social rituals; friends get together to watch races and matches, and talk about it with others later. It provides experiences in common for a large group of people, reinforcing shared values. It works as an arena of representation of nation and nationhood. Sports teams are always identified by the country they represent. There is clearly a strong relationship between television, sport, the big business that sponsors it and that buys time in the ad-breaks, and projections to the rest of the world of the characteristics of a nation. 'Corporate advertisers are aware of the importance and power of . . . national sense of identity, and exploit it in their campaigns,' explains Massey University sociologist Avril Bell.[17] She tells us how we are sold much more than a product, a 'version of the nation itself'. Sport as an arena for expression of nation is never politically neutral. Television does not simply show us reality, but an interpretation that is 'rah! rah!' for us. Newspapers are similar: one could quickly and easily assemble a collection of newspaper cuttings about sports events, in the manner of 'New Zealand came eighth' — and where the item never does mention who won. Media coverage of sport, then, is a popular venue for the stating of national mythologies, again and again.

The adventures of the America's Cup illustrate the power of television in guiding responses to 'national' events. Television was the driving force behind the America's Cup fervour; it could do the same on other issues, if it were in its interests. Imagine, for instance, if the same powerful factions were behind the peace flotilla that sailed up to Moruroa in September 1995 to protest at the continuation of French nuclear testing; or gave such rousing support to New Zealand artists and writers honoured at overseas biennales or awards events.

Collective egotism: national pride

Superficially, 'nation' sounds a positive, harmless enough term. Most of us think of our nationality as a central part of our identity, and see our country as unique and wonderful. This form of collective egoism is good for morale in an otherwise remote, perhaps globally insignificant, group of islands. Any nation's existence relies on some sense of loyalty to that nation, on patriotic sentiment, on awareness of nationalism. A sense of shared purpose, a pride in place, acknowledgement of national successes: these all contribute to a sense of belonging. Our imagined linkages with one another mean we perceive we have something in common.

Boosting the nation's morale is a constant process, to instil loyalty and to unite otherwise diverse groups. As the America's Cup illustration above shows, sports teams that achieve international success provide just such a boost. 'Our' team is claimed by whoever wants to make such a claim; hence any New Zealander can 'share' the success. A friend teaching intellectually disabled teenagers in Auckland tells me that these children have cottoned on to the America's Cup. In their work they were asked to draw a New Zealand icon. Whereas they might usually draw Rangitoto or One Tree Hill, with a sprinkling of kiwis and perhaps a sheep or two, this year *Black Magic* sailed well past the usual images in popularity.

Historically, rugby union boosted the national psyche, a sport linking provinces, players and supporters, and different ethnic groups. Great days of sport — important wins — are claimed to link the nation. Sport as a venue for promotion of national unity has fostered the idea of New Zealand being a sporting nation.

Similarly war has been a sphere in which New Zealand men could measure their prowess against those of different nations. Traditional links with Britain gave New Zealand involvement in two world wars, our economic dependence on Britain demanding participation. New Zealand men proved themselves on the battlefield, this 'proof' some sort of consolation for the huge loss of life.

To be a desirable trading partner and site for offshore investment we have to at least look stable. For instance, an election barely won by one seat can cause uncertainty in investors, who might decide to put their money elsewhere. Such an election result indicates a country divided, hence unstable, and therefore unlikely to be favourable to economic growth. Media coverage of great shows of national fervour are a way of showing stability. Look: one big happy family!

Throughout Pakeha history, the political and economic links with other countries have been used to manipulate versions of national identity. Even as children we learned about this country's superiority over others. At Sunday school we gave shillings to very poor people overseas. Pictures on the collection envelopes of black people with leprosy and nothing to eat showed us that, by comparison, we were very rich indeed. We were rich enough to give away money. We understood that we were very fortunate because in our country our government looked after us. We were nagged about our privileged status: 'You children don't know how lucky you are!' Or 'Eat up all your silverbeet, there are starving children overseas who don't get any dinner!' There was no suggestion that we should invite them here to share some of these great feasts of mashed potatoes and lamb chops.

So we ate up our dinner, and vaguely absorbed the messages that told us that almost everywhere else in the world was a political and economic disaster. In fact, it looked as if most people in the world were starving and had leprosy. We were lucky: we lived in the world's only perfect country. England was second best. It rained there a lot, and people couldn't go to the beach as often as we did. But we didn't have to send them money. We sent them butter instead. Unfortunately, it turned out that they didn't want so much butter forever, after all. The reduction of trade links with Britain meant that New Zealand had to look for other markets for its goods.

The mileage gained from national pride cannot be underestimated. The promotion of internal policies has to show other nations things to impress them. Once we described ourselves as 'the social laboratory of the world'; many years later we were 'nuclear free'. In 1995 we even have a postage stamp to proclaim this. These claims imply a national consensus across policy areas to make us that way. This is very good for the state, and for whichever party is in power at the time. Power and prestige are validated through acknowledgement from elsewhere.

New Zealand has a history of seeking external validation. For years there was a joke about asking newcomers the minute they arrived here, 'What do you think of New Zealand?' In 1972 Austin Mitchell described this as 'a major preoccupation . . . the rest of the world ignores it, so it compensates by more and more frantic exercises of national belly-button studying. . . . It is a request for reassurance, encouragement, admiration and all the other things assisted immigrants are brought in to provide. . . . When I arrived in New Zealand, the first words of my kindly boss were a warning not to be critical when asked how I liked New Zealand.'[18]

His comments mark about a century of this sort of thing. There is more than a subtle echo in them of a comment recorded in 1887: 'Nothing is more offensive to Colonial views than to have the dark side of things in the country fairly set forth. But should anyone write very favourably of climate, productions, commerce, institutions and the wonderful future of New Zealand, well then his future is made, he is a god out here.'[19]

Globalisation

The increasing dominance of transnational companies, placing internationally familiar items and services on the local market, makes it imperative to proclaim local national values. When the agendas of large companies in New Zealand are set by offshore owners, their relationships with the client base here has to be articulated. Hence international companies present their goods and services encased in local imagery, so that globally familiar products can be perceived as 'for us'. For instance, the huge international company Heinz now owns Watties, which began in New Zealand as a small

Hawke's Bay canning operation in the 1930s. For years the name 'Watties' was synonymous with canned food. Today, promotion of Heinz-owned Watties products includes some advertisements that sell a nostalgic New Zealand setting for their products. 'We love our Watties sauce' includes scenarios familiar only to New Zealanders: ladies-a-plate, and down-on-the-farm scenes that link the viewer, the buyer of the sauce, and the nation. In upholding local traditions, including the tradition of consuming Watties foods (especially tomato sauce!), there is no hint that the products advertised have anything whatsoever to do with one of the biggest companies in the world.

In advertising, the power of this recognition (of a population's primary interest in themselves) is manipulated for economic ends. By showing the product or service in a (romanticised, idealised) New Zealand context, it is suggested that not only is the consumer item appropriate to this place, but the consumption of it is somehow in the national collective interest. These notions are manipulated to sell products, policies, ideas, consumer goods, images — for the good of the individual New Zealander, and for the national good.

The style and imagery used in advertising may consist of an adaptation for local markets, as the drive by consumers to join the world in consumption of famous international products motivates their spending. Or there may be a deliberate reduction of difference between cultures assumed in the advertising, conveying the product as one that will be enjoyed anywhere, and that in consuming it, one is participating in a sophisticated international marketplace. Happiness, satisfaction and ownership as international consumer goals are attached to products sold with confidence globally. Differences between cultures as sites for consumption are brushed aside, or projected as positive. For instance, Bacardi shows us and tells us about places where Bacardi is enjoyed: on exotic faraway islands. New Zealand? North *Island*, South *Island* . . . And is that an actor from *Shortland Street* enjoying this drink? We only get a fleeting glimpse, but if we think he is familiar, the ad is further localised.

Small local producers must struggle to survive against multinational companies. In trying to reach the national market, the trump card may be the foregrounding of local origin. In competition with international companies the familiar traditional, local values are exploitable. The L and P campaign in 1995 claimed the little Waikato town of Paeroa as 'World Famous in New Zealand'. The fact that the drink has not been manufactured there for years is superfluous. The point is, the name of the town is carried in the name of the drink. A cute ad making good-natured fun of Paeroa (and by association, our own vernacular culture) totally localises the soft drink in a way that overseas soft drink manufacturing competitors cannot.

New Zealand cannot be economically autonomous and independent. It is part of a world-wide political and economic system. Rocketing change in media and communications, with the resulting time-space compression, means a permeation of cultural boundaries by the new technology, and an invasion of values from elsewhere. This, along with major political and economic changes, has meant increasing uncertainty about sense of place, and has undermined traditional local identification and diversity.

These complicated and interrelated changes have resulted in a desire in New Zealand to assert distinctiveness: by using the same technology, to proudly reaffirm our senses of unique local, regional and national identity. The same technology that swamps our culture with external values and information, can be used increasingly to transmit some of our values back out to the world.[20] In the late 1990s we are likely to see an expansion of this process, as technological advancement in communication perpetuates the process of claiming distinction. The 'electronic collapse of space', as one writer refers to it,[21] gives rise to a universal sameness, as nations across the world share cultural components; but it also gives cultures ammunition with which to fight back, and reassert difference.

Why this debate, now?

My generation, born after the war, grew up in the conservative, comfortable 1950s and early 1960s. It was a time when it seemed things would never change. Our 'history' was British imperial history. We were kept ignorant about the impact of Pakeha settlement on Maori. In schools we learnt nothing of Maori art, culture or tradition. Our literary references were to British writers. Children's books were about cute little rabbits, Noddy, the Famous Five and Biggles. The body of knowledge transmitted to us at school linked us to our British heritage. In fact, there was no sense of any other.

We did not look at anything published by the first New Zealand writers. We did not even know that such literature existed. It seemed that literature, like art and music, could only come from Europe. Indeed, all arts appeared defined by Europe.

Nobody explained to us at school that British culture was foisted onto the Maori. The racial tolerance we grew up with was no big deal, because Maori were largely invisible. The assumption was that Maori would increasingly assimilate and become more and more like Pakeha. This might take a couple of generations, but was seen as essentially unproblematic.

We instinctively knew that anything English was superior to what we had here. This was partly through the Queen as figurehead (it was quite usual for ordinary people to have framed pictures of members of the royal family in their homes); and also because we knew that an English accent was superior to a New Zealand one. The Queen had a *very strong* English accent, we thought: the ultimate example of perfect speech. But she also seemed motherly. It wasn't just that she had children. In her Christmas speeches, heard by the ordinary New Zealand family gathered around the radio on Christmas Day, she always talked about the Empire as her 'family'. The connection between us in the 1950s and 'Mother England' appeared perfectly correct.

BBC radio newsreaders also spoke the true English language. We understood and were slightly embarrassed that ours was an inferior, parochial sort. I well remember some of the girls at high school going to elocution lessons, their parents anxious to help rid them of their New Zealand accents. In school speech competitions and plays they sounded much like Margaret Thatcher. In everyday conversation they spoke like the rest of us. I often wondered which voice they used at home, in front of their elocution-fee-paying parents. The first television productions made here suffered from this attitude to local speech. 'Proper' television programmes (those imported from overseas) did not include people with voices like these. Local drama programmes *looked* amateur at least in part because they *sounded* local.

It seems extraordinary now that teachers at my all-girls school seemed to have the idea in their heads that they were trying to turn out nice English girls, rather than pleasant New Zealand ones. We learned embroidery and manners; both sets of skills imposed on girls who despite the unsophisticated culture might go on in life with at least a veneer of civilisation. 'Go on in life': back in the early 1960s it meant that these girls would become good wives and mothers, and bring up the next generation to be equally good citizens.

Training for a career before marriage would give us 'something to fall back on' if 'something happened'. But our destiny was to be wives and mothers. The apparent inevitability of that destiny was thankfully, and unpredictably, sabotaged by the arrival of the oral contraceptive pill. Then the 1970s new wave of feminism put a final end to motherhood as our only option.

We also grew up with an assumption of 'egalitarianism'. Looking back, it was a strange sort of egalitarianism. It was one which gave total priority to men. Somehow we vaguely understood that this was 'natural', because men owned the property and few married women were in the paid workforce. Women in the same jobs as men, for instance teachers and clerical workers, were paid less than men. Logically, because of the responsibility of property ownership, men had greater rights and ran public life. Politicians, generally male, were authority figures. Adults who were around when I was growing up seemed to assume that even if they personally disagreed with some government policies, the politicians knew what they were doing; it was for the national good.

It was considered bad manners in social situations to discuss politics or religion. So teenagers, or certainly those I knew, did not normally get to participate in political debate. A few years later, when the protests against the Vietnam War came along, there was sheer exhilaration in expressing resistance. Many of us had far more education than our parents. Indeed, for parents who had left school at twelve or thirteen, a priority had been that we had a good education. They now watched in horror as we behaved in ways they saw as 'subversive'. Where were the conservative, decent young citizens they thought they were nurturing?

Looking back, the 1950s and early 1960s seem such a naïve and innocent time. Divorce and illegitimacy were disgraceful events, to be borne with deep shame. Indeed, family secrets were so heavily guarded that we barely knew such things as ex-nuptial childbirth or incest existed. A litany of cover-ups kept the impressionable younger generation in the dark, and excluded them from adult society, in the interests of raising us to become respectable adults.

To counterbalance the silences were the celebrations. Bloke culture was celebrated in Barry Crump's book, *A Good Keen Man* (1960).[22] 'Rugby, racing and beer' as applied national stereotypes were readily recognised and accepted. There was a sense that the way things were was the way things would continue to be, pretty much forever. Adults kept telling us, when we were still at school, that 'schooldays are the best days of your life'. This was a horrifying suggestion: was this as good as it got? Help! Their lives looked pretty boring, but they seemed to accept the boredom. After the wars and the Depression, they were probably relieved to be at least comfortable.

People who had never been anywhere else kept telling us this was the best country in the world. We believed them.

An industry of books about 'beautiful New Zealand' celebrated these islands in glossy photographs. A newspaper columnist published a book in 1962 called *The Land I Love*. Aimed at New Zealand readers, her very first paragraph summed up the current popular sentiments: 'This land I love is New Zealand, and it seems to me that such a love is not a light to hide under a bushel; but a heart to wear on the sleeve. Ours is a green and blue and golden land, demanding not rosy-tinted spectacled indulgence. Yet one does not love it for being in any way perfect, but with all its faults, as one loves a child, or a lover, or as one would wish to be loved oneself. One loves the wildness with the mildness, the rawness with the richness, the rough with the smooth. And one loves it not always with logic or even with sanity, but stubbornly, instinctively, and deep in the marrow of one's bones.'[23] Throughout the rest of her book, she continues in this vein, innocently delighting in the country of her birth, happily blind to any experience than those that reinforce her view.

But times were changing. In the 1970s two very popular books arrived to dissect the anatomy and way of life of New Zealand: *The Half-Gallon Quarter-Acre Pavlova Paradise* by Austin Mitchell (1972)[24] and *The Passionless People* by Gordon McLauchlan (1976).[25] Both of these books were satirical observations about what it means to be a New Zealander.

Mitchell wrote his book as an 'outsider', a British academic and television personality living here for a few years, and about to depart. Each chapter is a letter back to Britain to his friend Keith. He opened with the following: 'It's a wonderful country. Not quite paradise . . . but probably the best country in the world. Certainly the best in the southern hemisphere. Having made this deference to New Zealand sales, I must in all honesty warn you. It's a funny country. The natives have their own tribal customs and ceremonies. They also have their own susceptibilities. If an Englishman . . . didn't find them different to the folks back home in all sorts of endearing little ways the natives couldn't bear it. Different means better. Let your indulgent smile turn into a laugh — once imply that certain things are better handled in Britain and you'll get the ritual excommunication: "If you don't like it here why don't you go home?"' [26]

McLauchlan wrote as an 'insider', someone who had been born here and had always lived here. He opened with the suggestion that New Zealanders must set about re-examining themselves. 'The time has come now to see ourselves as we really are — a racially and culturally homogeneous group of people who have nurtured in isolation from the rest of the world a Victorian, lower-middle-class, Calvinist, village mentality, and brought it right through into the 1970s. We have established a society in which we have been spared the disgusting sight of the poor and the sick, the dirty and, particularly, the different. Materialism has been the coarse fabric of our dreams . . . there was nothing else, just materialism. . . . New Zealanders have no moral or social philosophy, no dream of the future, beyond the orthodox good health of that pagan god, The Economy.'[27] His plea was to rid ourselves of drab sameness and look for passion, variety and a vibrancy that he may well still be seeking.

Both of these writers challenged the ideology which guided social values, but in a way that avoided heavy-handedness. They presented good-humoured, palatable versions of culture, the goal to amuse the reader rather than stimulate serious discussion. I recall that these books were laughed over and talked about. But they were considered more the work of two witty, slightly eccentric writers, rather than valid and serious criticism of the culture. For how could any criticism be valid? Nonetheless, they signalled a challenge to the old, long-accepted image of ourselves.

Moreover, as time moved on, a lot of things changed. Key

amongst them were events that led to a maturing of our perceptions of race relations. The 1975 Maori Land March from Pungaru (North Hokianga) to Parliament in Wellington, for example, drew attention to Maori causes, and began a campaign that met with increasing hostility from conservative Pakeha over the next twenty years. The 1981 success of protests against the Springbok tour and its subsequent cancellation had given liberal Pakeha something of a 'high'. The challenge from Maori was that Pakeha were more concerned with apartheid in South Africa then in race relations issues here.

With this focus on race came the realisation of a need for Pakeha New Zealanders to look at themselves as well as their actions. Pakeha writers began to seriously consider what it means to be Pakeha, not a transplanted European. For 'Pakeha' there is not the clarity of identity that there is, conventionally, for Maori.[28] In part because of this latter point, the process of 'invention' is a constant part of Pakeha society.

Further impetus to Pakeha writers came with Donna Awatere's text, *Maori Sovereignty*, published in 1984. This really was the 'big debate' book of that time.[29] Her work fuelled the Maori Renaissance; it also stimulated examination by Pakeha of who they are, and their own commitment to New Zealand, in the light of Maori identity.

Michael King's book *Being Pakeha*,[30] published the following year, also gained enormous attention. Then, as now, there was heated resistance to the term 'Pakeha', and to King's insistence that to be a citizen of Aotearoa involved necessary respect for things Maori. Anthropological and autobiographical, it described how the writer's experiences researching Maori history with people in Maori communities gave him both his personal and national identity. A new word was coined: 'Pakehatanga'. It did not catch on.

The debate continued with books such as Jock Phillips's *A Man's Country?*,[31] which tracked the development of male dominance in New Zealand culture; Claudia Orange's *Treaty of Waitangi*;[32] and *Honouring the Treaty* (1989) by a group of writers and activists.[33] Magazine columnists and newspaper articles that looked at how New Zealanders conceived themselves nationally, critically examined the ways in which institutional racism was prevalent in New Zealand.

Academics have continued the debate, noting the problem of

seeing Pakeha as a 'distinct community'. Where is the sense of solidarity needed to distinguish a group? There is little coherence or agreement on what a Pakeha is.[34]

In *Being Pakeha* Michael King explained that previous generations had not had the same concerns. New issues in the 1980s meant the need for self-examination. Biculturalism, for instance, was symbolic of an equity that had not concerned our parents or grandparents. Later, in *Pakeha: The Quest for Identity in New Zealand* (1991)[35] a group of liberal Pakeha writers stated their confidence in the possibility of a racially harmonious New Zealand. Some things have barely changed. Early this century the assumption was that Maori should 'assimilate' within dominant culture. Indeed, policy was set in place to help facilitate this. Vocal right-wing groups and much of the population in general still believe this. Talkback radio provides ample evidence!

This romp across colonial history, popular culture and personal biography demonstrates that an array of symbols and circumstances intersect to affirm Pakeha identity as dominant in this country. The analysis of Pakeha values has increased since events of the 1980s. Simultaneously, the articulation of Pakeha values has multiplied with the growth of television, that claims and expresses (Pakeha!) identity values on behalf of all, for everyday consumption. This book is about some of those current processes of showing what New Zealand is: representations claimed for us, to convey what and who we are.

2
Clean, green and beautiful
— the nature myth

A powerful concept of New Zealand is based on nature: clean, green and beautiful. The dramatic natural landscape, varied and picturesque, is a source of national pride. Unique flora and fauna feature as the dominant motifs in identity imagery. While most New Zealanders are urban dwellers, the experience of growing up here includes the experience of physical landscape and familiarity with distinctive birds, imprinted on perception and memory. We can also remember that our awareness of nature was always present.

When did we not know there was such a thing as a kiwi, for instance? Even though they did not trot about in the garden, we knew they were out there somewhere, and extremely important. The kiwi was clearly the most *special* bird in the world. It figured so large in public consciousness, in everyday language, on logos and on our two-shilling coins, that when I was small I always assumed it must be a very large bird indeed.

They ran about in forests at night. I longed to see one. I had in mind something about the size of a St Bernard dog, dodging hurriedly through the pine trees. (I lived in an area with little native bush, so the idea of forest was Tokoroa or Kinleith pine plantations, or rows of symmetrical conifers from pictures in children's books written and illustrated overseas.) We knew about English birds, because we had a whole children's encyclopaedia about them. Australia had lots of birds. We had seen them in photographs in the *Australian Women's Weekly*. The Americans only had vultures. No-one had anything as mysterious and important as the kiwi. It was quite shocking to discover eventually that these birds were rather small, very vulnerable, and that we'd probably never come across one in its natural habitat. Even so, they were still the most important birds in the world.

As one grows up, a sense of identity is drawn at least in part from nature. An individual is familiar with local land and plant forms, and local climate. Particular nature is understood as part of 'home'. 'Where are you from?' — this often asked question of one

New Zealander to another conveys in the reply some of these natural features, and the supposed way of life likely to go with them, such as farming on the Southland Plains, winter sports on the Central Plateau, the beach environment of the Bay of Islands, and so on. Investigation of our collective appreciation of nature helps us to understand its role in national identity formulation and patriotism.

The nature myth

Bio-physical nature is 4.5 billion years old. Nature as a human notion also pre-dates the first evidence of human conceptual activity (cave painting), and long pre-dates recorded human history. The past brings with it thousands of years of myths and legends about a nature untainted by humans, with visions of primeval forests, mysterious mountains, and modified only by the elements, not the hand of humankind.

For New Zealand, nature comprises pre-colonial history, and infuses it with historic attributes. To this is added the findings of modern science. In discourses on the development of a nation's identity, nature can substitute for or stand for the past. If the hunt for the root of Pakeha identity runs into problems with history (for instance, all Pakeha New Zealanders do not claim historic bonds with Britain); then turning to nature is another way of accounting for distinctiveness. New Zealand can claim itself a unique country, purely for its natural landscape and the plant and animal species endemic to New Zealand.

In New Zealand there are two versions of romanticised landscape. Landscape is either beautiful but potentially dangerous: sanctified, visited, enjoyed, photographed, then left; a vision to inspire. Or it is beautiful and beautifully cultivated, a tribute to both nature itself and to the efforts of human labour.

The first version assumes egalitarianism. Theoretically, every New Zealander has free access to beaches and national parks. As an Australian observer writes (with reference to Bondi Beach, but the same could be said here), 'egalitarianism is given by the sea, the sun, a natural democracy...'.[1] Part of New Zealand's egalitarian tradition has been assumptions of shared access to publicly owned natural resources. Recent challenges to this by Maori tribes as part of activism surrounding the honouring of the Treaty of Waitangi demonstrate the assumptions Pakeha people have made in terms of the right to nature. The stating of Maori grievances, expressed in claims for restoration of land and fisheries, couple Maori and nature, and undermines the myths of egalitarianism and a bicultural society. Maori culture is paraded publicly as indigenous New Zealand, conveying the idea of a country that is at one with nature and history. This is less to support Maori than to support the political agenda of non-Maori.

The second version valorises the antipodean success of transported British land-use practices, modified for conditions here. The land is developed to the point that New Zealand is acknowledged as one of the most productive countries in the world. At times (for instance in the 1880s and 1950s) the nation has enjoyed the status of having the highest standard of living in the world, and its spin-offs: in sum, 'the great way of life'.

Both versions of nature contribute to the national identity myths.

Sublime landscape

Early European depictions of New Zealand nature emphasised the majesty of the sublime landscapes. Especially popular were renditions of Mitre Peak, the Pink and White Terraces, Mount Aspiring, and Mount Taranaki. Artists such as Gully, Heaphy, Earle and van der Velden depicted New Zealand in its pristine state, according to European painting tradition. The eighteenth century concept of the sublime gave aesthetic value to mountains in particular; as Francis Pound writes, 'we've had landscape art full of them ever since'.[2] In the nineteenth century no new conventions of landscape painting had their origins here. The distinctive New Zealand landscape was conveyed in accordance with a received European painting tradition. These early paintings showed that this was a place unlike anywhere else in the world.

In New Zealand we have vast amounts of the 'sublime': mountains, volcanoes, avalanches, glaciers, the wide expanse of sky, the boundless oceans. Nineteenth century English people found in New Zealand splendiferous vistas to consume in the form of romantic landscape. 'It was as if . . . art had invented a type, and life had copied it, reproduced it in a popular form, like an enterprising publisher.'[3]

Many of these paintings went to Europe. Blomfield, for instance, produced numerous renditions of the Pink and White Terraces, often commissioned by visitors, who had him include them in the finished painted landscape. Multiple editions of other works by many artists were reproduced as chrome-lithographs to extend sales. When the subject was a town or a European settlement, a great deal of 'natural' detail was included, even though much of this quality was lost through settlement. It was as if displays of the untouched landscape would entice settlers to come and make their mark. From early on, 'beautiful New Zealand' meant 'exploitable New Zealand'. The natural vista could be consumed, and the sublime became a saleable bit of Arcadia.

These European beginnings in the eighteenth century introduced to the nineteenth century a vocabulary of the sublime in descriptions of the natural environment. By the late 1700s, mountains had been gaining credibility as places to visit, marvel at, and paint. The 'advantages' of this in the colonisation of New Zealand are obvious.

Artworks in Europe of dramatic New Zealand landscape promoted the country as suitable not only for the aesthetic gaze, but also for immigration and for tourism. The more spectacular sites (sights) soon became major tourist attractions, written about by visitors enthralled at the exotic nature found here. For instance, the day James Inglis visited the Pink and White Terraces at Tarawera (not long before Tarawera erupted in 1886, destroying the Terraces) was one 'surely to be marked with a white stone in the calendar of one's life. The memory of these marvels will haunt me to my dying hour . . .'. He described the Terraces as 'this masterpiece of God's handiwork in the great Art Gallery of nature'.[4] He also lamented the graffiti scrawled on the terraces: 'the apish propensities of multitudes of cads and snobs, who have scrawled and scribbled their ignoble names on every available inch of space . . . here on the exquisite enamel of these marvellously beautiful chalices were vulgar scrawlings, as if all the devil-possessed swine of Gadara had suddenly been supported bodily here . . . impelled to . . . deface with their hoggish hieroglyphics . . .'.[5]

Paintings established that there was a grandeur of nature here, to translate into art. Then came the new art of photography, and the 'view trade'.

The 'view trade' was first dominated by the Burton brothers, Alfred and Walter, of Dunedin, whose family in the English Midlands ran a photography business. In 1867 Alfred came to New Zealand to join his brother, who had arrived a few years before. At first they earned a living with their portrait work; but Alfred saw potential in the view business, and travelled extensively to collect images. By the 1870s they were also working in the North Island. Newspapers were happy to print their work. It is believed that Alfred's images of Fiordland helped persuade authorities to have this land set aside as a national park; the Fiordland pictures were very popular with tourists, who cruised to the fiords from Dunedin.

Other photographers were also cashing in on the view market. While the Burton brothers are remembered as probably the most prolific producers of nineteenth century views of New Zealand, their business was eventually taken over by the Muir and Moodie partnership in 1898. As Main and Turner explain, 'calling themselves Specialists in New Zealand Scenery, Muir and Moodie travelled the country to update the most popular views and anticipate the needs of a new generation of settlers and tourists, for whom the views symbolised material progress within a setting of inaccessible, if not tame, nature. By 1880 the time was ripe for Muir and Moodie to enter the profitable international trade in printed postcards . . . to meet public demand, hand colours were sometimes added: "penny plain, tuppence coloured".'[6] The tourist postcard furthered the same pictorial tradition, both in subject matter and motive, as the paintings. Postcards become mobile 'advertisements' for selected versions of identity. At 'penny plain, tuppence coloured', postcards were the accessible end of the commodified vista market.

Why do tourists like mountains?
There was no escaping New Zealand's inheritance of European cultural and intellectual movements. The comprehension of the Swiss Alps and the Scottish Highlands as 'sublime' places in the eighteenth century have had such a pervasive impact, that here on the other side of the world, mountains are an 'understood' sublime attraction.

There were differences in the ways classical and romantic thought perceived nature. Plato-influenced classicism referred to 'nature' with emphasis on human nature. The physical environment received far less attention. It was not until the Romantic period (from about the early eighteenth century) that nature referred to the 'natural' disorder of the wilderness: craggy mountain tops, threatening clouds, and so on. These could be 'tided up' beautifully in Romantic art.

In European literature at the beginning of the eighteenth century the mountain vista became part of the romantic imagination. Mountains were thought to enlarge and ennoble the human spirit, extend the sensibilities, expand visionary possibilities, and, in doing so, develop character. This implied that people who lived in environments without mountains might be limited in their outlook, so must seek some out. Besides, at that time industrialism was developing; mountains became sanctuaries from the excesses of towns and cities, a new part of the European Grand Tour. You only have to look at the romantic poetry and the Thomas Cook brochures of this period!

Early settlers wanted to discover potentially productive land. For this purpose some sorts of topography were more promising than others. Internal explorers also located objects of cultural significance such as rivers and mountains. They already had often lyrically descriptive Maori names; but part of claiming territory was name replacement. This process put places on a new map, an English one. It is clear that cultural appropriation of land was crucial. A colonising culture claiming land occupied by another culture defines or imagines spaces, on its own terms and in its own language, in order to conceive of it as *terra nullius*.

New Zealand's natural resources are a vehicle through which local, regional and national distinction is daily claimed and validated. The funny thing about the promotion of New Zealand is that most of what we promote we cannot really take credit for. The bush, mountains, lakes, beaches — our credit is in the conservation and preservation of these, which most of us as individuals are not responsible for. We bask in their glory. It is dead easy to point proudly to some mountains that we did not construct and are not responsible for, and say, 'They're ours!'

A wonderful thing about having nature as the main promotional imagery for a country, is that, if protected, the value of dramatic mountains and steep untouched bush or raging rivers cannot be depleted. In fact, as development proceeds elsewhere and many of the world's wilderness areas are destroyed, untouched nature becomes rarer and so more valuable. As tourism writer W. J. T. Mitchell explains, 'at the most basic, vulgar level, landscape expresses itself in a specific price: the added cost of a beautiful view in real estate; the price of a plane ticket to the Rockies, Hawaii, the Alps, or New Zealand . . . at the same time, landscape represents itself as "beyond price", a source of pure, inexhaustible spiritual value . . . an "ideal state" quite independent of "real estate" . . . the land, real property, contains a limited quantity of wealth in minerals, vegetation, water and dwelling space. Dig out all the gold in a mountainside, and its wealth is exhausted. But how many photographs, postcards, paintings, and awe struck "sightings" will it take to exhaust [the value of iconic natural landmarks]?'[7]

These sentiments underpin the establishment of national parks in New Zealand. The parks enshrine the iconic natural features which support local, regional and national identity, for instance Mount Taranaki, and Fiordland.

National identity based on physical geography, and on idealisation of lifestyles within nature, is persistently used as our claim to fame. We are far less notable for what we have in terms of everyday cultural creations that we have ourselves made, such as intellectual property, service, or glamorous or interesting towns. Most New Zealanders live in cities, well away from the sublime landscape. We know these cities are much like those of everywhere else, while our nature isn't. Nature persists in the imagery that shows our difference, and is a reality that can be affirmed by a short drive out of town, reinforcing the aptness of these representations over those of city life.[8] Perhaps it is because we feel we have little else to offer that nature gets such high mileage.

Portrayals of the magnificence of nature live on in the present: the postage stamps, the coffee table books, the calendars and the advertising campaigns (Toyota!), the array of postcards; and in company and government department logos. The imagery used for these follows the tradition of what is 'beautiful': landscape that is green, large, dramatic and inspiring. This is a readily accessible way of stating identity. Besides, the most famous New Zealander of all made his mark by climbing a mountain.

Colonisation

The dramatic New Zealand landscape was heavily drawn on in the earliest days of Pakeha settlement, as part of the New Zealand Arcadia myth. Through colonisation, Wakefield's company and other settler associations commodified the vista into saleable Arcadian plots. Settlers were promised a land of milk and honey. Early propaganda placed a lot of emphasis on the beauty and fertility of the natural environment, and its ability to sustain English land-use practice. To colonisers the apparently unused, fertile land invited settlement and development.

Historian Miles Fairburn explained in detail the importance of nature to the development of national identity. In *The Ideal Society and Its Enemies,* Fairburn wrote that 'of the themes constituting the Arcadian conception of New Zealand, the most common one was the notion of New Zealand as a land of natural abundance';[9] even where the *natural* nature had to be cleared to make way for productive nature. Fairburn tracked the romanticisation of the development of the pioneer family and their way of life in nature, as a foundation of modern New Zealand society. The mythical natural garden paradise was awash with almost spiritual values, and was one that contained a happy nuclear family, attuned to nature.

The pioneers wrested and conquered wild untamed nature, to turn it into richly productive agricultural land. It was important that the colony be immediately productive; free passages were available only to workers who could be self-sufficient, or readily employed, such as farm labourers. In return for their passages they would work for wages in New Zealand, the New Zealand Company guaranteeing employment if it could not be found elsewhere (though this guarantee was not later honoured). Records of the New Zealand Company's first ships show that one-third of all male emigrants were (or claimed they were) farm and general labourers, while one-fifth were building tradesmen. Half of the women were domestic servants.

This is a very Pakeha history, laden with aspirations and values achievable through male physical prowess. Historian Keith Sinclair described these physical efforts of the pioneers as central to the process of building a nation. Harsh, tough and lonely, it was believed that breaking in the land required a superhuman effort which formed national character. The climate (mild compared with that of Britain) facilitated year-round outdoor work, and values of outdoor life found their expression in terms such as 'honest toil', 'taking the wilderness', 'living off the land', and so on. Sinclair concluded that

New Zealanders look to the historic relationship with nature for their roots.[10]

Much of the land was already occupied. The Maori and nature were intrinsically connected, justifying the destruction of indigenous culture, along with nature, as 'progress'. To develop a new land as an antipodean version of the old one elsewhere involved conquering both Maori and the bush. The Maori people already living here were trampled in the mission to develop a distinct new white identity in New Zealand. Initially dependent on Maori for food, the settlers gradually adapted to their environment, developing as they did so a concept of what it meant to be a 'New Zealander'. This had a strong European flavour, and was a direct imposition on Maori, as the pioneers set about creating a history that included themselves and was unrelated to Maori history. Imported ideas of what constitutes a history drew from British tradition, and included nostalgia that mediated visions of the nature left behind: the carefully cultivated fields of a civilised nation. Could this be established on these islands, on this terrain, with this climate, and in the face of resistance by this indigenous population?

New Zealand was being constructed. Mastery of nature resulted in economic success, and a viable new life in contrast to the difficulties left behind in Britain. Labouring for oneself meant also labouring for the new nation, and by implication for the empire. Farms carved out of bush were testament to hard work, and to the emerging New Zealand 'character'.

The settlers saw themselves as conquerors, tamers and owners of the environment. The interaction of 'man' with environment ('taming' it — irretrievably altering it!) gave an impression of a close relationship with nature. The beloved wide open spaces and green pastures were all at the cost of what was there before, and who was there before. Since Pakeha settlement, the New Zealand ecology has been more altered than most others in the world. Such is the 'nature' of colonisation and 'development'.

This was a fundamental ideology of the development of national identity in New Zealand: a land of bountiful natural resources, and the inhabitants closely in tune with nature. Expression was not of the poetic love of nature so much as the Christian drive to civilise the pagan, and of the sense of pride and achievement in conquering such an unsympathetic physical environment, as land was 'developed'. This experience shared by early rural pioneers unified settlers and contributed to the development of a sense of national pride, and nationhood. The New Zealander was not defined as an intellectual, or by spiritual or political characteristics, but by the physical and the masculine: man against the elements, man transforming nature into nation.[11]

Flora and fauna: accessible symbols

There is still sufficient unspoiled bush for it to be a visible statement of beauty and uniqueness. This ready accessibility is central to the romanticising and mythologising of nature as a crucial component of national identity. Protected in national parks, it persists as the foundation of New Zealand's national beauty and diversity.

Flora and fauna are ascribed with great symbolic value. Identity needs are satisfied by claiming or adapting as symbol an emblem or object or creature that precedes society and human settlement. The more ancient the history of the claimed symbol, the more firmly its claim to be fixed as a permanent feature of national identity.

Symbols to represent New Zealand globally are drawn from nature's generosity. Richard Wolfe has extensively documented the kiwi and fern as particularly significant emblems. Wolfe explains that the need for a specifically New Zealand symbol arose as a way for the newly colonised nation to assert distinctive identity that separated it from the 'homeland'. Efforts to transplant here British national symbols such as John Bull, Britannia and the lion were discounted as 'imperialist connections hardly [befitting] a nation which even as this stage prided itself on its independence'.[12]

Various species of flora and fauna were exploited in efforts to claim a national symbol. The kiwi has persisted: it appears on currency, coins, consumer products, 'kiwi pride' campaigns, and is embraced as a popular colloquialism to identify New Zealanders: kiwis. We once had a Prime Minister who referred to himself as 'Kiwi Keith'. Some may ponder the bird's flightless, endangered and nocturnal nature. Yet New Zealanders are probably the only population of the world known internationally by a vernacular name that refers to the national symbol. We are referred to globally as 'kiwis'. Australians do not have similar ascription as 'kangaroos' and Britons are certainly not referred to as 'lions'.

Drawing from plant life, the silver fern's symbolism has remained strongly familiar in the sports arena. The 'silver fern' motif is sewn onto the garments of all New Zealand contestants in international sport — rugby, netball, Commonwealth and Olympic games. Wolfe supports this symbol as representing New Zealand as a fern-fringed land. He reminds us that in the early 1900s, New Zealand was often referred to as 'Fernland', the stories relayed home of tree ferns growing here in abundance coinciding with the Victorian mania for conservatories in which ferns were grown.

Wolfe's work shows the array of attempts to claim from nature a symbol to represent New Zealand, and the persistence of the successful symbols. National emblems draw constantly from nature to claim distinct identity. The national flag, still a version of the Union Jack and so demonstrating connections with Britain, includes the stars of the Southern Cross, a natural star formation that is consistently visible only from New Zealand (it can also be seen in certain parts of Australia, but only at certain times).

The drawing from nature supports Matthew Hirschberg's note that national icons in this country symbolise the natural environment, not the political or social components of environment as he observed in the United States. His examples demonstrate that national identity symbolism is learned, taken on board by individuals as they are socialised into belief in their nation.[13] While the claiming of kiwis, silver ferns or dramatic landscape may seem 'natural' to us, years of reception of messages telling us so has formed these beliefs — just as Americans grow up with repetition of their nationalistic messages as daily experience. When I was about eight or nine years old I was amazed to discover that other countries had glaciers and thermal springs with geysers and mud pools. Such a fuss was made of them here, I honestly thought we were the only country in the world to have such wonders.

For New Zealanders, praise of nature is readily supported by visual evidence. Superficially uncontroversial, the nature ethos persists as a dominant thread in national identity imagery. But why 'beautiful New Zealand'? Why not 'remote New Zealand', or 'distant New Zealand'? Clearly, because 'remote' or 'distant' by itself is not necessarily a positive attribute. If we live somewhere 'beautiful', we are somehow valuable by association with this context. International achievement is made much of, because of the small size of the nation, and its remoteness; but when it comes to enticing people here, 'beautiful' is more seductive.

'There is something about living on an island which gives a sense of smallness and isolation. One's island becomes one's separate world and the outside world becomes large and distant.'[14] Hirschberg reminds us that in fact New Zealand's land mass is similar to that of Japan or Britain; and that our perception of being 'small' is possibly because nations with whom we have some cultural values in common, in particular the United States and Australia, are very large.

New Zealand's composition of two major islands and many smaller islands suggests a physical distinctiveness which affects national character. These characteristics, with the distance from anywhere else, means New Zealanders can view their country as unspoiled, untainted, independent; a safe haven a long way from the bad things in the rest of the world.

Nostalgia for Nature

Memories of idealised previous times and childhood behaviour in the outdoors (a place in which to create an exaggerated mythical version of nature, or a 'hypernature') continue to validate retrospectively the nature myth. Nostalgia for the past and the romanticisation of nature entwine. (A regular example of this occurs every month in *North and South* magazine, which features a 'where I grew up' story. The most consistent theme in these articles is memories of the great time had on holidays at the beach.)[15]

Nostalgia for innocent participation in nature is articulated in an essay in *Te Whenua Te Iwi; The Land and the People*, where one writer longs for a New Zealand where the 'good, wild and sacred will be one again'. In short, he voices the classic nature myth of human 'badness' (cultivation of nature in unsympathetic capitalistic modes against nature) against the 'goodness' of untouched nature. This is an example of how readily nature may be romanticised.[16] The assumed pre-industrial, if not pre-agricultural, vision of nature presents a resource that is used non-exploitatively, a model of ecological harmony. In the face of evidence of human abuse of nature (for instance, species driven to extinction by humans), somehow we have managed, romantically, to invest in early humankind an innate respect for nature. It remains a convenient assumption underlying the nature mythology.

Perhaps a romanticised appreciation of nature is most likely to flourish in cultures with highly developed technologies. Nature is the one site for indulgence of our dreams of mastery over the earth, while we enjoy some kind of contact with the origins of life. These are experiences we do not foster very vigorously in urban settings. The natural world is the beautiful alternative to urban industrial civilisation. And in the urban world, a form of nature is cultivated, by dedicated gardeners and the ubiquitous motor mower, which keeps suburban gardeners mean, keen and dutiful.

Nature, identity and tourism

Like New Zealanders themselves, who contribute around 63% of all tourist spending here, overseas tourists submit to a process of acquiring concepts of New Zealand. As American tourism analyst Dean MacCannell puts it, tourism is not just a commercial enterprise, but an 'ideological framing of history, nature and tradition, a framing that has the power to reshape culture and nature to its own ends'.[17]

To attract tourists, nature is utilised mostly by nations where cultural history may be of less interest to visitors than the physical environment — the Pacific Islands; or Switzerland, which has over 50 million visitors annually. In New Zealand, images of mountains, rural pasture land, beaches, rugged coastline, forests, mud pools and so on reinforce tourists' expectations. The relative emptiness of the land is a curiosity, a luxurious contrast to the crowded cities whence many come. The place is 'familiar' to them from promotional material. They come to see the 'real thing'. To these ends attractions are promoted and sold.

Travel and communication are now faster, easier and more accessible than ever before. Tourism has become a $21 million per day industry for New Zealand, providing 170,000 jobs, and earning more than the income from annual exports of meat or dairy products or forestry or manufacturing. To achieve this, and aim at even higher yields, New Zealand has to compete with other destinations to offer something unique to the tourist that cannot be experienced anywhere else in the world.

In *The Culture of Nature*, Alexander Wilson explains that tourism reorganises perceptions of nature and our place in it, redefining the land in terms of leisure, at a time when most of the population is urban, with little direct connection with the land. 'It is no coincidence,' writes Wilson, 'that industrial agriculture, the spread of suburbs, and the growth of mass tourism all coincided in the mid-twentieth century.'[18] New Zealanders' national pride is stimulated by the same beauty and uniqueness that is sold to tourists: a reinterpretation and revaluing of that which is familiar, glossier on the brochures than in everyday reality, and removed from any context that might detract from the splendour. Selective items of nature imagery are compiled into an overall 'Beautiful New Zealand'.

This gains local support because it looks great; and also it promises to stimulate national economic growth while developing local employment.

The idea that nature is central to the way of life for New Zealanders allows further appropriation and manipulation: presentation of the 'way of life' itself is offered as a tourist attraction. This is acceptable because it is in the interests of the nation. The campaigns rely on people's concerns for financial security and employment — and the possibility that this might keep viable the way of life otherwise under threat. Regional authorities lend their backing to campaigns that might not only put them on the map, but also encourage economic growth and full employment.

Where once commodification was of the vista, or of the view translated into a painting or photograph to sell, people now expect to interact with nature. The present conservation ethic is to preserve whole ecosystems, rather than some visible exemplars of a species. Whale-watching at Kaikoura is a pivotal example of the inversion of historic relationships with nature. Last century Kaikoura was a whaling settlement, based on killing the migratory sperm and humpback whales. These days, selling the experience of seeing whales is more sustainable, and politically appropriate, than harvesting the diminishing numbers of whales themselves.

In the South Island in particular, a revitalisation of some small districts can be observed as the potential to exploit local natural resources is being realised. At Whataroa village in South Westland, a tourist enterprise has developed around the presence of white herons (kotuku) near the town. The fact that they are a breeding colony is tangible evidence that the visitor is viewing a viable 'authentic' ecosystem. This experience has been commodified in the form of local accommodation, a jet boat ride and a bushwalk:

a controlled 'adventure' component is paid for by the visitor. The herons have long been present in the district but the exploitation of them as a tourist attraction is more recent. It has been the 'salvation of the place', with spin-offs for hoteliers, shop owners, garage proprietors, and farm-stay hosts. The local entrepreneur and former farmer who set up White Heron Sanctuary Tours hints at more nature tourism events to come: 'I've got quite a few ideas, but we want to make sure we've got this one right first!'[19]

This entrepreneurial strategy commodifies pre-existing natural attractions. Anyone can drive up to the Fox Glacier car park then follow the track to see the glacier, for free. One simply goes for a walk, then stands and looks at the magnificent sight. I did this, for the third time, in 1994. The track to the glacier was very busy. A long row of yellow-clad people slowly and carefully trudged upwards in front of me. They were wearing matching warm parkas, woolly hats, sunglasses and hobnailed boots, carefully picking their way through the scree with identical walking staffs. This day of their fun holiday looked very serious indeed.

Against the stunning glacial backdrop, appropriately costumed, these actors were taking part in a real life eco-drama. The cry of keas offstage (back near the start of the track) added aural effects to the natural ambience.

The experience, which I'd remembered from previous times as an easy little walk, had now been mediated for these tourists by converting the placid (non-paying) traveller to a (paying) alpine adventurer, with all the correct garments and equipment required for such an adventure. By augmenting (artificially) the scale and danger, in effect they become participants in a recapitulation of nineteenth century experience of the vast and sublime. Literally, the fifteen-minute jog in track shoes has been transformed into a half-day guided 'expedition'. Simultaneously, a tourist company earns income and provides employment for tour guides.

The actual contact between visitor and attraction remains an uncommercial one. The commercial role of nature tourism or adventure tourism does not detract from the egalitarian access to nature, described above; the expenses are involved in getting there, and payment for accommodation, maps, souvenirs, guides, suitable clothing, film, and so on. Tourists themselves become promoters, taking home 'advertisements' for places they have visited: their own memories and stories, and the souvenirs and photographs that they bought to represent attractions that cannot be for sale.

An added benefit of nature as focus for commercial enterprise, is that various sorts of nature can be promoted for different demographic groups. Nature has something for everyone! And it doesn't matter if they don't speak English! Some visitors are content merely to look from a tour bus. Younger people often require something more dynamic than this. A range of nature tourism events responds to these needs. The 'outdoor adventure' industry offers the tourist a chance to participate in grand and exciting landscapes via white-water rafting, jet boating, bungy-jumping and various other thrilling sports. If held at a suitable location, some of these activities capture both sort of participants: those who, for instance, bungy-jump, and those who watch (delivered to the site by a tour bus, perhaps at the Kawerau River bungy-jumping site north of Queenstown in the South Island).

On the day I visited, over 400 people lined the banks to watch the bungy-jumpers leap off the historic Kawerau Bridge. Many aimed their video cameras at the jumpers, colourful active subjects to film against the barren grey landscape of the rock face on either side of the bridge. Amateur videos that pan across grand landscape can be very dull indeed; now, here was something to film! The riverside film directors/camera operators enjoyed a novel and satisfying experience, with the jumpers starring in the home movies of strangers.

A little later, once retrieved from the river below and still euphoric, the jumper is delivered back to the bungy depot and can immediately watch a video of themselves jumping. ('God, if I'd known my tee shirt was going to fall down like that, I would have worn a different bra!') They can buy the video, and a still shot from the video printed onto a tee-shirt — all within minutes of their jump. The bungy-jumper becomes a word-of-mouth and souvenir-bearing advertiser for both the event, and the magnificent scenery (sublime!) in which it takes place. Their tee-shirt also advertises the video in which they are the star. Many young people on tour post the video back to their parents. 'Look Mum! No hands!'

The movement of nature tourism to kinaesthetic experience — jumped into, paddled through, trekked across — has huge implications for tourism. The active tourist wanting (video-able) adventures in nature opens an array of possibilities for entrepreneurs. Imaginative ways to market nature can revitalise the small localities. However local community entrepreneurs have to compete with businesses operating outside, who may bring in their clients, enjoy what the locality has to offer, and then leave very few dollars in their trail.

At a small-scale local enterprise at Pukekura, near Lake Ianthe on the West Coast of the South Island, the exploitable resources of the local community includes two 'natures': the pastoral and the native bush. At the Bushman's Centre, set in an authentic West Coast bush glade, the visitor may look at instructive displays about traditional local land-based occupations, such as deer culling, possum shooting, eeling and farming. The centre conveys a nostalgia for mythologised, largely lost lifestyles of the West Coast. Through displaying these pursuits as heroic, and offering 'traditional activities' to keen visitors (horse trekking, deer shooting, bow hunting), it is ensured that the visitor can engage in 'real' activities that are to do with surviving in nature, and exploiting nature: all set in a magnificent natural bush setting. For the owners of the Bushman's Centre, who are no newcomers to trying to make a living in such a challenging physical environment, the hope is that by showing strangers these intriguing everyday local skills, they themselves might manage to survive the economic pressures of the present.

The ingenious 'consumption of nature' is taken a step further at the annual Hokitika Wild Food Festival. At this event visitors have the chance to consume such newly invented local delicacies as pukeko pâté, possum stew, goat curry and grilled huhu grubs. This attempt at the greening of the foodie is a new angle on 'nature to sell', and an example of manipulating and appropriating a (fictional) vernacular way of life as a novelty for tourists.

The ultimate goal of nature tourism, for local operators, is to make viable their own desired way of life. During times of economic difficulties, it is clearly apparent that the government will not save them. Local initiatives to try to sell components or representations of a remote vernacular way of life may enable those people to actually make a living there. They have grasped that, as Dean MacCannell tells us in *Empty Meeting Grounds*, nostalgia is 'a prominent feature of the motive for international tourism, and the rhetoric of cultural nationalism'.[20] While MacCannell worries that this nostalgia can be 'bad faith' celebrations of folk society (bad faith if they 'ultimately serve to promote artificial simplicity'), the move parallels aversion to the complexities of modern society; for instance the widespread problems of drug use, crime, and Aids. It is perhaps ironic that the rapid increase in global tourism may be an important factor in enabling small districts throughout New Zealand to maintain their traditional lifestyles, as they figure out ways to offer experiences of local nature for sale.

Eco-tourism, adventure tourism

People pay to view an authentic ecosystem. As one definition states: 'eco-tourism is purposeful travel that creates an understanding of cultural and natural history while safe-guarding the integrity of the ecosystem and producing economic benefit that encourages conservation'.[21]

The quality of the natural environment is what is promoted, to entice the eco-tourist to go whale-watching, dive with the dolphins, snorkel with the seal (a package of activities is a better proposition than just one thing!); to stay with farm home hosts; to take scenic flights to White Island or Great Barrier Island, and so on. Each year over half of the 1.3 million tourists who visit New Zealand include time at an officially designated conservation site. Other elements of New Zealand culture are marginalised, as the viewer follows the nature tour route. The 'real' New Zealand is the one promoted, paid for, photographed, and remembered.

Adventure tourism, like eco-tourism, takes place in nature, but the focus is adjusted to challenge and to victory over nature: a well established tradition in New Zealand history, after all. But in tourism it is not to do with land development, but with the new 'extreme sports'. Bungy-jumping, white-water rafting, parapenting, mountain biking, heli-skiing — all of these activities take place in stunningly beautiful, potentially treacherous surroundings. The activities are promoted as unique to New Zealand, through taking place in the unique landscape. Adventure tourism is set in places which may have accommodated tourists before, but are now marketed in a different way. For the intrepid visitor the new, invented, experience involves excitement, danger (but 'safe' because the guides are paid to take responsibility), and heroism. Admit it: would you bungy-jump?

Through this new catalogue of activities, new categories of tourist destination are invented. Places that may have lacked any claim to fame in the past become popular because these are the locations of the exciting new adventure sports.

All interconnections of nature and tourism are inherently ways of packaging, promoting and selling 'New Zealand'. The new marketing angle restates nature as representation of national identity. In the 'greenwash' approach, with its veneer of ecological correctness, nature as a commodity may provide an economic incentive to protect the environment. This aspect of New Zealand is advanced to the wider world. Nature imagery is New Zealand's commercial response to the global increase in tourism, a way of reasserting distinctiveness, for economic reward.

In this process of reinvention, nature is now more exciting and more dangerous than it used to be. New Zealand is a prime site for many extreme sports, which are not participated in very often, if at all, by most local people; but we all know about them, as they are heavily promoted in tourism advertising, and in television items purporting to represent New Zealand. The dangerous environment in colonial times was tamed; it has been made excitingly dangerous again. While some extreme sports have been around for a while, the constant addition of new variations (bungy-jumping out of a hot-air balloon or helicopter; rafting through a cave in the dark!) adds to the catalogue. And all take place against backdrops selected for their beauty. The landscape is once again sublime!

Tourism informs our identity?

These processes reaffirm the national collective imagination, starring nature as a dominant feature of national identity. The landscape is central to self-image, claiming distinction and superiority in the international contest for tourists.

The tourist wants to experience a culture different from his or her own, hence, as MacCannell explains, representing to him/herself 'the [broad] differentiation of modern culture'. That differentiation may in fact rest on nature. At the same time, he writes, tourism 'organises positive social sentiments: tourists seek affirmation of basic social values' which are not present in their daily work lives. Those values may well include a supposed love of nature.[22] Tourism that emphasises idealised nature satisfies those visitor needs. We have all heard tourists describe this country as 'so beautiful'. We want them to do that, because they will tell others, who may come here too, and spend more tourist dollars.

Most of us see landscape, wild or tame, from car or plane windows. But representations that glorify it are everywhere, as landscape is heavily commodified. Landscape used in this way can perhaps be dismissed as commercial convention, rather than any sort of conspiracy. How many North Islanders actually see the South Island mountains, apart from on brochures and as backdrops on television ads? Yet they clearly inform our collective identity.

Perhaps a glorious nature is also convenient, because it readily provides commercially valuable destinations for international visitors. These sites are unobtrusive, and fortuitously located away from centres of population, so that income can be generated by transporting the visitors and accommodating them. Different destinations compete for tourists; at the moment they have to arrive at the main centres, where the international airports are located. This spreads the tourist dollars, as a trail of expenses lies between them and the attractions they are most likely to visit. We tell them what to come and see; they then seek out those travel goals. Like the classic layout of any large supermarket, the goods most wanted and needed are far from the doors. While the trolley we take there is provided for free, we are encouraged to want to buy other temptations on the way.

Destinations, after all, are constituted by the advertising of tourism operators. New Zealanders' offerings fit the international pattern of representation of local culture for tourist consumption: the amplification of the exotic (for instance, commercial Maori culture shows); the glamorisation of the mundane (farm home stays); the strange made routine (the Fluteys' paua house at Bluff, with its endless stream of visitors); and the showcasing of the most aesthetic features that we have (natural attractions!).

So when a 'tropical paradise with friendly people' or a 'clean, green and friendly' place is promoted, the tourist expects to consume exactly that. The goal is an exotic experience compared with the tourist's own daily life; but it has to be safe, with a comfortable bed each night. Image-makers have to create a place that is interesting but not alien, exciting but not scary, and devoid of contentious local political issues. (Have a good time, and don't be taken hostage!)

In common with these contemporary tourism conventions, tourism in New Zealand is about building on existing myths, and generating and selling new ones. In its endeavour to commercialise, tourism says much about the public identity of a region and of a nation, and works to remythologise what was in danger of becoming quotidian.

New Zealand has heaps of things to mythologise! Nature, traditional Maori culture and successful, diverse agriculture and horticulture: together these have provided a unique space for visitors. Regional diversity of nature extends the scope and range of possible visitor attractions. We can read the process as manipulation of nationalist ideology. Representations of the 'egalitarian' landscape mask actual inequalities in social life, as tourists are sold the most sanitised version of a place.

It is easy, when overseas, to describe New Zealand as 'green', as if this is a generally agreed shortcut to explaining who we are, which saves us from bothering about thinking of something more evocative. Our own experiences may in fact be based on the grey concrete of cities. As Roland Barthes explains in *Mythologies*, such simple 'myths' function as systems of communication, containing meaning, concept and sign. A myth can be a 'whole new history', a handy distortion serving ideological purposes.[23] In New Zealand we can see that nature and landscape have become a powerful identity 'myth'. 'Green' is a splendid example of this; myth transforms nature into history and political expediency. We can then sell it to tourists as national identity; and half-believe it ourselves.

The status of nature within the notion of national identity renews a sense of pride in the nation. The authenticity of New Zealand's history embedded in nature is rarely challenged. The explorers, the pioneers, the gold miners and so on have left visible remnants; and there are still rural New Zealanders engaged with various forms of extraction from the land. Any travel around New Zealand readily authenticates national identity imagery.

Leisure in the age of technology calls for something more novel than technology. Fast-flying jets take tourists to consume nature. But it has to be good! Tourists pay a lot of money and take precious vacation time to travel, so want something worth the expense: natural splendour, enchantment, awesome nature, a more pure environment, untainted by industrialism, fascinatingly uninhabited, so therefore more 'natural'. Selling nature is selling an entire package, including anticipation, the experience itself, and the after-experience, as photographs and artefacts are displayed back home. To attract and please as many people as possible, a massive industry manufactures or constructs new experiences.

New Zealand tourism has a tiny 'niche' in the global choice of holiday destinations. Fewer than 1% of all global tourists come here annually, but the numbers are nevertheless significant to the New Zealand economy. In an industry hungry for novelty, with a particular 'branding' for each place, New Zealand is simplified for tourists as 'clean, green, beautiful — and remote'. These things clearly work as attractions.

Iconic landmarks

Landmarks are reproduced over and again to tell tourists who we are and also inform us. The iconising of some locations directs tourists to a few specific places, to fulfil their own expectations, and leave other places. Seeing the much-reproduced image affirms that indeed they are in the right place. This is New Zealand: look, you can tell because that is Mitre Peak over there! Familiar images in the tourist imagination drives the visitor towards the physical icons. Satisfaction is assured once the icons have been ticked off the list.

New Zealanders are actively encouraged to visit other parts of their country, to 'know their own country'. A lot of advertising is aimed at the domestic market, specifically at affluent Pakeha consumers. Through experiencing the famous landscape icons at first hand, we affirm the identity we have been socialised to believe in. Landscape features familiar all our lives have been presented to us as components of who we are.

I admit being very surprised on first visiting Milford Sound to see Mitre Peak, to find that the tide was out. I had only ever seen it photographed with the tide full in. Why did I then take such perverse pleasure in photographing it with mud flats and litter? The litter, by the way, was mostly cola cans and chip and chocolate wrappings, their international logos humbly juxtaposed against the national icon. The expected tranquillity was supplanted by the roar of small planes — six in the air at once — taking visitors out over the fiord. I hadn't expected a toilet block in the foreground, either. All this: and a congested car park, too!

Success in tourism affirms and validates the distinctive nature of specific localities, reinforcing local pride in the area and subsidising the drive to conserve the locality. Even if all New Zealanders do not live next door to the most stunning, heavily promoted chunks of nature, they can still claim this as their heritage. They believe the egalitarian myth that they share ownership of national parks, and have the right of access to the land if they wish.

Since the 1960s some observers have considered there must be basic limits to the potential scope and scale of tourism. The costs to the environment would necessitate restrictions, and congestion would degrade the quality of the experience to the visitor, as tourists ruin tourism. There has also been concern at the inherent conflict between tourists, their necessary infrastructure, and us, the non-tourists. Tourists might seem like useful low-impact money-carriers; but as they view the nature, might they not change it by their physical impact, and also change the culture? Would much of the population have to adapt, and work primarily in service of those who had come to view?

There is also the potential for conflict between tourists now, and future tourists. Will the next generations want to cover, again, the territory that bored them witless when shown it on their parents' holiday amateur videos? Will viewing nature go out of fashion; or demand even more extreme ways of interacting with it? What will be new and exciting to visitors next century?

Green tourism

The growth of nature tourism runs parallel with the growth of industrialism. In unhealthy industrial society, nature takes on spiritual values, and is claimed as a salve to metropolitan life. Commercial enterprises aimed at the nature-lover are prevalent in societies with sophisticated technologies. Dissatisfaction with 'unnatural' urban industrial society and its destructive and unaesthetic impacts on the landscape gives impetus to forms of tourism that purvey the opposite kinds of environments.

In New Zealand around 200 operators can service visitors seeking to fulfil this need. These numbers indicate the adaptability of tourism to commercial possibilities, following overseas examples. The New Zealand Natural Heritage Tourism Guide lists operators who specialise in natural heritage tourism: birds, wildlife, marine life, forest ecology, World Heritage Park sites. An expert guide accompanies each tour, ensuring the educative value of each experience. The goal is conserve and promote, and maximise visitor enjoyment. This industry has to compete internationally with other holiday destinations.

'Green' has a range of implications. 'Green', 'natural', 'organic', 'unpolluted' — these are 'added value' to products and services, recognised as morally and politically superior for consumers. Through 'green' marketing, conservation values are commodified. The particular natural quality of a product receives emphasis, superseding less desirable attributes, which may not be mentioned. In this way conservation values are exploited and promoted, to appeal to a greater number of discerning consumers; and providing opportunity for a slight political gesture on their part. Conservation policies may be expressions of awareness of concerns for the planet; but they are also effectively used in the economic interests of business and nation in promoting New Zealand and its goods overseas.

Until the mid 1990s the goal, regardless of impact, appeared to be a record three million visitors per year by the year 2000. Very recently, this has been proffered less eagerly, and an alternative plan has been to aim not at such high visitor numbers, but to encourage smaller numbers to stay longer and to spend more.

Bio-tourism, eco-tourism; however it is named, this has a huge world-wide market, with New Zealand a popular site for eco-tourism experiences. Perhaps it could be sold, some suggest, as 'exclusive, expensive tourism', like that in the Galapagos, where tourists pay around $3000 per week to visit, and numbers are firmly restricted. In this way, visitors enjoy an experience of enhanced quality through smaller numbers; they can also enjoy the status of a more exclusive experience. The suggestion is to move from 'old tourism' to 'new tourism', away from the standardised packages sold by promoters, to the customised tours designed for individual visitors or small groups. It is a solution that would address the collision between conservation and tourism in New Zealand.

The Department of Conservation has responsibility for all publicly-owned land in New Zealand, totalling five million hectares, or nearly 19% of the total land area. Its mandate is 'to protect natural and historical resources and foster recreation but only allow the use of these resources for tourism where this is not incompatible with the act's central purpose of protection'. Government commitment to this has apparently been declining, if we measure this by budget allowances. DOC's budget has been cut 23% since 1987. The department has to generate income to recover the shortfall, and aims at achieving a target of 20%. To earn income, it grants concessions and leases to private companies such as tourism operators; and markets tracks and walks as revenue-generating attractions. It is forced by economic need to do this, even though it is a contradiction to the philosophy of free public access under the National Parks Act and Conservation Act.

This 'user pays' philosophy places DOC in the ironic situation of being official custodians of the national estate, in daily charge of management of the iconic landscape and its preservation, maintenance and mediation. The under-funding and decreased income of DOC means it is forced to on-sell guardianship of some of the land under its jurisdiction. In effect, this means that as the resources which are the generative constructs of national identity are effectively sold, DOC stops being the guardian and becomes more like a pimp for national identity.

Pollution

Lost in the myth of 'beautiful New Zealand' is the ugly true story of pollution. In an economy that relies on agriculture and forestry, water and landscape abuse, erosion and contamination by toxic substances is widespread. Many pesticides banned elsewhere are in common usage here. Information from the Ministry for the Environment shows that over 10,000 sites in New Zealand might be affected by toxic wastes.

There appears to be limited concern nationally for this. There is no clear programme or strategy for resolution, and no basic standards to control waste disposal set in law. New Zealand is not a world leader in waste disposal. It is estimated that in New Zealand 2 kg of solid waste per day is dumped for every individual (compared with 1.8 kg for New Yorkers, for instance). While some local bodies encourage recycling, as a general policy this has not been implemented.

Most coastal towns and cities discharge raw sewage into the sea. For instance, in Wellington the solids are removed, but the rest is dumped. Industries are also to blame: tonnes of effluent from meatworks are dumped into waterways daily. An estimated ten tonnes of organochlorides are released into the Tarawera River each day by Tasman Pulp and Paper; and eight tonnes of gaseous and particulate fluorides emitted into the air daily at the New Zealand Aluminium Smelter.[24]

These few dramatic examples indicate a culture in which environmentally sensitive waste disposal is a low priority. Short-sighted and short-term solutions to waste disposal have been driven by economic, not environmental, considerations. Historically these strategies have been tolerated because of the relatively low density of population. Yet the clean green imagery survives this: first, because it is restated so often. and second, because a superficial glance out the window affirms this is so — even though the lush pasture has been drenched with chemicals, and the bush we see is just remnants of a far, far larger forest.

We are able to sustain this 'clean and green' image far better than we sustain land use. The concept grew out of nuclear-free slogans and activities, when the bombing of the *Rainbow Warrior* (1985) and New Zealand's stand against France made this little country a big (environmental) hero. By denying or ignoring environmental problems a myth is accepted into national consciousness, even though it would be better understood as a marketing slogan. Ironically, the more effectively the problems are resolved, the closer we will come to making the myth match reality: restoration of the environment which gave rise to the myth in the first place.

Central government does not develop and enforce policies that care for the environment, but 'shares' responsibility with local government. This is less conducive to sustainable environmental policies, and does not include a central and recognised system of penalties for those who do not comply. However, in a market-led economy the costs involved are the primary consideration. Green parties insistently explain that responsible management is possible, to protect the environment for present users and future generations.

Against these neglects and failings, New Zealand still romanticises its environment, drawing from history and the present to place the New Zealander in a scenic landscape from which is drawn an emotional and perhaps a spiritual response. Aha! This is one that can be commodified. If earning dollars from the environment is the priority, then the interests of tourism might serve to protect the environment; or not.

The 'beautiful New Zealand' myth has been sustained simply by having a small sparse population, and through negative comparisons with other places. New Zealand's boastful claims suggest that other western nations have little nature worth mentioning. The public celebration of nature implies a 'natural order' in which nature is good, in harmony with the population. When the population identifies with nature, then by association this implies positive things about the population. Nature as a source of national identity serves up a simple story: it simplifies history, it simplifies economics, it simplifies politics.

The tourism version benefits some groups economically and politically. It is also a delusion that the general population can believe in if they wish, because it is far more palatable than other versions of New Zealand. As observers of the tourism game, we know there are discrepancies between our own national cultural experiences and the images presented so gushingly to tourists.

A tour around New Zealand affirms this. Clean public facilities can by no means be taken for granted; and friendly service is not always present. But anyone making such statements is instantly howled down. Part of the national public relations exercise is to say only nice things (even if there is poor food and coffee in many towns, and limited service in some places). Negative comments make a visitor a 'moaner' or 'whinger'. New Zealanders refuse to acknowledge the validity of critical comments.

Tourism promotion is a means for the overt expression of culture, and its conscious reproduction. On a global scale, cultures are promoted for tourist consumption. The tourist coming to New Zealand 'consumes' the country, seduced here in the first place by images of identity. These have to be pleasing, commercial images, that will happily find a place in the tourist's imagination: unspoiled, unpolluted, natural, charming. As globalisation increases at the end of the twentieth century, assertion and celebration of national identity becomes more desperate. The manufacture of these images to feed the visitor's imagination is an on-going strand in the 'invention' of New Zealand.

3
'My grandmother had one of those!'
At the museum

Showcasing identity

Museums, reconstructed historic houses, cottages and villages are part of the process that tells the viewer about Pakeha culture. While the exhibitions are of artefacts from the past, they inform the present by the values inherent in the displays. In acclaiming local or national culture, the curators as guardians of the past undertake a public relations job for New Zealand.

The first museums were privately housed, eclectic collections of objects, often bought from travellers, who brought them back together with strange tales from distant lands. These museums were ad hoc recapitulations of British imperialism on a small scale in the Wonder House. As colonial processes infiltrated far-off countries and threw up curios and artefacts, the collections showed off the status of the owner, who could afford to house and own such wondrous objects.

New Zealand has had museums of sorts since as early as the 1840s, when there were collections of curiosities and antiquities on display for the public; for instance, at the Mechanics' Institute in Taranaki. Gradually, museums opened in various localities. Today there are around 160 museums in New Zealand.

Museums show us the past in the present, and tell us a version of national identity. Local and regional curators, as trustees of the public memory, select 'suitable' display material to represent the past. The local museum reminds us there was a past, and articulates the general shape of this past. This is often based on particular occupations, such as kauri forestry as represented at the Otamatea Pioneers' Museum at Matakohe, agriculture at the heritage museum near Hamilton, or whaling at the Kaikoura and Russell museums. The past becomes a resource to underpin present-day identity: valorisation of the past conveys pride in the present. In these reconstructions historic objects are props, used to represent a past that conveys distinctive local significance.

For those who donate the goods and set up the displays, or just live in the area and claim the museums as 'theirs', it is a statement of association with the district. For residents not involved in building the local museum, identity and history are claimed for them. They have an assumed role in the wider collective locally, and their historic sense of themselves is articulated without their input.

Many labels on objects at museums acknowledge the name of the donor of the item. That their names are present states family connections with the locality's past. In this venue older people in the community, and their predecessors, can leave a tangible mark. Through the display of their objects in the local museum status is added to mundane objects, which also carry the sentiment of memories of personal use.

Ancestors have a way of becoming heroes. As the personal knowledge of them fades, their lives are given a glory that may not have been present, noticed or toasted during their own times. Retrospective recognition for their contribution to an era of the locality, and of the nation, awards them the prize of names that live on through time. In commemorating specific personalities who lived in the district, the past itself is celebrated, and so is New Zealand. Local people contributed to building this nation, and the museum ensures their efforts are acknowledged.

Just who were the personalities of the district who are remembered in this way depends a lot on which families hung onto the artefacts of the past. If one simply tossed granny's mementoes away, then her memory may fade more quickly than the neighbour's granny, where the neighbour kept a whole household of possessions. Besides, some grannies had stuff that was evaluated as more worth saving. Some families value old possessions of their forebears more than do some others. These are the families more likely to be commemorated in local museums. They are also more likely to be actively involved in the representation of local history. Hence although the past status of some families may have been modest, it enhances the status of descendants if they offer objects for the collection, and have their forebears celebrated.

One (voluntary) museum curator of a reconstructed family cottage told me how good it had been for 'the community'. 'It really brings people together. There is a sense of common purpose.

It's a brilliant retirement hobby. Older people really have something to contribute to the community, and are happy to see their family treasures put to such a good use. They know that through these treasures their families cannot be forgotten. It means the younger generation, even if they don't think they are very interested now, get an idea about their great-grandparents' lives. That will stay with them.' This person was clear about his role as safe-keeper of public memory, quite determined that the history of the locality would not be lost.

The publicly imagined past is described by American writer Jo Blatti as 'a vast and rolling field or plain that is populated by clumps of symbolism that are mythical, experiential, and nostalgic'. She adds that for the viewer of reconstructions of history, their goal is to 'locate oneself or community selectively in time and space. It is not to use history as an analytic system for understanding time and space as socially constructed concepts, but as absolute places of another time.'[1] The more aesthetic and uncontentious the construction of the past, the better.

Visiting a recreated historic village or cottage is a visual experience, dependent on authentic objects to look at. The display should be appealing in its presentation. Cultural history becomes material history. In the case of rural re-creations, the goal is that they should be appealing in their rusticity. Old cart wheels and ploughs casually arranged in the garden contrive a rustic aesthetic: a tranquil ambience that conveys all is well.

Visitors are not only invited to remember. At these sites they are instructed on what and how to remember. The more picturesque, charming and novel features of the past are chosen, with any unpleasantness eliminated. As Game explains, '... there is nostalgia for the authenticity of craft production, the memory of which is itself being mass-produced. While memory is being mass-produced the notion of memory as individual or personal is constantly appealed to.'[2] The museum display, which echoes the currently extensively promoted 'country style' decor, is such an appeal to mass-produced memory.

Surveying the past

Between 1991 and 1995 I visited as many local museums around New Zealand as I could. I wanted to see how local history and identity were displayed to the public. What were these small local museums trying to tell us about themselves, about their local history, about their community's identity? Did that also inform visitors about national identity?

The buildings and objects at each site demonstrated several ways of conveying the past: through preservation of objects (the object in its original condition, unrestored); restoration (the genuine historic object made to look and work the way it did when it was built); re-creation (new objects made to look like historical artefacts); illustration (depictions of the past); and fabrication (invention of a plausible but fictitious past). Enthusiastic volunteers had put enormous numbers of hours of their labour into creating a tangible memorial to early settlers in their districts. Visitors who knew little or nothing of the locality's history could learn about it here; and the history of the families of the volunteers themselves would be preserved. Future generations would have an array of artefacts, appropriately housed, to convey to them the history of the area.

The 'past' at these sites usually began with Pakeha settlement of New Zealand. A few had some minimal reference to Maori residents of the area; but in some places it was hard to tell whether or not Maori had lived there at all in the 1800s.

I saw many similar tableaux of domestic interiors. These were always immaculate, and eagerly displayed the dignity of genteel colonial indoor life. Each tableau or diorama maximised the comforts and superior taste of the idealised colonial dweller. The piano or spinet implied refinement and leisure; the Sunday dinner-service, large lidded serving tureens and silver-plated accessories on the table implied a comfortable, indeed bountiful, life. The well dressed mannequins were clad in heirloom garments: clothing important enough for the family to preserve, so probably Sunday best. Grand fabrics and handmade lace represented women of elegance, taste and affluence.

These tableaux imply an unquestioning distinction between vice and virtue: good citizenship, stable family life, cleanliness, good health, and Christianity (there was always a Bible) as the characteristics of citizens. In this contrived reality inequalities are glossed over and the past looks charmingly innocent.

I discussed this with my companion on some of these visits. He'd agreed to come with me to Otamatea Kauri and Pioneer

Museum at Matakohe, about two hours north of Auckland, because I'd promised him lunch at the Gumdiggers' Café. Besides, I told him it was a splendid museum. We stood peering through the glass protecting the mock-up of the drawing room, in which the well dressed family members ostensibly went about their daily domestic occupations.

'No sleaze!' I observed. 'They really are a perfect family.' By this time I had been to a lot of museums, and seen a lot of perfect families.

'What would you expect?' asked my patient, good-natured companion.

'I'm just noticing that every one of the mannequins is on their best behaviour, because we are visiting. There is no suggestion that there might be a daughter or niece somewhere, on the game; or a son or nephew blowing the family fortune on card games.'

'But the real people then wouldn't have told us about aberrant family members, either!' he suggested. 'So these shop-window displays probably do convey quite accurately the public face of family life back then. Apart from being entombed in these glass cases, they are entombed in moral virtue!'

These interiors supposedly convey the private domestic life of the bourgeois colonial family but in reality show its public face. We happily speculated about ways in which a less well behaved family might be displayed. But who would want to claim such ancestors? The museum is expected to maintain its role as public relations agent for the past.

The domestic tableaux have predictable emphasis on the gender zones of the household: the father in the big chair, relaxing, the mother frozen in time as she bustles in the kitchen. The displays convey that their makers had unquestioningly accepted this style of representation familiar from museums they had visited. The presentation, as a romanticised and nostalgic view of happy family life, demonstrates emphasis of those values as more important than representing the contentious information of history. In early family photographs, convention and technical requirements (keep still!) had everyone posed and smiling. A similar convention is evident in these representations of domestic life.

Besides, orderliness and quiet gentility look good. The selection of middle-class interiors provides opportunity to display a far greater range of attractive domestic objects, in a prettier setting, than could presentation of a working-class interior. Many families' possessions go into each tableau. It is a good place to store heirlooms where they are appreciated, looked after, valued, and seen by thousands. For the donors of the objects, this also suggests that one's own family ancestors were genteel and refined: ancestors one can be proud of.

The emphasis is on the commodities they owned, and the leisure they enjoyed. There are indoor amusements evident in the spaces. These families were affluent, with time for leisure pursuits (whatever the mythology tells us about the slash-and-burn going on outside). They enjoyed great comfort, with plenty of material possessions. The family past is attractive: a palatable imaginary past; an invented past. The arrangement of objects must be decorative, to satisfy an aesthetic of interior decor understood from contemporary interior design magazines and televisual fictional interiors. This is less a tranquil past than a past tranquillised.

As French cultural theorist Roland Barthes sums up, 'myth acts economically: it abolishes the complexity of human acts . . . simply, it purifies them . . . it gives them a clarity which is not that of an explanation but that of a statement of fact'.[3] The enshrinement of ancestors in domestic museum tableaux places those characters beyond any possible criticism.

Praise the workers!

Regional difference in local history is probably most noticeable in the careful indoor or outdoor representations of workers important in the history of each area: for instance, the gumdiggers at Matakohe, gold-miners at Ross, and coal-miners at Westport. Workers are valorised at these sites, illustrating all the properties of the mythical New Zealand pioneer male described by Jock Phillips in *A Man's Country?*[4] There is often an extremely strong contrast between the way of life of workers conveyed at the museums, and the domestic interiors, which must have belonged to someone else.

The outdoor physical workers are always male in the reconstructed life-sized tableaux. That unpaid labour of wives and children upon which the early 'independent' settler was so dependent is not shown. Where women and children are included, they are encased in glass in immaculate interiors wearing their

Sunday best. Hence the history of women's contribution as workers is erased. Their role in nation-building is relegated to the reconstructed kitchen and elegant lounge. (Similarly, in the collection of outdoor murals depicting Katikati's history, even the mural marking the Suffrage Centenary shows a woman with her baby in the kitchen — not out voting!)

My favourite tableau of workers is of two life-size figures at the Matakohe Kauri Museum, modelled on actual people drawn from the history of the district. The two gumdiggers are set artistically in a corner against a mural backdrop of the gumfields, artfully drawn to convey the vast barren fields, thoroughly dug over by workers in search of gum. A framed poem on the wall beside the tableau tells a romantic version of the way of life of these gumdiggers. Here are some of the verses:

> The happy gumdigger who lived in shack
> Ti tree rails for a bed and a mattress of sack
> He worked at times just when he wished
> For meals were eels from a creek that he fished.
>
> Butter and bread he took in a sack
> For miles each day he'd walk from his shack
> With spear and spade to dig out the gum
> His washing plant was an old oil drum.
>
> An era has gone of the gumdigger's boom
> — and the ti tree brush he used for a broom
> To sweep out his shack — that was the way
> For the happy gumdigger of yesterday.

These poor gumdiggers are primarily picturesque. The surrounding opulence of the building itself and other magnificent, abundant displays deny the physical misery that must truly have existed for those diggers who camped in damp fields with little food and limited domestic comfort. Maori presence in the district at this time receives scant reference. This museum is unashamedly a memorial to Pakeha pioneer settlers, whose families donated or lent the goods displayed. Current political correctness has not yet caught up with the curators at Matakohe. One of the very few photographs of Maori in the gumfields is accompanied by a caption that tells us that the gumfield way of life was very suited to the Maori 'temperament'. And for the 'temperaments' of the other ethnic groups there, too? Or not?

Downstairs, in a glorious treasure trove of trinkets and other objects fashioned out of kauri gum (sailing ships, lighthouses, birds and animals) there is a near-life-size caricature of a Maori chief. As a valid historic artefact, it represents the view of Maori at the time it was made. The accompanying label tells us only about the maker, not the subject. This is 'telling' history!

As visitors arrive at this museum the person at the desk advises them on the best route around the displays. This is partly to enable visitors to 'tour history', but also to reduce congestion at the front of the building, where the shop and domestic interiors are situated. We are advised to start at the rear of the building, where the machinery and the tree-felling tableaux are set up. From there we move past the photographs and the tableau of the gumdigger's hut, past the jinker and big logs, through the alcove into the corridor of domestic tableaux, into side rooms full of toys and small artefacts made of kauri gum, then into another side room of kauri furniture, then downstairs to the gum room and gumdigger tableaux. The journey ends at the shop. Having looked at the displays one can then relax, browse and buy. Then one might cross the drive to Gumdiggers' Café.

Clearly, there is a 'way to look at history'. This is prescribed at this museum, to assist us with our imbibing of the past. The routes through museums aim to ensure one correct reading.

Lurking around, eavesdropping on reactions (research!) it was easy to tell that overseas visitors saw this museum as a representation not particularly of the district, but of New Zealand. While local people might protest that kauri trees only ever grew in the north of New Zealand, to visitors this appeared a trivial point. On their travels they had seen bush elsewhere in New Zealand; regional botanical specificity appeared to be of little interest. Though a far more impressive display of locality than most, the museum was seen to stand for 'New Zealand'.

'See one and you've seen them all,' one visitor told me. 'They all have the same things in them!'

Mining local history at Ross and Shantytown

Ross is a tiny village on the West Coast of the South Island of New Zealand. The population of about 360 is spread around a large rural district. The people who run the local historic society work hard to insist that, even if it doesn't look a fascinating, colourful place to people passing through today, well, it used to be.

At Ross a small number of local people have been working with the Department of Conservation to re-create an historic gold-mining village. They have put great effort into this, in the belief that nothing of Ross's present will attract tourists, so they must draw from the past. Much of their display material is donated family memorabilia. These artefacts link present Ross inhabitants (and museum developers) to those early miners who settled there, and produced descendants.

The reconstructed gold-mining village project has now been under way for some years, with original old buildings from the district moved onto the site and restored; and existing old unused buildings nearby (a church and a cottage) converted for inclusion in the gold-mining village.

In 1995 there was cause for alarm. Gold prospectors announced that the little town of Ross was probably sitting on around $700 million worth of gold.

'It's terrible!' a member of the restoration project told me. 'They want to dig up the town. After all our work on the [reconstructed historic gold-mining] village!' He explained that local people were unlikely to receive direct benefit from the gold claim. 'It's okay for the young ones, they'll be compensated for their houses, and will be able to afford to move somewhere else. But for us old people, it's a disaster! The gold licence will be sold to an Australian company, they'll make a fortune; and we'll lose our homes and our historic village!'

In this analysis, the reconstruction of a gold town of the past is far more highly valued than a gold town of the present. History is colourful, a form of recreation for those reconstructing it in the present; in this process of reconstruction, history can be controlled. The historic village belongs to those who live in Ross, and who built it. A new gold-mine on the same site belongs to somebody else, from outside: anonymous, exploitative, capitalist, with no sentimental links with the place and its past.

Further along the West Coast, and far larger than Ross, is Shantytown. But because Shantytown is fabricated history, and not really an historic town at all, and does not even have a 'real' name, Ross residents see their village as 'authentic' (a term laden with righteous moral values). Shantytown demonstrates that 'colonial' is a style, as much as a period.

The problem for Ross is that Shantytown is much more popular than Ross because it is more 'fun'. It has add-on attractions that are not historically accurate, such as fun rides, fast food outlets, and contrived 'photographic opportunities' (visitors can dress up in period clothing and have their photographs taken. The final picture, in sepia tones, looks authentically Victorian). These activities are viewed with some indignation from Ross, where the town promoters are finding tourism is a competitive business.

To their surprise, it seems that simply conveying local history is not enough for fickle passers-by, however much pleasure it provides for those developing the project. At Shantytown the developers have found that commodification of the past is more commercially viable when offered with popular consumer goods and novel experiences, such as steam train rides and the opportunity to actually handle old tools and household appliances. The enterprise is consciously aimed at all age groups. Their theme park approach presents West Coast history as a consumable exotica for tourists, with 'something for everyone'.

Both of these gold town re-creations start with the same theme. The gold-miners of the past and the farmers supplying them with food become historic heroes. Hard manual labour is praised as 'real work', character-forming not only of those individuals, but an inherent quality required for the making of a (colonial) nation, precisely as described by Jock Phillips[5] and Keith Sinclair.[6] The supposed wholesomeness of that way of life is assumed to have created the national character. Rural pioneers are claimed as the real pioneers: the ones who slashed and burned rugged bush, turning it into Gardens of Eden, and in the process generating national Pakeha mythology.

At Ross (and elsewhere), miners laboured for specks of gold in freezing rivers, and a few are survived by descendants who celebrate them. These descendants, mostly people who have retired from paid employment, have taken as their mission the keeping alive of local myths. With groups of volunteers working in this way all over New Zealand, the mythologies common to Pakeha New Zealanders are maintained, and willingly consumed as New Zealand 'history'.

Clydesdale Museum

Agricultural industries and a rural way of life are displayed at the Agricultural Heritage Museum at Mystery Creek near Hamilton, generally known as the Clydesdale Museum.

Again, in these buildings and outside display spaces, one is directed on a specific route around the exhibits. In this case, because the period displayed is not fixed, as at the kauri museum, the journey follows the passing of time and the development of innovations in the agricultural industries.

This museum tracks changing technology from colonial times to the present. It does not locate colonial dairy production in a remote or disjunctive past, but gives us a continuity from the story of the six cows that were brought to New Zealand by Samuel Marsden, to the impact of scientific twentieth century butterfat analyses and sterile production methods. Its credibility regarding access to the future of knowledge and innovation in agricultural technologies is enhanced by the placement of the museum at Mystery Creek. Over three days each year more than 100,000 people visit the agricultural field day at Mystery Creek to see the cutting edge of agribusiness, and to place their orders for whatever of the very newest technology they now need. In turn, the field day is set against the history of industry, which has preserved, restored, recreated and fabricated items from the rural myth, a central part of national identity.

Rangariri Battle Site Heritage Centre

A new enterprise about forty kilometres north of Hamilton is the Battle Site Heritage Centre at Rangiriri. This small roadside business, still in its infancy, aims to redress the present limited understanding of the local battles of the bloody land wars, which took place on this site in 1863. The site has always been preserved, and is marked with a monument to the Maori warriors and British soldiers who were killed here.

The owner of the café has undertaken extensive research of the events that occurred on this site. Concerned that Pakeha histories have always told just one side of the story, he has set out to reconstruct the actual site, including the redoubt and outworks. However, most of this is yet to come. At present, the visitor can enjoy a snack at the café, look at the dioramas (still in the process of being assembled as I write this), and see the growing collection of memorabilia on display. Best of all, for a mere $2 visitors are escorted into a purpose-built cinema and shown a 20-minute documentary about the land wars. This is presented as a triple slide show, drawing from paintings, drawings, lithographs and newspaper material of the time, with an appropriate soundtrack. The sites in the old pictorial material are also shown as they are in the present, juxtaposing the events of the past on the present visible landscape. Visitors actually see in the slide show, then later walk on or park next to, the same sites as those in the old images.

This is a completely different representation of history from any others I have visited, because it deals with Maori-Pakeha conflict, the displays put together after a rigorous research of chronological events. They are exactly located in the contemporary physical landscape, and within the historical cultural landscape. This enterprise demonstrates that it is possible to integrate Maori and Pakeha history, even with regard to such contentious events as land wars.

The past in real time

Some museums have 'live days'. Costumed performers demonstrate blacksmith skills, bread baking, woodwork, iron forgery and perhaps ploughing with draught horses. Colonial skills are shown as romantic historic artefacts, celebrated for their contribution to present-day New Zealand.

Live days combine aspects of theatre, museum, and amusement park, but do not wholly replicate any one of these. At Shantytown and at the Museum of Transport and Technology (Motat), Auckland, on 'live days' the actors as tradespeople explain the processes and use of their goods to visitors.

At Motat a volunteer posing as a baker told me that the scones he offered were made from the genuine original recipe, followed from a cookbook found in the cottage drawer.

'It's the real thing,' he explained. 'I just changed it a bit, and I use far better quality ingredients than they would have had. And I always use margarine instead of butter.'

The authenticity of the historical experience is automatically betrayed, both by the adaptation of the past to the more expedient present, and as their pedagogical function requires the actors to explain their activities to the audience, rather than theatrically reenact what might have been daily-life conversation. Howick Village is perhaps the only reconstructed colonial village in New Zealand where volunteers research individuals from local history, and act them on live days, or on special live evenings open to the public. Aircraft and traffic noises are explained away: 'a shooting star'; 'a storm coming'.

With massive numbers of visitors to support them, some outdoor museums overseas go a lot further than this in the re-enactments. At Williamsburg in Virginia, a reconstructed eighteenth century city employs dozens of actors. These 'People of the Past' assume the identities of town residents, and offer visitors the opportunity to 'debate matters of philosophy with Thomas Jefferson. Share the latest gossip with Grandma Geddy. See history through the eyes of the free and enslaved African-Americans who made up one-half of the town's population. Eavesdrop as the "residents" of Williamsburg discuss religion, slavery, Indians, politics and tobacco prices.' As well, visitors can enjoy 'the best shopping in history', the Williamsburg shops promising to sell exactly the same kinds of goods as were sold here 225 years ago.

We can readily see the difference between historical and other amusement parks. In the historical attractions the first agenda is the archiving and production of the historical setting (for instance at Howick Historic Village). The production of amusement is secondary, as the curators believe history is interesting in itself. At theme parks, superficial reference to history is made as a resource for 'themes'. Dreamland in Queensland has a reconstructed old gold-mining village, where hundreds of sheets of rusty corrugated iron have been assembled to create a makeshift mining town.

But the emphasis is firmly on entertainment. Rides, 'photo opportunities' (cute things to stand next to for family snapshots — helpfully labelled 'shoot from here'), distorting mirrors and participatory activities have priority over educative information. 'Gold-mining history' functions as a picturesque backdrop to activities that could be adapted easily to any setting. History as stage set is also demonstrated at the 'state of the art' shopping mall at Surfers Paradise, Pacific Fair, where one section of the mega-mall is a series of shops housed in brand-new reproduction colonial streets. Designer goods of the present are for sale in an environment that promises the supposed goodwill and honesty of the past.

Pakeha past

The selective constructions of the past in museums and restored cottages dotted around New Zealand may be described as a Pakeha folk-history. While Maori have their own ways of preserving history, the clash or entwining of cultures during settlement appears too difficult for curators to address in these exhibits. The only exception I noted was the still-developing Rangiriri battleground enterprise. It was different, too, in that it is the work of an individual, not a local committee or historic society. The owner's agenda is not primarily a public relations effort for the local community, but a passionate drive to restate this particular era and strand of local history.

Elsewhere, the displays appear determined to bowdlerise political issues, offering 'untainted' versions of the myth of colonial life. They show that the settlers worked hard on arduous tasks, but in a Garden of Eden context. Any actual garden will be filled with traditional English cottage garden plants (for instance at the Putaruru Timber Museum, and at the Wagener Museum at Houhora), representing a trans-planting of a romantic British rustic lifestyle. Poverty is recast as modesty or simplicity; wholesome, frugal, warm, clean and cheerful.

Maori reproductions of the past are usually totally separate events, at separate venues, the content unconnected to particular events of Pakeha colonisation. Maori cultural displays such as haka, poi dances and wood carving are popular with tourists for their aesthetic content, not their political significance, which is not stressed, for instance at Whakarewarewa, Rotorua, and at the Auckland War Memorial Museum.

These commercial representations of Maori culture do not underline the fact that the traditional culture being conveyed is no longer the everyday experience of Maori people in New Zealand. Ethnographic museum displays of Maori artefacts do not recognise the fact that Maori now live quite differently from when these objects were collected. Displays imply a static culture. Most museologists do not seem to have found a way of displaying contemporary Maori culture, or its relationship with Pakeha culture.

What we find is that the material in museums tell only one fragment of a single story. Museums lack, at present, ways of telling very many other stories, as preference stays with a decorative version of the past. An illustration of this is a series of beautifully crafted inlaid wood pictures displayed in a row on a wall at the Otamatea Pioneer Museum. The pictures are replications of famous New Zealand scenes from history, recognisable from paintings that have been reproduced numerous times: the signing of the Treaty of Waitangi, the first church service conducted by Samuel Marsden at Russell, the burning of the *Boyd*, and so on. These painstaking versions are identified by the name of the maker; but there is no information at all about what they depict. For locals their familiarity means no extra information is required; for visitors they are probably barely worth a glance. The inclusion of these objects is apparently for their crafting; not for the historic events to which they refer, or to the paintings from which they are derived. In this way, history is merely a series of motifs for decoration.

Romanticisation of the past appears perfectly acceptable, especially in a culture where so much romantic material is consumed daily. The fictions of television are consumed as leisure for many hours per week, and escapist home computer games have quickly grabbed popularity. Most viewers or users see nothing odd about spending so much time absorbed in fictional worlds.

For the visitor, the journey around the museum is similar to window-shopping (another form of fiction!). The historic period called 'colonial' becomes a place to visit. Walking through the 'sets' is like participating in a television show, where such sets and props are familiar. With a village reconstruction we can walk into the sets. For instance, at Shantytown visitors actually *become* the actors in the huge set with 'authentic' props. This is less passive than watching television; but also less exciting than television, where diverse characters and exciting plots provide action against this backdrop. At some overseas museums now the addition of plots and contrived action adds to historic reconstructions. For instance, at Williamsburg visitors become researchers, interviewing people from the past, played by live actors. They can also become actors themselves, donning costumes to join the daily domestic routines, or to participate on a jury or in the gallery of a mock trial. And at the Museum of the Moving Image (MOMI), in London, visitors are encouraged to participate as actors in a movie, with costumes provided.

At the New Zealand museum village, dates and facts are less

important than the context or the overall effect. The history of historians does not have much of a place here: this is a visual nostalgia. Tableaux are often constructed as representations of a period called 'colonial'; not relating to any specific year. The appeal is to sentimental memory. The production of public memory is juxtaposed against the appeal to private individual memories and associations of objects. At the same time, the reconstruction is a guarantee of authenticity: material evidence states a plausible past. Together, these museums represent the materiality of New Zealand history.

'My grandmother had one of those!'
In all of the sites described above, everyday, mundane buildings and tools of colonisation — of civilising the wilderness — become heroic icons. Old tools and cart-wheels, wagons, water pumps and domestic items are symbolic motifs of another time, the objects quaint and interesting, so therefore the times they represent similarly so. There are hierarchies of valuable qualities in the objects themselves: age, curiosity, or clear connection with local or national event carry varying status.

Through the display of objects, abstract historic concepts become myths. For the viewers, an analytical reading is hypothetically possible (under the paradigm of objective history). Usually, however, recognition of the buildings and objects is located in the viewers' own biography. 'My grandmother had one of those!' This often-heard comment articulates the way the viewer connects to the items on display. The viewing is mediated in the present by nostalgia. Hence the museum depends to a large extent on the familiarity of some objects, to maintain interest. Totally foreign objects would not be meaningful. Besides, the viewer will readily recognise these objects of the past because many of them are now mass-produced as commercial nostalgia objects in the present. Visitors are also likely to have some understanding of how the objects work, or are used: far more simply that the complex technology of today, that is difficult to comprehend or explain.

Usually little actual explanation is offered with the objects. Many of the items are already familiar, from contemporary reproductions and from advertising images: antique tools, household goods, clothing and old buildings are often used as photographic props, decontextualised. And if one really wants them, many shops stock new brass miners' lamps, and reproduction colonial kitchen accessories. But museum items have the added value of age. Antiquity itself becomes a commodity with enhanced value and status; purely because they are old, some items become objects of our attention.

It seems that through displaying objects as representation of an earlier stage of our culture, the idea is reinforced that the objects contain desirable qualities. Thus the positive story of material progress becomes a positive reading of history. Historic displays teach materialism as they implicitly promote the interests of the business and manufacturing classes. Those classes produced objects that can be preserved, compared with the home-made disposable solutions to practical problems made at the same time (the famous No. 8 wire object! the kerosene tin furniture of the Depression!). Their significance is lost in displays celebrating and commemorating the New Zealand colonial way of life. Rugged colonial rural dwellers' dependence then, as now, on urban manufacturers is never spelt out; nor is the reverse relationship considered. Museums do not analyse production, agricultural export history, or rural-urban tensions. Most displays of New Zealand popular history and national identity include an array of rural references as aesthetic objects, but the implications of this reach further, to convey positive qualities of national character.

There are inevitable historical discrepancies in the commercialisation of history. For instance, we understand that the objects produced in the museum shop as replicas of the items in the museum display are not sold to be used as they were originally intended. The hand-dipped candles displayed for sale may match historical processes in their making; but they will be bought as gifts for people who use electricity to light their homes. The candles have aesthetic and romantic appeal, rather than any real consumer need for their original function. And New Zealand's only qualified wheelwright — trained in an English working museum — finds his customers in tourism, garden centres and the film industry, the original use for these handsome wooden wheels no longer present. This form of nostalgia is also ingeniously manufactured in the current crop of souvenirs for tourists, in picture frames and other objects crafted from lichen-covered fence posts. In buying these objects the purchaser is taking away a symbol of the New Zealand agricultural tradition.

An interesting variation of this is represented by items for sale in the Otamatea Pioneer Museum at Matakohe, where one may buy a turned kauri bowl. The bowl may look like any kauri bowl, crafted on a lathe, but an accompanying certificate identifies the bowl as being made from local swamp kauri, carbon-dated at 1700 years old. Hence the bowl is not just a casual consumer product, but the delivery mechanism for reified time: the consumer is buying literal antiquity, as well as an object representing New Zealand. In fact, the bowl is *older* than 'New Zealand'! By contrast the granite cladding on a city high-rise building, which may be seven million years old, is not seen to validate the building, because the building is not read in a museum context. Yet both the bowl and the building are contemporary artefacts. The age of the granite is not revealed; and the building is not a conscious symbol of identity.

One writer described this process of symbolically acquiring and possessing the past in a British context: 'The tourist can hunt for a bargain ... history is a repository of artefacts to be consumed. The hunting for bargains, whose associations with the past can be quite tenuous, becomes a metaphor for the consumption of history, the old.'[7] To illustrate: at New Lanarch, Scotland, I saw old spinning bobbins recrafted into objects for sale in the tourist shop. One can buy toys, bird feeders, and other decorative objects, not for the need of such items, but to recall Robert Owen's social experiment at New Lanarch. Reprocessed into the consumer item it has a function, making it more saleable. But simultaneously abstract concepts such as the social ideals and values of Owen, and the charm of the New Lanarch village, are reified and become consumable in the form of these saleable objects.

At New Zealand museum tourist outlets, as well as consuming history by making purchases, the shopper also, symbolically, buys New Zealand. The objects, once taken home, are tangible representations of place. 'New Zealand' is permanently represented in the kauri bowl, or in tourist kitsch: sheep and mountains trapped in glass domes with fake snow; kiwis crafted from possum fur; plastic tiki; disposable paraphernalia of tenuous function and dubious design that exist solely because they can be sold as mementoes of place. The kauri bowls sell well, I was told; so do the fur kiwis and the 'Beautiful New Zealand' coffee-table books. These objects are uncontentious, aesthetic, and portable: representations of nation that function as takeaways for itinerant shoppers.

Touring the past

In 1994, 1.32 million tourists visited New Zealand. Of these, 47% (more than 600,000) visited at least one museum during their time here. Serious history was not usually the focus. The museum experience has to be intellectually undemanding, and the more entertaining the better. Visitors rarely wanted much more information about the objects on display than they brought to the encounter, or could quickly see. Often no information at all was required. Those I spoke with wanted to have fun! Participating (panning for gold, riding on a horse-drawn wagon), and taking photographs or videos that visually place the family in picturesque history, were the most favoured activities. Two popular sites for photographs were outside the picturesque colonial cottage at Motat; and at the entrance of the Otamatea Pioneer Museum, where the museum's name would appear as information in the photographs. The colonial wooden cottages appealed far more to overseas visitors than to New Zealand visitors; after all, many of us live in such houses, or drive through streets of them daily (and, sadly, have some idea of their inconveniences and what it costs to maintain them!).

The past presented to tourists had to be inoffensive, simplified, with clean toilets and a cup of coffee to hand. I asked the manager at one well-attended local museum to account for the museum's popularity: it was packed with people the days I was there. His instant answer: 'clean toilets! People get to know. It's the main thing a lot of the older tourists, specially, think about!'

For those really interested, historic facts can be sought out elsewhere. Meanwhile, the experience at the museum offers a conservative history for undemanding consumers. The exhibits create and perpetuate the most popular perception of New Zealand history, uncritical and positive. This becomes a pervasive form of national public relations.

It is clear that overseas visitors read symbols of the 'local' as representations of national identity. Those I spoke with at museum sites often could not remember the name of the place where we were at the time ('where are we now?' has a 'does-it-really-matter?'

ring to it), and saw the displays as 'New Zealand'. As I lurked inconspicuously around the displays the most often heard comment (in English) apart from 'My grandmother had one of those,' was 'We used to have one of those when I was a kid'. This came from non-New Zealand visitors as well as New Zealand viewers. The objects conveyed 'meaning' to the viewer: familiarity or nostalgia was apparently sufficient.

At the sites I visited, the shop (if there was one) was often more popular with visitors than the displays. I watched four bus-loads of visitors at the Otamatea Pioneer Museum, for instance, and noted that most of them spent more time in the shop and at the café than looking at the museum. 'I've seen dozens of museums! They are all the same!' I was told by one (New Zealand) shopper. So much for efforts to emphasise distinctive localism in these regional presentations!

Processes of historic reconstruction demonstrate the fundamental principle of capitalism, that anything can be commodified. This includes local and national culture, history, manufactured 'traditions', and tangible mementoes of place. The sites I visited around New Zealand showed that local people were hopeful about the potential of history as a small industry, with possibly large returns as the tourist industry grows. In places that have not participated in the much-vaunted economic recovery; where unemployment is high; where the local population looks as if it will never again grow, the tourist is seen as the potential saviour.

Development of a local museum is a way of restating the value of place, both to those still living there, and to visitors from elsewhere. The retrospective view articulates its historic importance: perhaps for an early industry, long gone (gold-mining? whaling?); or perhaps for the uniqueness of its settler group, for instance at Puhoi, which was the only Bohemian settlement in New Zealand; or at Akaroa, the only French settlement. 'We're on the main road, there is constant traffic. But we have to have something people will stop for,' I was told at the Putaruru Timber Village Café. 'As a small town we don't have a lot to offer. The timber museum makes this a more interesting place to stop. Gradually, as we develop it, people will come here especially to see it.' The Otamatea Kauri and Pioneer Museum could well be their model for this.

The reconstruction of buildings and machinery of the coal-mining industry at Westport, and the gold-mining village at Ross, are but two examples of attempts to 'sell' the past, to increase income in the present. In those areas where unemployment is very high, rather than allow a town to die altogether, this form of resuscitation just might give the town a tenable new life. The sense of exclusion from an active role in the national city-driven culture is being addressed.

The past: a journey

A more literal journey into the past can be taken on heritage tours, guided journeys around historic sites, which sometimes continue for several days. We are invited to visit, view and experience attractions that the organisers have selected, to fit a theme of local history around those remnants of the past that are still visible.

The organised journey is offered as a way of maximising the ratio of time to attractions, the best deal that promises as many 'destinations' as possible, and as little uneventful landscape. The organisers will plan the journey of discovery for us, because their local knowledge means they can edit out for us the boring, less historic, or less physically accessible possibilities along the way.

'Heritage Tours' and 'Heritage Trails': the use of the very term 'heritage' conveys a version of the past that should be valued in the present. It has an 'official history' ring to it. Any competing (un-heritage?) histories are dropped away.

Usually heritage tours mean us to literally take a journey, the journey contrived to take the visitor 'back in time'. The Gold Trail tours out of Dunedin in the South Island invite us to 'travel in the comfort of a modern mini bus' to visit old gold-mining sites, travelling through spectacular landscape. During the journey one may pan for gold, and stay at an historic hotel. Part of the mystique of the past is present in the old road names: the Pig Root; Moonlight Road. There is also the opportunity to pick fresh fruit in season, see the Roxburgh Dam, and the new dam at Clyde, and have afternoon tea at an 'historic' hotel. Everything possible to do along the way is added to the itinerary to increase value for the tourist.

The promotional material for these tours sets a general historic tone. The main image might be an old gold panner, or an antique vehicle: the latter suggesting transport across time, perhaps by horse-drawn wagons. These illustrate how we can physically move into the past, where we may encounter representations and icons of another time. For New Zealand visitors, we are not so much 'tourists' as descendants connecting to 'our' past. Anything old is seen through respectful eyes. Disused buildings are historic evidence of an 'authentic' past. And on the journey there is also the landscape in which that history took place, sliding past the bus or train window much as television images change before our eyes.

Local histories: written

Parallel processes of invention take place in written local histories. Local history is reinvented to comply with notions of appropriate local versions of national identity. The writer's local ancestors become 'heroes'. There are dozens of these, including *Early Manukau: Secrets of Yesterday* (1990),[8] (its first chapter is 'Utopia — The Garden of Eden'); *Sam Chapman's Coromandel in the Golden Days* — 'a town of intrigue and romance' (no date);[9] *Waves of Change in South Warkworth* (1987);[10] *Song of Two Waters — An Early History of Waiatarua* (Wade, 1979).[11]

These works inevitably romanticise the struggle to success — always success — as new settlers tamed the wilderness into a bountiful (Pakeha) Eden. Drawing on the traditional appeal of Arcadian visions, a spirit of co-operation and community solidarity is projected onto the settlers. This is then shown as 'the way it was'. If there were upheavals such as war, depressions or natural disasters, utopias were not threatened.

Any written history is a perspective on what happened, not a record of reality. Only some things that happened are chosen and included. Lay people possibly assume that historians write about universally agreed-upon historic facts. Museums reinforce this notion. Historians are image-makers as well, as they select the 'bits' they want to represent or portray as history. As New Zealand historian Jock Phillips explains, 'although the historian strives for objectivity, the interpretation and even the facts the historian looks for are to a considerable extent a reflection of his or her own background and prejudices'.[12] Along with meticulously researched, useful material, further biases or distortions are added to the national collection.

For instance, national heroes are mainly male. They have more status in their lives, and there is more documented information available about them. Women are often not integrated into historic narrative. Did women have so little part in building this country? The heroes who thread their way through the history books show that inequalities exist in written history itself. In fact New Zealand history as a sequence of eras is often recited in terms of male occupations: first the whalers and sealers, then the labourers who came to farm; then the gold-panners and gumdiggers, then the coal-miners, and so on.

The style of written history known as 'local history' usually starts with Pakeha settlement, or with a description of the local natural landscape. Geographic areas determine the subject matter. The added value for the local historians is the personalisation of history, with the naming of actual characters who lived locally, and who would not be named in national history. Usually these personalities — often the author's ancestors — are central to the text. Inevitably some individuals and groups of people are excluded; for instance, itinerants in the district who may have played a significant role in blending populations from different parts of New Zealand, but who were not part of important established local families.

The goal in local written histories appears to have been to escape traditional formalistic sequential histories, which concentrate on policy and status. This is the sort of official history probably familiar to most local historians from their own schooldays. The local history genre has tended to largely ignore national political issues even where they impinged on locality. The elimination of powerful external forces puts the place in something of a time-space vacuum, with no larger context, as local folk history is explicated.

Nevertheless, if a local society is to be considered 'local', this implies that it must also belong to some bigger national body. No community in New Zealand is completely autonomous or tidily deployed on the ground, without overlap in personnel. Even community boundaries may be unclear, as residents are perhaps employed in one location, and send their children to school in another, in the opposite direction. There may be defined cultural edges, for instance by ethnicity, history or economic circumstances, such as at Kawakawa, gateway to the affluent tourism resort of Paihia; and just six kilometres away Moerewa, a town suffering depression since the closure of the local freezing works some years ago. Generally identity is labelled by geographic coherence and shared cultural association. Within this space are some residents who, over a long period of time, are aware of, and wish to emphasise, distinctiveness from everywhere else.

New Zealand's Pakeha history is short enough for some old people to be able to link, by memory, to a generation whom we would call 'pioneers'. A person in her 80s may remember stories told to her in childhood by her grandmother, of that grandmother's own childhood; this takes us back to about the 1860s. Memory and oral history shorten the past into something that involves direct family connections. And because New Zealand is about the same age as photography, we can see photographic images of some of the first Pakeha people to live here. This relatively short history, readily retrieved, means that many local histories have been compiled that go back to documentation of the start of their communities. This has been helped by the punctuation of the time frame by the official New Zealand Centennial in 1940, when much archival material was compiled in permanent form.

If the local community appears insignificant to the outside, one of its strengths is in the valuing of itself. Through documentation of events in the locality, even where explicit details are limited to the parochial, a flavour of nation is implicit. As the particular place was developing, so was the nation. Major events, such as war, that impinged on the locality, may include discussion not of large international political movements, but of the impact on the community of local men going off to fight. The implicit parallel with national history cannot be obliterated. A strong strand of national history can be read from the sum total of local community histories.

Concrete myths

All of these processes make concrete the myths of colonialism. An imaginative, reconstructed, colonial domestic life is made physically present to viewers. The collections of objects and written histories become aesthetic repositories for material mementoes of local families, reinforcing their affiliation to place. Instead of manufacturing new goods, 'heritage' is manufactured. Each site celebrates picturesque components of the past: a past that is superficially plausible, and where the viewer does not seek closer investigation, which might reveal the distortion.

Perpetuation of the myth of the ideal past (implying a positive present), is demonstrated at the sites cited above, spread throughout New Zealand. Mythology binds the volatile present to the (unrefuted) regularity of the past; to a nostalgic version of that past. Myth is definitively collective, across generations, over time and space. Inherently conservative, emphasis is on the continuity of society and its organisational features, acceptance of tradition as a behavioural guideline, and authoritative reinforcement for attitudes and beliefs. As British anthropologist Anthony Cohen reminds us, 'myth confers "rightness" . . . by extending to it the sanctity that enshrouds tradition and lore'.[13]

The goal does not seem to be to change popular perceptions of the past, but to affirm and illustrate preconceptions. Displays rarely reinterpret or challenge conventions. For the viewer, looking at 'authentic' buildings and objects becomes equated with learning about New Zealand history. In historic village re-creations, history can be imbibed (an acritical taking-in) in comfort, the viewing mediated by nostalgia.

Nostalgia has a highly functional role in the perpetuation of mythology. Nostalgia does not denote so much despair of the present and future, perhaps, as yearnings for times that are safely, rather than sadly, beyond recall: those days are out of reach, so nostalgia is a safe fantasy. Envisaged is a past that was (apparently) unified and comprehensible, unlike the confusing, divided present. And so nostalgia becomes a pro-active and aggressive tool in reconstructing the past. This 'wilful nostalgia'[14] appears to derive from the impacts of globalisation that seek universal sameness. Nostalgic use of cultural artefacts is a way of addressing defiant insistence on visible uniqueness of identity; whether for the nation, or for the small locality.

Dean MacCannell explains that 'every society necessarily has another society inside itself and beside itself: its past epochs and eras and its less developed and more developed neighbours. Modern society, only partly disengaged from industrial structures, is especially vulnerable to overthrow from within through nostalgia, sentimentality and or tendencies to regress to a previous state, a "Golden Age", which retrospectively always appears more orderly or normal.' He adds that the loss of local traditions stimulates an appetite for relics of pre-industrial life, an appetite that accounts for the hugeness of the tourist industry. 'Remnants of dead traditions are essential components of the modern community and consciousness . . . reminders of our break with the past and with tradition . . . nature and the past are made part of the present . . . as revealed objects, as tourist attractions.'[15]

New traditions are invented, as we will see in Chapter Five: town festivals to celebrate locality and history appear to be taking off in New Zealand in the 1990s, as they are in Europe. These have their own history, leave their own imprint, and over time intertwine with, or become, local history. The manufactured sites in fact create a tradition that would not otherwise be there. During my visits to local history projects throughout New Zealand, organisers were very eager to tell me the background of their reconstructions. Most had documented stages of the process: scrapbooks were shown and progress related with far more attention to detail than the history of the place itself. The goal, over time, is for these reconstructions to become important local institutions. It is a process that, in creating buildings and inventing activities now, at the same time invents local cultural history. Hence both retrospective and present identity are simultaneously invented and reinvented.

Each example mentioned above draws from and perpetuates nostalgic notions of colonial mythologies, reinforcing national identity values in the present: the love of the land, joyful community life, satisfying family life, the rural aesthetic ideal, the nature myth, conformity. There is no critique of actual conditions, no political voice but the status quo, and no expression of a drive for change. These events and processes are attempts to encapsulate a culture, telling observers, 'Look, this is how things should be, this is the proper, ideal pattern of social life.'[16] The viewer is guest: one does not show guests the skeletons in one's cupboards.

Museums and national identity

The inherent nationalistic and patriotic sentiment of museums — in celebrating history and locality, nation is also acclaimed — invites individuals to have an historic sense of themselves as part of a wider collective. When we feel some connection with the objects on display, the implied reading is that we have a shared history. Through the museum the nation is covertly articulated; an identity where people look backwards to the controllable and uncontroversial past, rather than forward to uncertainty.

We understand that the concept of 'nation' is not politically neutral. Neither are museums neutral spaces: how can they be, if national museums represent nation? Many representations of the past appear to demonstrate history as a simple process of evolution; a naïve acceptance of history as 'natural' and shared. There is a lack of alternative information. In these *tableaux vivants* the viewers stand and look, descendants of the disenfranchised who are observing an inclusively-constructed history as if their ancestors were enfranchised participants. All of the clues to the myths are arranged there in front of them.

Though objects of capitalism are preserved as museum artefacts, the impact of that same process is not examined. In this way dominant ideology is underpinned, as the 'more important' groups in society are generally those who are commemorated. Critical analysis not encouraged in the displays, which try to remain firmly apolitical to perpetuate popular, uncontroversial versions of history.

Museums see it as their mission to be educational: the International Council of Museums' definition includes the goal that 'a museum . . . acquires, conserves, researches, communicates and exhibits for purposes of study, education and enjoyment material evidence of man and his environment'.[17] One can readily see that visitor enjoyment outweighs education. The showing of not just what happened, but how and why, is a complex of ideas and historic circumstances that does not reinforce popular perceptions of a picturesque past. Displays that strive to be attractive, tasteful and uncontroversial inherently limit scope for dealing with complex political issues. By displaying a bland past, national unity as a permanent feature of New Zealand history is implied.

The relating of the past in this way, and linking it to the present and future by stating *who we used to be*, tells us about *who we are now*. This is simultaneously identity construction, maintenance and reconstruction. Museums reinforce the notion that history is a set of universally agreed-upon facts. Eric Hobsbawn, a British writer on cultural issues, reminds us that 'getting history wrong is part of being a nation'.[18] Drawing from the past means reconstructing past events, policies and attitudes — from whatever is known, selecting, decontextualising, recombining, and inevitably distorting. Hence museums add to the process of national myth-making.

Reconstruction of historic buildings and villages is on the increase. And existing collections tend to grow rapidly as people donate no-longer-required relics and archives for safe storage and public display. Will these continue to be presented in the manner described above, as superficial ways for the public to experience a sanitised version of the past? Will the various strategies of museums themselves one day fit into a museum of museology?

By the end of the 1990s it is surely urgent that we try to develop an historical understanding that allows for greatly expanded definitions of a multicultural society, and tracking of its historic development. 'There are in fact many stories to be told if we are to understand the truths of past times with any complexity', suggests Jo Blatti.[19] While no site will tell all, each site will allow some exploration beyond artificial displays of artefacts. The current lack of recognition of multiple interpretations of the past and current change in New Zealand is a way of insisting that New Zealand is a Pakeha culture; the museum displays are attempts at Pakeha preservation. As David Lowenthal reminds us in his extensive commentary on representations of the past, 'Memory, history and relics of the earlier times shed light on the past. But the past they reveal is not simply what happened; it is in large measure a past of our own creation, moulded by selective erosion, oblivion and invention.'[20]

4
One million dollars worth of hokey-pokey ice-cream
Expo 88

Expo at Mangere

The Pavilion of New Zealand was designed and built for the World Exposition that took place in Brisbane, Australia, in 1988. Our pavilion was the dazzling sensation of the Expo — or so we (New Zealanders!) were told. We read of the queues of visitors lined up outside it, around the clock, dying for a peek inside. We were told how the visitors simply adored our superb food, and were blown away by the Maori concert party. New Zealand newspapers and other media reports at the time made much of the stunning popularity of the New Zealand presentation. New Zealanders at home could be proud of 'our' efforts at Expo.

The agenda of the Expo pavilion when it was designed and built was to operate very specifically as a site for expression of New Zealand identity, constructed for overseas consumers. Repatriated, to 'bring the magic back', the pavilion is now landscaped in a park near Auckland International Airport. While fewer and fewer people visit the resited pavilion, it nevertheless persists as a concrete display of an intentional interpretation of national identity. Built as a representation of the nation's sum achievements over time, it may be described as a physical landmark of history, culture and progress. The stance taken assumes that within this is even more progress to come! The pavilion has been kept intact because of its past success as a representation of New Zealand culture, and therefore (it was hoped!) as a permanent tourist attraction.

The pavilion is close to the airport, but its operators have not found this is a good situation to attract overseas visitors. A pavilion spokesperson told me that 'they arrive, go to their hotels, then head off for Rotorua, or Waitomo, or somewhere. They don't want to turn around and come back out here.' Tourists logically want to get on and see the real New Zealand; not a simulation of it.

Taken out of the context of its original site and agenda at Brisbane

Expo, the pavilion at Mangere is no longer seen as a national display to compare with others at an international venue. Instead it is translated to something far more prosaic: just one option amongst many as a place for an outing. Its audio-visual roller-coaster cannot compete with the real thing, not far away at Rainbow's End. And as venue for a weekend family outing it has to convince potential visitors that it is more interesting than a museum trip, more appealing than watching or playing sport, and more fun than a day at the beach — all of which are free of charge.

The Pavilion of New Zealand is open to the public at weekends and public holidays, though it will open specially for school parties and other large groups on weekdays as required. Newspaper advertising lets people know that it is open seven days per week throughout January. But it cannot compete with other visitor attractions.

As a staff member explained, 'Places like Kelly Tarlton's Underwater World change all the time, as they take on new features; they get better. This doesn't. It was first displayed in 1988, so it was designed before that, say in 1986–1987. It is now nearly ten years old, and using technology of that time. Everything is getting a bit old and tatty and dated. The slides have faded, and the city scenes shown have long changed. If people have seen it once, they'd have no reason to want to come and see it again. Visitor numbers have been dropping by 60% each year.' Usually just two hostesses are sufficient staff at weekends.

There are no plans to upgrade and actively promote the displays; or to dismantle them. What looks much like a time warp now will eventually become a time capsule. Meanwhile it is a suitable centrepiece for the new life of the whole complex as a conference venue. Dunlop, Amway and other large companies have launched new products in the theatres, in these surroundings the idealised images of nation contextualising their products. The environment represents the assumed collective New Zealand population to whom the products are to be sold; at the launches, salespeople are shown the product in the context of fabricated New Zealand. They now have to go out and confirm those hypothetical sales. The venue is also used for weddings and other functions, the landscaped lake a photogenic backdrop. This attractive environment well suits the wedding photograph nature aesthetic: catered nature for hire.

Brisbane

The motto of the Brisbane Expo was, 'Together we'll show the world'. This in fact meant more of the world than ever before could have seen an Expo, as satellite television flashed footage of the Expo experience around the globe. It also meant 'to show the world' a country celebrating its Bicentenary. For the entrepreneurs who put together the whole Brisbane Expo, the main thing on display was Brisbane: a display to the world of all that this city and state could offer to international tourism and potential investors. In keeping with twentieth century Expo practice, the exhibition was a chance to promote a second-rank city (preceding Expos had been held in Vancouver, New Orleans, Knoxville and Montreal; this century, Expos have not been held in capital cities).

For the host country, boosterism adds status to the host city and promotes local businesses, while stimulating the service sector. In itself, this commercial process reflects the times, as the service industries increasingly replace manufacturing as a major source of income. Each display for each country links various industries, producer boards, tourism operators, hotels, newspapers and transport services, for their common benefit in the drive to enhance their own image, both to themselves and for outside. Commerce and idealism combine.

When Brisbane won the right to stage the Expo, they were successful not only in their bid against other countries, but also against other states of Australia. Brisbane as venue was also fought for against bids by other Commonwealth countries. At that time the Australian economy was in recession, and the Australian Bicentenary celebrations had first claim on funding. Most of the funding for Expo had to be borne by the government of the state in which the host city was located. While Expo's brief was to have a national focus, it could only be staged if it was likely to be a profit-making event. The Queensland private sector lobbied strenuously for the Expo, driven by the lure of short-term rewards: private company profits, increased tourism, a money injection into the local economy, and the chance to redevelop the Expo site after the big event. Private companies' involvement was encouraged by awarding naming rights (just as the Aotea Centre in Auckland acknowledges funding with its Levene's Foyer, Countrywide Bank box office, ASB and BNZ Theatres, and so on). This tells us that despite messages to the contrary, Expo was not a demonstration of a population's celebration of national identity, however vigorously it was promoted as such.

Like previous Expos, Brisbane Expo provided an opportunity to build new public facilities. Australian writer Jennifer Craik explains, 'short term political motives and outcomes, especially naked opportunism, are the only predictable features of expositions. Brisbane's Expo 88 typified this pattern with an aging premier seeking to hold onto office to launch Expo, another concerned to oust him and take the credit, and a public tussle between a new premier and opportunistic lord mayor over the pecking order for the opening ceremony. . . . Expositions have been marked by basic motives and grubby politics — opportunism and a potential real estate bonanza.'[1] The site of the Brisbane Expo was a large derelict area on the river, across a road and foot bridge from the central business district. The South Bank site was adjacent to the Queensland Cultural Centre, the new museum and art gallery that had opened there a couple of years previously. This was a part of town where formal exhibitions of Brisbane's culture and history were already displayed, in modern buildings that showed this to be indeed a cultured, progressive city. The site could be viewed from the top floors of corporate offices on the other side of the river. Hence it can be said that Brisbane itself was the primary witness to Expo. For all its role as a site for international display, best of all was the fact the city itself was on display.

Brisbane Expo organisers claimed their event as the centrepiece of Australia's Bicentennial festivities, a deliberate attempt to run against the historical meaning of the Bicentenary, which commemorated two hundred years of white settlement of Australia. Local squabbling aside, Expo's public agenda was to spotlight Australian unity, quality of life, and achievements. The theme was 'Leisure in the Age of Technology', which seems arbitrary. While the brief was clear that Expo was not a trade fair, how could an exhibitor translate the slogan into a pavilion exhibition? With this theme was the Expo primarily to promote international tourism? Indeed, many exhibitors focused just on this.

Like other Expos, the Brisbane event ended up with a large debt. Creative accounting methods make the actual amount unclear, or possibly unknown; but it is estimated that the whole enterprise cost well over $400 million. (Montreal was left with a one billion dollar bill; Vancouver with 400 million; New Orleans with 100 million. Most of these debts had to be carried by the public sector.) At Brisbane fewer than 10% of visitors were from overseas. Most were visiting Australia anyway, timing their already-planned trip to Australia to coincide with Expo. There is no evidence that Expo was, by itself, an attraction for overseas visitors. In sum, the Expo was expensive, with few short-term pay-offs for the host city, very few guaranteed long-term benefits; and little evidence of sustained economic growth or increased tourism resulting from it.

Brisbane sensation

Our huge success at Expo, so our local news programmes told us, was the greatest overseas promotion by New Zealand, ever. Television gave plenty of mileage to this event. Coverage of this 'success' involving 'our' sensation linked New Zealand viewers with an event to feel proud of.

Over two million people were claimed to have visited the pavilion in Brisbane, including 300,000 New Zealanders. Some New Zealanders went to Brisbane Expo especially to see the New Zealand pavilion, we were told. 'Many expatriate Kiwis left with tears in their eyes. One man even visited the pavilion fifty times!'[2]

Why the New Zealand visitors? This is not surprising, because so many New Zealanders visit Australia every year. Over 276,000 New Zealanders live in Australia, which means many New Zealanders have friends and family members living there. Timing a holiday or family visit to fit with a trip to Expo adds an international event receiving massive media coverage to a holiday. Curiosity about how 'we' present ourselves to the rest of the world can motivate people to want to see for themselves, especially when we are told the displays about 'us' are outstanding, the star attraction of the whole Expo. Our own culture is made visible in the context of the Brisbane Expo, encapsulated and simplified in a form that disentangles it from complicated everyday things that cannot (or should not!) be displayed. When someone has done this for us, and it is a hit, then we are stars by association, and want to bask in the glory. Going to Australia to see the New Zealand pavilion (along with all the other displays with which we are competing) is to be reassured of all the positive things about being a New Zealander.

Rave reports told us how many people had experienced the 'kiwi magic' (of the eighteen million who attended the Expo); facts and figures were recited to impress us: at Expo more than 100,000 cans of New Zealand beer were drunk, half a million servings of seafood sold, and over one million dollars worth of hokey-pokey ice-cream licked.

New Zealand design: children

As preliminary investigation for the design of the New Zealand submission, New Zealand school children were invited to suggest ideas for the pavilion. How could 'we' best convey a sense of New Zealand? What themes were appropriate to represent us?

Earth, sea and sky were apparently the favoured themes. The children knew that New Zealand is clean and green, with Maori and European culture. Obviously, they were recapitulating what they had been told. Children recite received ideas, telling adults what is expected, what children think they want to hear. Involving children is an interesting ploy: a way of getting the public on-side. Children represent the future, and legitimate design decisions, demographically greening the image of the actual designers. The 'innocence' of children untainted by sophisticated agendas means any concepts taken 'out of the mouths of babes' can be manipulated to suggest an innocent view of New Zealand.

What children inevitably suggest is a recapitulation of the media's self-generating version of New Zealand, subsequently reconstructed by the pavilion builders. The pavilion is then valorised by the media. The pavilion constructed is an instantly recognisable New Zealand, and every New Zealander is primed to recognise it by years of exposure to these versions by the media.

In another context, recently I saw the effects of this process of recapitulation of media-generated versions of culture literally acted out in a school concert. The concert was staged by an Auckland inner city primary school. Children representing eighteen different ethnic groups attend this school, which has strong Maori immersion and bicultural units, and a lot of emphasis on teaching Maori language and culture to the whole school. The children strutted their stuff according to their ethnic identities: a wonderful performance of Maori action songs and haka; Pacific Island children dancing with drums; a glimpse of Greek, South American and Thai

'We won!' The welcome-home parade up Queen Street, Auckland, for the Black Magic team and the coveted America's Cup.
New Zealand Herald

Tableau of gumdiggers at the Otamatea Pioneer Museum, Matakohe. Modelled on actual people, Steve and Bob represent gumfield workers in Northland from the 1850s to the 1970s. Claudia Bell

Interior, Blenheim Cob Cottage. In displays of reconstructed history, visitors can identify objects similar to those remembered in their own family past: 'my grandmother had one of those!'. Claudia Bell

Myrtle and Fred Flutey's paua house, Bluff. Media attention, including a starring role in a Tip Top bread advertisement, promoted the Fluteys from charming local eccentrics to national icons. Courtesy Allied Food

The fibreglass forest: magnificent artificial kauri trees at the Expo Pavilion, Mangere, re-sited from the Brisbane Expo of 1988. John Lyall

Roadside war memorial featuring George V, Matakana, Northland. Most New Zealand small towns have a war memorial, once celebrated, but now often taken for granted. Claudia Bell

Visitors put themselves in the picture, joining children lined up in the mural of the original little Waitekohe Schoolhouse, Katikati, 'The Murals Town' in the Bay of Plenty. John Lyall

dancing. The main event for the Pakeha kiddies to show 'our' culture focused entirely on sport: a re-enactment of All Blacks and Silver Ferns training, and a race in a cardboard *Black Magic* yacht by named America's Cup heroes around six marker buoys dotted across the stage. There was also a lively piece about Hillary conquering Mount Everest, with Weetbix cartons littering the stage. The concert showed us that the children understood that ethnic groups have *culture* (singing and dancing), while Pakeha have sport.

The pavilion in Auckland

As noted earlier, after stardom at Brisbane, the pavilion was not allowed to fade gracefully into memory. The entire edifice was shipped back to New Zealand. Resited at Mangere on land owned by BHP, it was placed on permanent display. In its new incarnation it was open in time for the Commonwealth Games held in South Auckland in January 1990. This was part of the Sesquicentennial, marking 150 years since the signing of the Treaty of Waitangi. Over 10,000 people visited the pavilion during the first week it was open.

The pavilion is accessible by a side road off the motorway to the International Airport at Mangere. One takes about a kilometre drive through farmland along Montgomerie Road, and there are the gates. The gates feature the pavilion's logo, a neon Maori face, much like the Warriors league team logo. This motif is repeated throughout the display, on buildings, pamphlets, tickets, and in the carpets in the pavilion's office. On the gates, wooden taniwha flank the neon face, providing a contrast of old and new. From the gates one can hear the recorded sound of tuis and other birds, a sound effect that grows louder as one enters the grounds.

Tour of Expo

Once inside the grounds, visitors advance up the landscaped driveway, park their cars, and wander through the turnstile ($10 each) into the grounds. Everything is immaculately tidy, but has a barren air about it. The empty octagonal pavilions were once shops and food outlets. The offices are deserted, the centre courtyard quiet, and the outdoor tables and benches surround an empty concert rotunda in the middle. A playground helps make the place suitable for family outings, though the designs for the wooden climbing frames are puzzling: (a *lumbung*, or Indonesian granary; *kumano nachi* or Japanese gateway; Italian courtyard; and a New Zealand Victorian home, 1880s–1890s). The playground is an add-on to the pavilion in its Auckland location, an addition to keep the children amused. At the Brisbane Expo live entertainers were a continuous attraction. At the Mangere version, Maori and Pacific concert parties perform at lunchtime, weekends. Other than that, there is piped Muzak.

Visitors can wander around for a look outside the main pavilion, as they wait for the conducted tour. An extensive boardwalk takes the viewer alongside an artificial lake, with weeping willows and green fields beyond. People may try their luck at fishing for catfish off the boardwalk jetty. Exploration along the boardwalk to the rear of the grounds leads to a small animal farm (one pig, one calf, one guinea pig and about twenty hens, on my most recent visit). A grass mini-golf course and summer buggy tours through the orchard provide further activities.

At the Brisbane Expo food was a strong feature of the New Zealand display. New Zealand restaurants offered 'food flavours which have become Kiwi emblems, or identities, like hokey-pokey ice-cream, lamb burgers, kumara chips, whitebait fritters, paua patties and L and P'.[3] At Brisbane the seafood chowder, brandy snaps and hokey-pokey ice-cream 'drove the people wild', an Expo publication tells us. This was the first incarnation of food associated with this pavilion: menus aimed to showcase New Zealand specialities.

Most of these products are not available at the Montgomerie Road version. When I visited two years ago, fast food suitable for family outings was on sale: burgers, chips, ice-creams. But most of the food outlets have closed. One lunch place survives, dependent on the convention trade for business, not the weekend visitors.

Once back in New Zealand the showcase of New Zealand food loses its relevance. Here, mussels and hokey-pokey ice-cream are available everywhere, whereas at Brisbane these and kumara chips would have had novelty value. People wanting to eat out in Auckland look either for familiar popular fast food, or for whatever is trendy now. The discretionary dollar that goes on eating out can be spent on a far wider selection than meals of iconic food. At Brisbane the iconic food was required to represent New Zealand, its purveyors jostling for attention against the presentations of food from other countries at the Expo site. At the New Zealand site there is no such contest. Local day-trippers have other needs.

The famous paua wall deserves a special mention. The pavilion brochure tells us, and television footage shows us, that in Brisbane the pavilion was further enhanced by 'a giant waterfall cascading over a luminescent paua shell wall'.

Paua's distinctive patterns are used extensively in manufactured tourist artefacts: crafted into jewellery, and used with other materials such as black resin to make little kiwis, and domestic decorative objects such as ash trays, trinket boxes, and so on. It is chosen because it is pretty, readily available, inexpensive and distinctive. Apart from at the famous Fluteys' house at Bluff, where whole shells are displayed (easy: Fred Flutey simply hangs them on nails banged into the walls!), the shells are not generally used in interior or exterior decoration. The pattern of paua has not been adapted for things like wallpaper or bench tops or bathroom wall surfaces; though whole paua shells used as ash trays, soap dishes and casual receptacles are a nostalgic feature of New Zealand baches.

When I first visited Expo at Mangere, water was flowing down the paua wall, just like we'd seen on TV footage of Brisbane Expo. On the recent visit the only thing cascading down the wall was bird droppings. The previously iridescent paua effect had faded. The pump is no longer used, because the low visitor numbers do not justify its continuing expense; and the place is gradually being turned into something else, where a simple blue wall suffices. We can sympathise with this economy, and appreciate the lack of currency of paua as novelty here.

The pavilion

The *pièce de résistance* is the grove of replica kauri trees. One takes a short walk through these to the entrance of the pavilion. Native ferns are arranged 'naturally' in the undergrowth. Recorded native bird song punctuates the air, from speakers perched at tree-top height amongst the bird's-nest ferns (in competition with the piped Muzak from the rest of the complex). For those who never get a chance to walk through the magnificent and fast-disappearing kauri forests of Northland, this provides something of a substitute. For while the smells, texture and coolness of the bush environment have not been captured, the scale and grandeur of the trees with their dappled patterned bark is conveyed with convincing accuracy.

An intercom announcement draws us into the kauri bush walk, to begin the tour through the pavilion. A friendly hostess is not surprised there are only two of us. 'Sometimes no one comes,' she tells us, quite cheerfully; and leads us into the first display room.

The first theatre is called 'This is New Zealand'. Visitors are shown a multi-screen presentation much like any tourist promotion of this country; but bigger. The slides that flash onto the twelve screens invite the viewer to wonder and marvel at the grandeur of New Zealand's nature. The ephemeral vista flashes by, the landscape accelerated by heli-skiers and white-water rafters. The sublime is revisited, as quickly as possible. There is no time for contemplative immersion! This is New Zealand as utopian playground in beneficent nature. Boredom-prevention and thrill-seeking tactics insist that a quick swoop through the landscape can show us everything in minutes.

When it is over, the smiling hostess reappears and escorts us to the next theatre.

In the next space the spectacle attempts ethereal effects of the mists of time, as nature and mythology entwine as a creative part of early history. The floor has been built to look like wavelets; the walls are thin curtains of falling water. Viewers sit on ocean-blue benches and face the screen, a thin continuous stream of water, on which the images are projected for a ghost-like effect. The aim is to immerse the viewer in a time capsule that takes them to a mythical past, unmeasurable by rational chronology. Volcanic sound-effects add to the drama. A dream quality is encouraged. The obliging tourist must go along with the invitation to suspend belief, and honour the mythology of Maui fishing up the islands of New Zealand.

Next, the Hall of Celebrations is traversed on a moving walkway. The visitor on the conveyor belt glides (stern instructions: no photographs!) past a succession of mock ice-sculptures, tableaux of early settlers and famous New Zealanders. Video images are projected onto the surface of each.

In this display around a dozen tableaux illustrate various themes. 'Navigation' features Maori canoes arriving in Aotearoa in the same tableau as Captain Cook, with the caption *'On the water, Maori navigators and European explorers kindled a tradition still alive today.'* 'Flight' is marked by references to Jean Batten and Richard

Pearce. 'The Father of Nuclear Physics', Ernest Rutherford, is represented by a model of the atom with a dove in the middle to represent peace (presumably suggesting peaceful uses of Rutherford's discoveries in atomic science); 'Sports' shows All Blacks, cricketers, and netballers; 'Women' are represented in depictions of suffragettes. The last tableau represents 'The Future', and directs the visitor into the next theatre: *Our Children and Yours Will Inherit the World. Come and Meet Them But Mind the Step.*

The final theatre is designed to represent a New Zealand woolshed. Life-sized woolly sheep are arranged in rows as seats for visitors, and face another large screen. The hydraulically operated floor tilts, to match the movements on the screen: when the image of a roller-coaster roars above us, we too tilt forward. The tilting floor is a way of activating kinaesthetic senses, making a novel experience for visitors, who by now have spent about forty minutes looking at things.

The big screen fills with images of sheep, and actor John Clarke in Fred Dagg mode. His black singlet and gumboots mean 'farmer'. He makes a few references to things rural ('Gidday! Get out of there, dog!'). The rest of the screening shows children enjoying outdoor activities, roller-blading, surfing, on a roller-coaster, all generally having a great time. On a more serious note, some of them tell us what they want in the future: new bicycles, a good education, world peace — that sort of thing. These healthy, active children represent the future of the nation. They tell us what is good about living in New Zealand.

The final exit on this one-way journey (in national identity displays there is no going back!) is through a glow-worm grotto: along a twisting track through stalagmites and stalactites, past a reclining moa skeleton, with twinkling simulated glow-worms high above (lights piped through fibre optics). As simulated nature gets more and more sophisticated, representations of ten years ago look decidedly unconvincing.

The succession of display theatres is supposed to convey a total environment, one which demonstrates New Zealanders' collective triumph of human will through politics and technology over nature: 'In mixing portrayals of life in New Zealand with myths and legends in a way that gives visitors a sense of what makes this country tick — its history, people and spirit' (statement in the Pavilion newspaper by the Chief Executive of the Pavilion of New Zealand). When it opened at Brisbane it was described in the *Sydney Morning Herald* as 'an exciting exhibit, a wondrous journey through New Zealand's past and present'.

The journey completely controls the route the visitor takes. As at Disneyland, the spectator must look in the right direction, with no ambient noises to break the spell. The magic world removes every possible trace of the real.

Making an impression

The pavilion after all is about image-making, not historic and social accuracy. For its original purposes, at Brisbane, its goal was to combine amusement with public relations. The version of New Zealand shown at Expo is inevitably clean, green and beautiful. Why show any features marring this, when it is so abundant?

The displays include little sense of any cultural diversity in New Zealand; Polynesians and Asian groups are almost entirely absent. Most of the people depicted on the screens are affluent-looking Pakeha, enjoying enormous quantities of leisure, in cities of bright lights and elegant restaurants. It looks as if this range of tourist activities are those engaged in every day. The mundane is bypassed, and the reality of working life excluded, as the glossiest imagery possible is presented for tourists. Where Maori are shown, it is as performers of traditional cultural rituals: the karanga, the waiata, the haka. Maori are shown as historic cultural artefacts, acting out traditional cultural practices against a late-twentieth-century backdrop.

Maori imagery in the pavilion site is presented in the company logo, the decorative gates, the audiovisual shows, and by occasional concert party performances. This is the populist, safe view of Maori culture, the tourism version that presents indigenous populations as live ethnographic museum exhibits. Studies carried out in Australia, Canada and New Zealand show over and again the utilisation of indigenous people as living artefacts for tourism, as 'added value' readily exploitable in accessible form. In post-colonial tourism, exotic cultures are attractive to tourists, but only of interest if they 'go native': wear traditional costumes, perform traditional songs and dances, and are photogenic.[4]

Indigenous people go native! This internal colonisation, or

reconstructed ethnicity for tourism, is questioned by American tourism writer Dean MacCannell. He considers how the boom in tourism internationally calls for re-colonisation of indigenous peoples, inviting them to act out their traditions in a context for tourists, when otherwise largely excluded from mainstream dominant culture. Visitors can photograph Papua New Guinean mud men dancing on the lawn outside the hotel at certain hours; see real Navajo Indians selling contemporary versions of traditional crafts in New Mexico; or buy replica didgeridoos at The Rocks in Sydney. This fictional recreation goes unquestioned by visitors, as ethnic identity is pragmatically reconstructed and sold as entertainment and consumable items for international tourists. At Expo, Maori culture is not the focus; rather, a Pakeha version of New Zealand culture is presented. This includes a limited Pakeha view of Maori culture. In its original incarnation at Brisbane, the Maori culture party was a much-publicised feature of the display. This reflected extremely well on the display as a whole. Having to address deep-seated difference about the meaning of the national experience for non-Pakeha groups is averted by these tactics. For tourists, it is a case of 'what you see is what you get': indigenous culture as novel entertainment, devoid of politics or controversy.

The use of indigenous people in this way is but one illustration of the inherent contradiction between the Expo event as a rhetoric of progress, and no-longer-tenable values underlying some of its content: for instance, colonising the natives, but refusing to show the indigenous population in their present-day incarnation.

Another contradiction is the insistent preservation of the display, which by its nature and purpose was an anachronism the moment Expo was over. As Australian cultural theorist Tony Bennett explains, 'At expositions, the idea of progress has typically been thematised technologically via the projection of a line between past, present and future technologies . . . in summarising the course of mankind's advance and plotting its future path, expositions allow — invite and incite — us to practise what we must become if progress is to progress, and if we are to keep up with it. They place us on a road which requires that we see ourselves as in need of incessant self-modernisation if we're to get where we are headed.'[5] Nostalgically hanging onto the 1988 Expo pavilion now in Auckland is not a way of forging ahead.

Technology in the New Zealand display was used to present ideas about nation, and was compared with the efforts by other nations at the same venue. A similar comparison is made by Umberto Eco, with reference to Montreal's 1967 Expo, but as valid for Expos since then. He writes, 'Each country shows itself by the ways in which it is able to present the same thing other countries could also present. The prestige game is won by the country that best tells what it does, independently of what it actually does.'[6]

What Eco did not realise then was that as time went on and technology grew more sophisticated, Expo displays of nation would have to compete against the charismatic technology itself. At Brisbane Expo, both IBM and Hitachi had pavilions where they demonstrated state-of-the-art technology that takes little notice of geographic boundaries. Their goal was to foreground themselves, not any nation state. Nations trying to compete are at the mercy of the technocrats, who will inevitably show the most advanced technology of all to represent themselves. This also had to be dealt with at the next Expo, at Seville, Spain, in 1992.

A problem at Brisbane was that while a huge number of people visited Expo, 65% of these were Australians. Many of the local visitors had season tickets, and made non-profit-making repeat visits. For instance, many took their own lunch. The site was not accessible for Europeans or Americans, the biggest consumer groups in the world. However, for New Zealanders the success of their own pavilion at Brisbane encouraged sponsorship for the next pavilion at Seville Expo, held at the same time as the Olympic Games in Barcelona. For the Seville Expo, the Dairy Board chairman said, 'Our clean and green image and the less definable but in a marketing sense more valuable, uniqueness which the New Zealand pavilion will highlight, is a key asset for our marketers to exploit.'[7] The Seville display was now New Zealand's most ambitious promotion ever.

An article in *Export News*, 23 May 1991 (during the lead-up to the Seville Expo), said that, 'New Zealand has clinched a privileged zone location for its pavilion at Expo Seville . . . because of the spectacular success at the Brisbane Expo in 1988.' This spot was near the entrance, next to the 'biggies' like the United States and Britain. The brief for the designer of the New Zealand display was stated by the Expo 92 Commissioner: to say in visual terms, 'This is our lifestyle, our culture, our business and trading patterns. We're clean and green. We produce food that doesn't glow in the dark. We're an action-packed tourist destination and for a small place we achieve a high level of excellence over a wide field.' At an event closer to Disneyland than a trade show, 'We are trying to say something memorably exciting about New Zealand.'[8] $30 million was spent on the New Zealand Seville Expo pavilion.

At Seville, as visitors went through the main entrance, their first glimpse of the New Zealand pavilion was of a 12.5 metre high replica of ocean cliffs. The facade represented Young Nick's Head, the first New Zealand land sighting by Captain Cook. Covered with life-sized fibreglass pohutukawa trees, and with mechanical gannets flying and nesting overhead, a continuous fifteen-minute show simulated waves and blowholes. The display included rock pools, starfish, model fish and kelp. As people queued to go into the pavilion, they watched a large screen showing images of the New Zealand landscape and products. To one side a stage featured performances by New Zealand entertainers, including Maori concert parties. This was to be another notable event in the history of displaying New Zealand.

Progression from the museum?

Perhaps with so many other ways of displaying culture and trade goods, the Expo is a dated concept? This experience, as progression from the museum, has its limitations, as an orderly, systematic, static and controlled event is offered, with no chance for spontaneous discovery or active participation. Expo at Montgomerie Road is a sad little residue of an acclaimed display, showing above all else that things built to be ephemeral are probably best not kept. 'International exhibitions held around the world from 1851 . . . were spectacular gestures which briefly held the attention of the world, before disappearing into abrupt oblivion, victims of their planner temporality.'[9] Survival may make them greater victims: victims of a later re-reading, and re-analysis in the context of different times. In a closer reading at our own leisure we are able to pierce the façade and see the inadequacies. Away from the euphoric environment of the original Expo site, the hype has gone and the response is far cooler.

The pavilion at Mangere offers a version of New Zealand, a brief glimpse, as a declining commercial activity. The promoters of this enterprise have recycled a successful construction and event into a static and unsuccessful tourist attraction. After the attention is received when it was first opened at this site, its role has drifted to that of backdrop for far more viable enterprises.

The 1980s were a time of increased assertion of national identity by New Zealanders, observes Paul Spoonley.[10] The Pavilion of New Zealand may be seen as a material culmination of this self-promotion by Pakeha. The 1988 Expo gave publicists the opportunity to elaborate on a version of identity, then sell those ideas back to the crowds, to re-absorb into notions of personal identity. While all individuals have multiple identities, according to ethnicity, locality, region, gender, occupation, religion and so on, national identity as a single collective was the one being invented.

Expo-sing identities, over time

Thirty-four countries participated in the first Great Exhibition of the Industry of all Nations in 1851. The Crystal Palace housing the display in Hyde Park, London, was a major attraction. The glass — over nearly nineteen acres — was architecturally unique. Queen Victoria's husband, the project's driving force, described the Exposition as 'a true text and living picture of the point of development at which the whole of mankind has arrived'.[11] The event was attended by over six million people.

The Great Exhibition was a loud self-congratulation of industrialisation, modernisation and internationalisation. Exciting new innovations such as the first sewing machines and telegraph systems were displayed. At the Philadelphia Expo in 1876, Alexander Graham Bell's telephone was the main attraction. The Eiffel Tower was built for the Paris Expo in 1889. But as Jennifer Craik explains, unfortunately most of the records of these events are the official literature, public speeches, reports, and media articles: all in the rhetoric of Expo promotion, hype rather than analyses of actual events.[12]

In early Expos, between 1889 and 1914, indigenous peoples were brought in from all over the world to be part of the display. For instance, in 1900 at the Exposition Universelle in Paris, 'native villages' were displayed, the inhabitants living there for the full six months of the display, near native villages from other cultures. Real people doing 'normal' things, they performed religious rituals at set times of day, and demonstrated arts and crafts. Up to 200 people might populate such a village.

These displays were wildly popular with the public. They were romanticisations of another world, an exotic display to transport the viewer's mind from the mundane. Objects and cultural practices that were previously unknown enthralled the viewers, for whom these exhibitions were one of the few ways to learn anything of cultures outside their own. Artefacts from cultures seen as 'primitive' proclaimed the modernity of the culture of the gazer's eye, reaffirming colonial conquest and the imposition of 'civilisation'.

For Britain the first huge exposition displayed the empire, and celebrated progress. The diversity of countries participating augured well for 'progress', with their potential for growth of the empire, their need to be made modern, and their dependence on Britain for investment capital. Their presence showed off the vastness of territories claimed, and the huge range of exploitable raw materials available. Expo conveyed both anthropological difference and British imperialism. For the host country, this was also a chance to add glory to their own history by presenting the grandest Expo. For those sovereign states not part of the British Empire, it was a place to display their nation.

In contrast to the earlier Expos, recent Expos have been less concerned to demonstrate progress. Far more attention is paid to innovative display. Many countries now produce similar goods and use international standardised technology. In themselves, the products of these technologies have limited display value. Therefore the style of display receives greatest attention, both by the creators and their audience. Increasingly sophisticated display technology is used, this itself a statement of the nations nonchalant ability to accommodate whatever new technology the contemporary era can invent. Old fashioned museum-style displays at Expo would reflect a lack of progress in the late twentieth century. Similarly, countries represented only by traditionally costumed concert performers are effectively announcing either their rejection of, or peripheral involvement with, the cutting edge of display technology.

Visiting now

Visiting the New Zealand pavilion at Mangere again in late 1995 it is not easy to imagine, now, that this was the sensation it was claimed to be back in 1988. The dated look is in part a function of the technology it uses. In the 1990s visual media romps ahead monthly, rather than by the year or decade. If, as some observers suggest, the goal of Expo is 'to signify to the world, the nation, and the local area that the "international", in the form of the appearance of advanced modernity, has arrived',[13] then that helps explain the tired look at Montgomerie Road. There, the message overwhelms the media: the insistence on a tacky, transparently propagandised version of identity thrusts above any chance to impress visitors with the technical ways in which this is presented. The whole display area is quite ready for a new and vigorous life as something else.

1990 was the year of the Sesquicentennial in New Zealand. This did not turn out to be a time of outrageous celebration. Events to mark the occasion were thinly attended, and are but a dim memory for most people; though some will at least recall the commemoration slogan, *Huia, Tuia, Tui Tuia — Our Country, Our Year*. That most of the events are forgotten is in the nature of modern ephemeral celebrations.

Historically, the state's involvement in a rite of celebration for national regeneration first occurred during the critical stages of the French Revolution. Inspired by legends of festivals in ancient Greece and Rome, republicans created festivals to engender patriotic fervour in the masses, and to plant memories and imaginings of a great historic epoch. In the late twentieth century, this is far harder to achieve. An educated population is likely to be suspicious of the organisers' agendas. These days there is a supersaturation of events. The highly mobile population with more dollars and leisure, and better transport, than ever before, has a strong understanding of consumerism, including the consumption of events. Their place as participants or audience at local amateur events makes it hard to avoid the transparency of the displays at Expo, and to suspend disbelief. Expo becomes just one of many hundred available events in a supersaturated events environment.

Jennifer Craik noted from her research, for instance, that the people who most enjoyed Expo were people who had not travelled widely outside of their state, and elderly people, who enjoyed the excitement. She concluded that most of the population are probably busy doing other things; or satisfied simply to watch events on television; or content to have some 'down time' and retreat into quiet domesticity.

So why continue to stage events such as Expo? Just as we have inherited the physical form of the town monument to war, we have also inherited the event genre. On the whole, it continues without much critique. Designers of ephemeral events have inherited the previous form of the genre, and they replicate it. If it does not work too well, people are generally too polite to say so. Or they simply stay away in droves.

Public celebrations about place are increasing in the late twentieth century, according to Dutch writer Jeremy Boissevain in *Revitalising European Rituals*.[14] New celebrations are being created and older ones revived on a scale that is surely unmatched in human history. With the growth of leisure and consumption in societies, national anniversaries and celebrations are cultural productions that are emblematic of the modern world. Like the Expos, the rituals and displays themselves articulate leisure and consumption, in a form which is itself a leisurely consumable event.

There are growing numbers of celebrations of formative national events as, in this era of global competition, national governments strive to cultivate a sense of identity amongst their citizens. These rituals to reaffirm national identity are created by humans, quite arbitrary contributions to the invention of the culture. Like most popular cultural artefacts, such ceremonies do not make it their role to offer critical analysis of where the culture stands and where it is heading. The uncritical celebration of the present is a politically safe way of enlivening that present, promoting consensus about identity for the public, while creating temporary industries to service the event. For that part of the population more inclined to consume the culture than consciously create it, these events may be described as an easy resource for bread and circuses.

Whether most of the population attends them or not, Expo and special anniversaries like the Sesquicentennial have a lot in common. Both are managed by cultural entrepreneurs, who decide just what to celebrate, and how best to do this. Both promote the nation state and our identity. Both strive to show, in fact have their origins in wanting to show, that we are totally unique in the world, a one-off experiment and experience that is still being worked on, and will get even better in the future.

At both events corporate advertisers reconstruct and exploit our national identity to sell products or their corporate image while (in the case of the New Zealand Commission, which was set up for the Sesquicentennial) selling a state version of the nation itself. While both events are to show what is different and special about us, to differentiate us from other nation states, both also effectively work to construct a nation in certain images: to prescribe an 'imagined community'. For most of the population, these are uncontroversial forms of image-building.

Architects of these events have a commitment to the idea of a national culture, even though a consensual view of nation is not possible. The political conventions expected in an Expo display call for an imagined community, a politically and culturally happy society, an exemplary multi-ethnic collaboration which will guide its population through a future of rapid and uncertain change, forever one national community. National cohesion can far more easily be displayed than lived.

Media coverage of each event represented New Zealand's past and present in a highly favourable light, listing symbolic inventories of achievements (the same achievements as those reconstructed in three-dimensional form in the Expo pavilion ice-carvings). New Zealanders were expected to accept these inventions as their own: 'We conquered Everest/split the atom/invented Plunket', etc.

Expos can be described as 'hallmark events': enterprises put together by image-makers are special events to tell the world about a destination, while generating economic and cultural activities and enhancing the profile of the place for the future — mostly by valorisation's conservative versions of the past. Like world fairs, major festivals, and major sporting events, the central goal is to attract as many people as possible, and persuade them to part with their money. In this suspended time zone, visitors can have a great time, and affirm pride in their own nation.

From recorded birdsong at Brisbane, to electronic gannets at Seville: where next?! We know that gannets can fly in koru formation via computer graphics. Will there be a new incarnation of gannets to represent New Zealand at the next international Expo?

5
Have you seen the giant roadside shearer at Te Kuiti?

Local museums, discussed in Chapter Three, are not the only sites for overt expression of locality and nationality in small towns around New Zealand. Drive through almost any town, and casual observation will find numerous expressions of identity. Buildings, signage, statues and symbolic artefacts in towns and rural districts are some of the ways in which the locality's connections with the nation are literally stated. There is a giant fibreglass shearer at Te Kuiti, celebrating not just the local shearers who have won international awards, but marking the contribution of sheep farming to the nation. In Hamilton it is dairy farming that is commemorated, by a bronze farm family and animals as a town monument. In towns all over New Zealand, local history is displayed in murals. And is there a town anywhere in New Zealand without a war memorial?

Local monuments, idiosyncratic road signs, colourful town murals and original vernacular architecture tell two stories. One is about that which is unique, locally. The other is about how this place has contributed to the building of New Zealand.

The ongoing process of inventing New Zealand does not just take place in city television studios, advertising company offices, on tourist brochures and at Expo 88. For many people living outside main centres, there is a sense that the daily national identity fabrication excludes them; or that they are not explicitly included. How can local values be incorporated into or linked with representations of the whole? How can the distinctive worth of localities be made visible? Those anxious to address this, and state local identity, have to decide for themselves what their autonomous stance is, and find a means of expression.

The primary agenda: to make their towns visible. Throughout New Zealand one can see evidences of do-it-yourself identity creation exercises in competition with, and complementary to, the powerful, pervasive images coming from sophisticated marketing companies in the cities.¹ These features of the 1980s and 1990s are becoming familiar items in small towns, along with community halls, public parks and war memorials.

Before we look at the newer items, we can check back over time and see that the recent constructions continue a process long present in small towns and districts: processes that linked local achievement to national events, to state the town's contribution to the whole.

'Lest we forget'

In almost every small town there is a war memorial. These ornamental statements about the past preserve an aspect of history that links towns to nation and to significant international events. For Pakeha culture that lacked a sense of tradition here, and whose historical roots were in another land, the building of war memorials was an important process in stating a sense of belonging. Pakeha possession of the land and establishment of tradition was imperative to the new colony. In communities Pakeha had built, the monuments would be a permanent statement of community, and a public record of collective communal loss. The monuments announced not just the tragedy of personal loss; but tied imperial loyalty firmly to local pride.

War memorials as announcements of local sacrifices did not all spring spontaneously from individuals in small places, who wanted their dead brothers and sons visibly commemorated. They were encouraged by the New Zealand government, which gave out grants for memorials to the New Zealand Wars (usually built about fifty years after the events they commemorated), and subsidies to build Second World War memorials. In *The Sorrow and the Pride*, Chris Maclean and Jock Phillips explain that the community fund-raising required for memorials of the Boer War (nearly all erected within five years of the war) and the Great War were important projects for the strengthening of community bonds. The prime movers in these projects were leading businessmen, prominent citizens, mayors and councillors.²

While Maori recalled wars in whakapapa and in carvings denoting past warriors, Pakeha continues the tradition and style inherited from Britain. New Zealand has a large number of monuments to war. They range in form, including obelisks, statues, arches, gates, plaques and public buildings which today still fulfil their intended function (swimming pools, halls, etc.). Evident throughout New Zealand, these were built to be permanent monuments to glory and sacrifice. As the lives of those they commemorate were fleeting, these objects were built for permanence. Their sheer physical solidity — they were usually built in concrete, marble or granite — symbolised the weight of their significance.

Many are now deteriorating. The materials of which they were built has aged; their sites have become isolated as communities have changed; and upkeep has not always been a high priority. Deterioration of the physical memorials suggests the sentiments with which they are imbued have faded. The patriotic stances about wars that they symbolise have declined.

After the First World War, in many districts there was support for monuments that would have a practical function to the community. New halls were the most popular propositions. This idea was resisted by some who were concerned that as people busily used the hall, they might forget the commemorative function of having it built, compared with a non-utilitarian decorative monument, with just one mission: to express commemorative sentiments. Nevertheless, after energetic fund-raising some halls were built, the first three opening with much ceremony in 1919. Rolls of honour were generally mounted on the wall. Sometime photographs of local soldiers were included. Later, sports trophies might also find their home here. The buildings were both a source of local pride in the heroes commemorated, and a way of claiming something distinctive for the particular district or town.

After the Second World War there was no urge to duplicate the ornamental monuments of the previous war. While some new monuments were erected, there were far fewer than for the First World War. Sometimes names of soldiers who died in the Second World War were simply added to the first monument. The Labour government then in power was more interested in 'living memorials', functional buildings that would benefit communities for years to come. For these sorts of buildings, the government would provide half the costs, the local community to raise the rest (preferably not by raffles: these were firmly disapproved of by Department of Internal Affairs as inappropriate and 'disrespectful' to those being honoured). Community halls as monuments were most often built in rural districts and became important social centres. The monuments, whether halls or ornamental constructions, linked the locality with a national event. The soldiers whose names are listed on the roll of honour or carved onto stone may still have relatives in the area, who can remember this contribution to national history.

The wars in which New Zealanders have fought since the Second World War — in Korea, Malaya and Vietnam — involved mainly enlisted soldiers. The only monument to participants of these subsequent conflicts is in the army town of Waiouru; though in some home towns their names have been added to existing monuments. Those more recent wars were not about the defence of empire, so did not extend the imperialist monument tradition.

The New Zealand Centennial in 1940 was also marked by the building of utilitarian civic buildings. Plunket rooms, rest rooms and swimming pools, often in the art deco style current at that time, are still present in many towns. For instance, at Inangahua in Westland, an art deco rest room is like a little time capsule, with photographs of soldiers in the tiny sitting room. Where a community hall was built, it was sometimes a 'centennial memorial hall', commemorating local soldiers and the centenary in one edifice (the money collected in just a single round of fund-raising).

Civic consciousness began to develop in New Zealand at the turn of the century, explain Maclean and Phillips.[3] Founding generations had reached old age, and people had been here long enough to have established a sense of their family belonging to a particular community. The need for some physical manifestation of this attachment to place, that would express local loyalty, could be expressed in this built form via monuments and public buildings. While large monuments to each war were built in cities, there was a strong drive to mark local pride, honouring the wartime sacrifices of families in smaller districts. Indeed, some competitive spirit entered into this: towns tried to outdo their neighbours by building more impressive monuments, or by erecting them more quickly.

Today many of those monuments are still dotted around the countryside, whether decorative stone constructions, or civic buildings in small towns. They are largely taken for granted by the next generation, for whom they have little meaning. The objects are usually of very limited architectural appeal, and no longer tied to any annual rituals. Their original instigators and supporters have long died, or have moved elsewhere. Most of the objects have ceased to function as important statements of patriotism and local identity.

As times move on, fashions change, and new expressions of locality are invented. In the 1980s and 1990s this has apparently become more urgent, as efforts to pronounce distinction have been boomed up, and a new range of identity symbols has sprung up. It cannot be a coincidence that so many towns around New Zealand have been, and are, putting vigorous effort into asserting identity.

Methods used include quite modest road signs, colourful murals, roadside objects and newly invented festivals that gain publicity for the local, as they support and act out national mythologies with new style.

Road signs

In any small town we will find familiar service items, such as the standard design for telephone boxes, and the national flag which indicates the whereabouts of the local post office. Internationally consistent signs are a shorthand for giving and receiving instructions, such as the Transit New Zealand road signs. Advertising signs are ever-present, with some regional variation (Waikato Beer, Speights Beer); but many are as familiar in Invercargill as they are in Kaitaia, such as Mobil, BP, BNZ, Tip Top, Kodak, Coca Cola, and so on.

While I am quite sure most pedestrians do not gaze meditatively at signage on local businesses and think, 'That's a multinational, that's national and that's local,' my research on semiotic landscape has shown how small a statement of locality is required in this sea of signage to signify local distinction. The mass of signs does not swamp anything that makes a direct connection with the familiar or distinct locality.

A colleague and I investigated this at Pokeno, a town preparing to be bypassed by extensions to the southern motorway that zips from Auckland towards Hamilton. Over the years, as this motorway has plunged on through the farmland towards the Waikato Valley, small settlements along the route were forced from the wayside. Te Kauwhata, for example, was once a busy little centre where people on State Highway One could stop to buy fresh fruit, vegetables, petrol, wine, lunch, and so on. Now few motorists detour off the motorway to visit it. Remnants of it struggle on; but most former business premises are now vacant. A road sign invites motorists to detour into Te Kauwhata, but few take the trouble.

We checked out every sign at Pokeno, to see the ratio of local to national to international signs. We walked the length of town, both ways, and photographed every single piece of signage, however apparently trivial or obvious. The town has only about ten shops (thank goodness we did not choose a bigger place for this exercise!), but even in such a short commercial stretch there are several hundred different pieces of roadside text aimed at the traveller. Later when we sorted them we found we had over 400 images. With this collection as our database we could analyse the distribution of international, national and local signage. From this we would see what 'spelt out' Pokeno.

For years Pokeno has been well-known as the first town at the end of the motorway; or the last before the motorway begins, if one is heading north. Over 12,000 cars go through Pokeno each day, forced to slow down by the 50 km signs.

The town did well with its petrol stations, dairies, hot bread shop, and bacon and cheese speciality shops. Jolly pink pig signs invited travellers to stop in the town: 'Welcome to Pokeno — Bacon Country'. There were three pig signs in total: one beyond each end of town, and one in the middle of town, beside the bacon shop. There are hundreds of signs in any small town; even in towns as small as Pokeno. The highly localised signs were the ones that enabled motorists to make a specific association of a product with the name of the place. In the context of nationally distributed and official signs, the vernacular local sign was the one which stood out. Its visibility in the sea of signage was because it was unlike a sign anywhere else. While most travellers probably see Pokeno as primarily a motorway service town, a sensible place to buy petrol or an ice-cream before heading towards the city, the pink pig motif reclaims and localises the national rural tradition. The illustration style chosen links the 'country' with children's story-book pictures of animals, attempting to provoke nostalgia for a mythical country charm; even though this is contradicted by the roaring motorway nearby.

Familiar road signs are often welcome on a journey because we need whatever service they promise to guide us to — food! petrol! toilets! The signs which are distinctive to place are the ones that tell us that all is not the same out there. This refusal to remain anonymous while serving the needs of motorists is a strategy for survival; a way of insisting that the highly localised is valuable, distinctive and worthwhile. Unique road signs engage in competition in the semiotic landscape, gaining attention as the one sign that uniquely, often colourfully, refers to that specific locality, and no other.

It has been known for some years that the extending motorway would eventually bypass Pokeno. What we need to watch for now is whether Pokeno, like Te Kauwhata, will fade away; or whether a revitalised season of signage or other events will try to entice motorists to detour into town.

Much further south, near the centre of the North Island and still on Highway One, Taihape is a town not expecting a bypass. It is essentially a rural service town for the large surrounding farming area, a place for travellers to stop for petrol and a meal, with motels to take the overflow of skiers wanting to play on the mountains further north. As one enters town a sign tells us 'Welcome to Taihape, New Zealand's One and Only Gumboot City'. A cheerful little Fred Dagg-style figure painted on the sign grins happily, beckoning motorists into town.

In the main street amongst all the usual sorts of small town shops and businesses one item stands out: a neon gumboot mounted on a shop awning. At the top of the boot the familiar Lotto sign instantly shows where to buy one's tickets. Juxtaposed against these two symbols (local and national) are numerous other signs, advertising national and international companies. In this little set of messages the gumboot is the unique locality sign, the one that adds local character to the streetscape, in the company of those hundreds of mass-produced signs seen in any town. Like the original welcome signs on the outskirts of Taihape, the gumboot makes a statement about unique local identity.

I was told at Taihape that local people did not want to look like 'country hicks', by taking on board the Fred Dagg figure as town symbol. But I was also told that they believed it helped people remember the town, and had given the place good-humoured recognition unlikely to occur otherwise. An annual gumboot festival each Easter attracts big numbers and wide media coverage. If only someone can throw the gumboot further than the present world record, the town would wind up in the *Guinness Book of Records*.

This innovative attempt to promote the town illustrates the need, locally, to assert visibility. Mileage is gained for the town by claiming nationally recognised icons — Fred Dagg, gumboots — as local symbols.

While the town wants to show it is different, it also shows that it goes along with the nationally popular mythologies: the pervasive rural myth evident in other Pakeha identity mythologies discussed in this book. In the 1970s comedian John Clarke personified those myths in his famous Fred Dagg figure. He — Fred Dagg, John Clarke — had a hit record with 'If it weren't for your gumboots where would you be?' John Clarke left New Zealand, years ago, for Australia; but his character lives on in Taihape. The Taihape example demonstrates that signs that denote place are more than useful geographic referents. They often also assert an aspect of the character of the place that might otherwise not be recognisable to the casual passer-by.

In some towns the sign has been relegated to a large mural, that shows details of the town and its environs. By putting the map on the town, the town hopes to put its town on the map, by having people stop, look, and take an interest in places on the map that invite closer investigation. 'You are here!' maps are found in dozens of places, often in small towns where there are very few streets, so it is in fact quite easy for the motorist to find their way around — if they are not simply passing through.

At Waimate in South Canterbury there is a particularly colourful example. Waimate is about five kilometres off the main road, so first there is the problem of enticing motorists to detour. Immaculate signwriting on a large yellow barn tries to do this, by promising that if we detour into Waimate we will find a 'lovely, clean' town.

A detour into town, and we find that this is true. Better still, we find some fascinating Victorian architecture. It was well worth the detour! There is also a very large map of the town painted on a wall. We followed our road map of all New Zealand highways to get to Waimate; now here is a highly localised map. This must be for an audience who either already live here, as a colourful wall decoration; or for people who already know where they are, because they've just followed another map to get here. It is on a wall in a side street, not readily apparent to strangers. It seems that the collective authors of this map are celebrating their particular place in the universe, as much as showing the viewer where they are.

At Morrinsville in the Waikato the town map has evolved into a large mural. This shows a picture-book town set amongst a landscape of farm scenes, with perky animals and colourful vehicles chugging through the landscape. Alongside the image is the legend 'Welcome to Morrinsville — the Cream of the Country'. This is very flash indeed compared with the former town welcome sign, a concrete erection reminiscent of the most basic war memorials, and bearing a simple 'Welcome to Morrinsville' message.

The new slogan carries a message its originators hope is meaningful to travellers: a gentle pun that links both the traditional products, and the implied quality of life in Morrinsville. This came about with the development of a committee to consider new promotional tactics for Morrinsville. Everyone else was doing it, so they must, too!

The first big event from this new public relations effort was a country music festival. Gore in the south of the South Island has long called itself 'country music capital of New Zealand'. Perhaps Morrinsville could be the North Island country music capital? That way it would not be competing with Gore's established tradition; but it could generate new interest in the town, from people living outside. This strategy attaches a country music festival to local land use. For Morrinsville, the clear agenda is to promote the locality; not to promote country music.

Morrinsville's first country music festival in 1995 was extremely successful. The committee organising it intends to continue, and gradually invent a lively new identity for the town. They want to take the town into a new era with the 'Cream of the Country' slogan: an era that is prosperous, lively, and gives the town another claim to fame on top of its traditional reputation based on high-yield dairy production. New Zealand is famous for its dairy products; Morrinsville seeks to both state uniqueness, and continue to link to this national claim to fame.

At Katikati the Open Air Art committee goes beyond one or two signs and a mural. It participates in the same currency as other towns, but strives towards something far more ambitious. The first warning of what lies ahead is a road sign advising motorists to 'slow down, murals in progress'. Motorists are told they are entering 'murals town'.

In the main street you can hardly miss a series of large images covering every available wall in town. Someone in Canada in a dying milling town called Chermainus first had this idea as a contemporary strategy for attracting attention to place. At that little town dozens of murals depicting local history were painted on town walls, until each year over 300,000 visitors were coming to have a look. Someone from Katikati saw the Chermainus murals and decided that this was just the sort of project that would work well back home.

Murals depicting Katikati's history have been commissioned since the project began in 1990. At first local artists painted the murals, but as more and more murals were needed the committee advertised widely for participants. (Who can paint kauri trees? Who can paint horses?) The murals project has been a concerted effort to beautify the town, to make it distinctive and attract visitors. This project is also a way of resisting imminent change. A new highway will eventually bypass the town. The collection of murals, in progress well before the bypass is in place, is a way of establishing that this is an attractive, go-ahead town, and in future one sufficiently interesting for the traveller to detour into from the new highway.

The project is not so much about art, as about local identity. Most of the murals are copied from old photographs and show actual named people and places from the town's history. Alongside the murals that show people (for instance, a mural of the original little schoolhouse with the children and teacher lined up outside), the names of those depicted are listed. Other images are of picturesque flower-covered cottages and colonial bush and farm scenes. A mural to commemorate the 1993 suffrage centennial places a Victorian woman and her children firmly back in the kitchen (whatever changes the fight for suffrage hoped for, or its centennial celebrated). A very life-like old garage interior is praised for its attention to detail: there is even a dead moth visible in the (painted) car radiator.

The organisers of this project are proud that they deal with 'authentic' history. It is noticeable that the town murals concentrate almost exclusively on Pakeha history. To date, a mural of one unnamed Maori canoe is the exception. This image is in striking contrast to the rest, the Maori paddling the canoe not specified by name, suggesting this is a 'generic' canoe, less solidly grounded in the past than the images up the road of Pakeha. The impression gained is that the project foregrounds Pakeha claims to the business street of Katikati, over Maori who also live in Katikati and use this area.

The town is unlikely to become an art mecca for international (or national) artists, wanting to contribute their work for posterity in an outdoor gallery in this small Bay of Plenty town. The actual work runs counter to the whole of twentieth century art practice, and drags art back into premodernist photographic depictions in the service of this spurious Pakeha revisionist history. In the case of Katikati, it is not so much a case of 'home is where the heart is', as 'home is where the art is'. Where do tourists interested in contemporary art practice go to look at it? Not to Katikati!

The on-going project is extremely well organised, and has gained positive attention for Katikati. The town has won several annual 'Best Small Town' awards since it established its murals programme. In this example, external forces (Transit New Zealand's highway plans) have worked against the maintenance of the locality (the loss of custom through decreased numbers of visitors to the town centre). In response, a committee of local people has sought their own solutions, by adapting an idea that worked elsewhere. They want to be included as a not-to-be-missed spot on the itineraries of tourists, the hoped-for saviours of many small towns. In showing their own history, they are also showing the traditional conservative version of New Zealand history: from Maori canoe to Pakeha settlers, and bush clearing to farming. This broadens its appeal; it offers a localised version of a familiar national story, requiring no further interpretation than the colourful figures and landscapes displayed on each mural.

The same mural conventions are evident in many towns, though never as part of such a considered long-term project as at Katikati. Elsewhere the same mythical history is depicted with some local detail: kauri-felling at Silverdale; historic riverside buidings at Ngaruawahia; a stage coach crossing a river at Rai Valley.

Perhaps the longest single local history mural is at Riverton, on the south coast of the South Island. The Riverton mural illustrates history with a Gondwanaland sort of landscape at one end, through the successive stages of retelling conventional New Zealand history: the arrival of Maori waka to the land of the long white cloud, Captain Cook's ships, whalers and sealers, the first Pakeha settlers, and so on, until a contemporary beach scene is shown. The mural makes history aesthetic, keeps it uncontentious, and broadcasts very similar messages to those at Katikati, but localised at Riverton by the whales and ocean scenes.

Roadside objects

Town welcome signs with idiosyncratic claims appear to be on the increase. 'Welcome to Te Kuiti, Shearing Capital of the World': this sign on Highway 3, about 68 kilometres south of Hamilton, might be memorable; but the slogan makes nowhere near the impact of a giant roadside fibreglass shearer. At Te Kuiti they have both. If the locals in Te Kuiti don't tell us of their claim to fame, then who will?

A far older sign is also still visible, a remnant from another time. It reads, 'Welcome to Te Kuiti, The Caring Community'. That did not say anything different from what any town might claim about itself. It was certainly no incentive to detour off the main road to check out evidence of 'caring'.

At Paeroa the mayor claims his town started the 'big thing' trend. A giant Lemon and Paeroa bottle on the outskirts of town stands on a plinth flanked by explanatory tablets, war memorial style. (One could argue with Paeroa's mayor, reminding him that in fact Patea, South Taranaki, got in first, with its beautiful concrete canoe of Maori warriors paddling over an archway in the main street. It has been there since 1933. I wonder if he knows that?)

The big L and P bottle began life as a space rocket in a Christmas parade in 1967, then was placed in the centre of town in 1969. It has become a famous example of kiwiana, along with jandals, swanndris and pavlova, saying something familiar, unique and nostalgic about 'New Zealand'.

Although it has been in Paeroa since the late 1960s, in 1994 the big bottle gained new attention for the town. This came about through a colourful advertising campaign by Saatchi and Saatchi, which promoted the L and P drink in a series of send-ups about Paeroa itself. 'It ain't famous for its restaurants' said the ad, camera posed in front of a humble fish and chip shop. 'It ain't famous for its royal family' — and there was the mayor and his family waving from a dilapidated shop verandah. 'It ain't famous for its fast bowlers' — and some gentle elderly people are shown having a sedate game of bowls. A few more of these, and then, 'but it *is* famous!'

— and we see a close-up of the iconic big bottle.

While the advertising campaign gave publicity to Paeroa, even more publicity was gained when people in the town complained about the ad. Arguments flared in the local paper: was this great publicity for the town, or was it plain embarrassing? Were the comments in the advertisement really good-humoured; or were they derogatory? A television news crew went to Paeroa to check it out. The interest generated showed that the big bottle may be a symbol for Paeroa, but this piece of kiwiana was of sufficient interest to other New Zealanders for a news team to chase the story. It also showed that in a small town without much big news, a silly story is more likely to gain attention than a serious one. In about September 1995, for instance, a 'news' item was shot at a haunted hotel in Tirau (South Waikato) about a supposed ghost no one could see, or film. About a month later, another invisible ghost was sought on film at Vulcan, South Canterbury.

The Paeroa bottle was an isolated 'big thing' for years. Then a crop of these phenomena began to appear in the 1980s and 1990s. Their design is less explicitly reminiscent of war memorials than the L and P bottle. But in other ways they bear a resemblance to the war memorials, continuing a similar process with a contemporary agenda. The new signs and 'big things' are ways of localising experiences and occupations that are nationally valorised, making strong statements about the positive value of specific small places as they do so. As they become well known, like the L and P bottle, they do not simply represent the local place; they also represent the nation. The whole collection of these things is a coherent representation of who we are.

For instance, that giant fibreglass shearer at Te Kuiti, twenty metres tall, is hardly a parochial curiosity, meaningful only in the one King Country town. Sheep, and shearing, have been extremely significant in New Zealand history. The first flock of merinos was farmed near Wellington from 1834. Wool has been the longest sustained pastoral export. The shearer at Te Kuiti joins a small collection of monuments to this segment of the agricultural industry, including the statue of a Romney outside the Creamoata factory at Gore, and the bronze border collie at Tekapo, which honours the contribution of this breed of dog to developing sheep farming in the Mackenzie country.

I was told the giant shearer at Te Kuiti was great for the morale of the town. It was built when a local resident, David Fagan, held the world shearing record. This achievement, part of a sequence of successful competitive shearing bids by Te Kuiti shearers, was impetus to build the statue. The giant shearer has to be seen as a monument. It commemorates something special locally, that can be appreciated by local people and outsiders alike.

To raise the money to build the shearer, the promotions committee bought 120 young calves, which were then fattened by local farmers and sold on to the freezing works, the proceeds returned to the project. 'Probably about 80% of the money for the statue came from the farming population,' I was told, 'because they could see that the big shearer was representing their industry. In this way, it is not just about Te Kuiti. It is also about farming.' In that sense it goes beyond representation of sheep farming, despite its town site, to valorise all rural occupations, and the rural way of life.

There are growing numbers of examples of large roadside objects in towns around New Zealand: a brilliant green kiwifruit slice at Te Puke; a colossal carrot at Ohakune; leaping fish at Gore and Rakaia; a giant paua shell at Riverton. These are initiatives carried out by local people wanting to try to push their towns ahead. Their commitment to the locality, and to their schemes, is evident in their efforts to raise often quite hefty funds for project development and construction.

In some cases, the object seen to represent a particular place is privately owned. At Te Puke in the Bay of Plenty the big kiwifruit slice draws attention to a commercial horticultural theme park. It doubles as an architectural landmark, and a lookout tower from which visitors may gaze out over the property, Kiwi Fruit Country. At Riverton, on the south coast of the South Island, the large paua shell was built by the owners and staff of a souvenir business. A showroom and shop are attached to a small factory which makes paua and other shell jewellery and objects. The idea of building the big paua shell was to promote their own business; but because the shell has been installed on the main road, some distance from the souvenir shop which is on a side street, the paua shell is read as an identity statement about Riverton itself.

These processes appear to be a response to various events and conditions occurring in New Zealand at this time. The objects show that small towns want to visibly participate in the making of a nation, in creating cultural artefacts that contribute to the total way of life and imagery of New Zealand. In this way these towns add to the store of impressions of New Zealand as a whole that the traveller experiences (whether overseas tourist or New Zealander). For while the local is being spelt out, at the same time this collection of signs, slogans, murals and objects as a whole conveys a version of New Zealand constructed from regional variations.

The result gets ongoing exposure, not just in one's own journeys across the landscape, but also through media attention, such as the Saatchi and Saatchi television L and P campaign referred to above; in television programmes about small towns (*Heartland*); in newspaper and magazine feature articles: these are the mechanisms by which this agglomeration maintains a place in both the present-day perception and the collective memory of New Zealanders. Through media coverage, viewers and readers take a journey around vernacular culture. This keeps it alive and perpetuates it, as other towns take a 'me too!' stance and fabricate more of it.

When city-based media shows or writes about small towns, they look for the unusual, the quirky and the memorable. These conditions seem to be necessary for a story to appear — unless disaster strikes, then places get attention very quickly indeed. People in towns learn to work out recipes to get them on television, or into newspapers. A recent newspaper note, for instance, told readers of the first-ever Wild Taste Festival at Tolaga Bay at Labour Weekend, 1995. And every year the highly idiosyncratic food (such as goat kebabs, marinated albacore tuna, pukeko pâté and manuka wine) at the Hokitika Wild Foods Festival draws positive attention to the West Coast South Island town.

Festivals

The new Tolaga Bay Festival and the Wild Foods Festival at Hokitika: these two vernacular food festivals are attempts to invent new traditions. The woman at Tolaga Bay dipping huhu grubs into chocolate, then freezing them for a festival a month away, knows she is not cooking traditional food. What she is doing in creating these 'half pai grubs' is weaving a new strand into local legends, while drawing from the old tradition of families in the community getting together for a good time. One grinning grub eater, Mrs Hime Papuni, said, 'In my day we ate them raw. The fresher and fatter the better. These days we dip them in chocolate — well, that's just the Pakeha way.'[4]

The festival becomes a new pivot around which to organise the community, the focus of renegotiation of community values and resources.[5] By reproducing customary practices, even with new details (for instance, chocolate huhu grubs), the organisers and participants develop a renewed sense of community spirit. As many individuals and organisations as possible are invited to join in. In doing so, they are not only putting their names down for a good time; they are restating their relationship with the locality, by knowing it is 'appropriate' that they participate. The 'we' group is reaffimed as those wanting to eat, drink, clown and laugh together. The considerable effort it takes to make the event actually happen reinforces this sense of solidarity.

The celebration of locality by 'insiders' fosters an image of social continuity, as the event draws on the skills, experiences and goodwill of people who reside in the area and have shared experiences in common. At the same time, the new event engages with the modern trends of social change: the need to assert identity against excluding economic reforms; and the need to have this event reported in the media as a unique regional cultural event. These elements interconnect, as the people at Tolaga Bay, or at Hokitika, find a way to revitalise their own community, and ensure inclusion in a wider cultural context through the national attention they hope to gain.

Through inventing their own event and persuading the media to report it, people in communities are deciding how they want to be seen. What they choose to show, and footage that television then selects to show, informs viewers' visions of them. Eliminated from the televisual medium will be any analysis of why the community wanted to be in the news in the first place; or how the camera presence actively encouraged the acting out of the ritual representation. For both the place getting the attention, and for would-be entrepreneurs in other small towns wanting a special event, media coverage both legitimates the process of town identity celebration, and stimulates more of this activity. For urban-based viewers, watching the invented rituals of small places being acted out for the cameras, what they see is slotted into an overall impression of their own nation.

Town and district special events have become so popular throughout New Zealand that a national organisation helps co-ordinate them.[6] What might look like utterly spontaneous events springing from the locality are often now structured into a larger network of similar events. These events are used to promote identity, and generate some income for specific projects, or for the local school. They vary from gruelling sports events, like the Coast to Coast endurance race (from Kumara Beach on the West Coast of the South Island, to Christchurch), to highly localised fun events which receive little attention outside, such as the Round the Pub Kokatahi Triathlon, or the Whangamomona Republic Day. The most ambitious events are those that aim to capture as big a crowd as possible.

One of the oldest that is still running is the annual Alexandra Blossom Festival, which attracts over 25,000 visitors. Since 1956 this has been an important promotional event for the town. Other local produce festivals were instigated in the 1980s and 1990s. These include the Te Puke Kiwifruit Festival and the Ohakune Carrot Festival. Like the local fishing contests which are also increasing, all of these events add a special community day to the calendar. The Bluff Fishing Contest in February 1995, for instance, offered many activities to join in apart from fishing. Street stalls, a fun fair, street-side food sampling and games for children were just some of the options, aimed at as wide a range of participants as possible.

Through publicity about these events, messages are broadcast to the outside world about the distinctive qualities of the places being celebrated. The festivals are another way people in communities establish their own image, drawing from the mundane (carrot growing! kiwifruit packing!), then reframing it as a special event.

For instance, at Te Puke during the packing season, workers stack up the trays of kiwifruit and strap them into piles on pallets. This is an everyday job, just another occupation employing seasonal workers in the industry. During the festival this undergoes a brief transformation. The 'stackers and strappers' contest becomes a spectator sport, extremely popular with the audience, who cheer the contestants on in the race to see which team can carry out their task the fastest. The competitors normally do it every day, with no special attention at all. The event is only appropriate to people working in the industry. The contest is recognition of the skills involved; the winners are featured in the local paper and another occupation in the kiwifruit industry is acknowledged. When publicity for the unique event reaches beyond the town, the Kiwifruit Capital gains further affirmation of its status as the important producing area for this fruit. This restates its very specific place on the nation's export producers' map.

A far more upmarket festival is the annual Air New Zealand Marlborough Food and Wine Festival. At this festival, local gourmet food and wines are showcased. Visitors who attend come not just from throughout New Zealand, but also from overseas. Many of them are food and wine writers who will take back information that will be published to further promote Marlborough and its products. Only food produced in Marlborough may be sampled at the festival. The use of 'festival francs' as currency implies a European ambience, adding a sophisticated veneer to the event. While other local festivals consciously celebrate the vernacular, at the Marlborough Festival the style is definitely cosmopolitan.

Such a festival moves well away from the folksy styles described above, to a polished professionalism with full-time paid staff to co-ordinate and manage the event. The venue is Montana's Brancott Estate vineyard at Blenheim; the weather can be counted on to be perfect (usually!); and the crowds are admitted by ticket only, limited to 12,000. The event always sells out of tickets well beforehand.

The selection of delicacies available to sample at this festival is vast: locally farmed mussels and salmon; trout and whitebait from Marlborough rivers; snapper, blue cod and scallops from the ocean. Dairy products, fruit, vegetables and a huge selection of local wines ensure that the event lives up to its claim, 'New Zealand's Best Epicurian Event in the Country's Sunniest District'.

While specifically located at Marlborough, the festival works to establish a reputation for New Zealand produce. Its goal combines a celebration of the good things available locally with a clear eye on the export markets for these items. Most of the food products are also available in other parts of the county; but at Marlborough the whole range is produced in one region, along with a rapidly growing wine industry that is known internationally for its award-winning wines. This combination of place, products and local style (a landscape of pretty vineyards and fine architecturally designed houses) calls for a festival that denotes these things. The festival aims to place the products at a market level where eventual consumers engage in international high style: the smoked salmon and bagels of the urban café set; the sauvignon blanc and chardonnay of fine restaurants.

This is a long way from the sort of festival Ohakune organises around its carrot industry. A single prosaic product such as carrots, however perfect, has nothing like the marketing appeal of the gourmet smorgasbord of Marlborough. And Ohakune carrots probably look and taste similar to carrots grown anywhere in the world. At Marlborough the wines offer unique flavours, combined with a range of foods distinctive of that region. Hence the festival is a showcase, still celebratory of region, but moving a little closer to a trade fair, with products displayed for overseas consumers who may well read these as 'Marlborough'; and who will certainly read them as 'New Zealand'.

Stereotypes

In a curious cycle, these baits for publicity — roadside objects, festivals — gain attention by the invention of new local attractions and traditions. This in turn ascribes towns particular sets of characteristics. People living there are then stereotyped by this, reinforcing popular mythical notions of what happens in small towns (for instance, the worry about being labelled 'country hicks' in Taihape). This process can be of concern to some locals who feel that the promotion project is not really about them at all. The nation is similarly stereotyped, by visitors passing around snapshots and buying mementoes of these novel objects on the landscape.

As in the case of the war memorials, a group of local people taking on a leadership role for the community are the ones to make it happen. But the result can be more contentious than a war memorial. A giant roadside carrot that is easily subject to derision, for instance. . . . And in September 1995 the *New Zealand Herald* reported fear and panic at Masterton, Home of the Golden Shears. A proposed new road sign incorporating a logo of a pair of shears could be misread, and the town might become known as 'Testicle Town'. 'Do you really want a symbol of castration hanging over the town?' one resident asked.[7]

The economic recession in the 1980s had a harsh impact on many small towns throughout New Zealand. There was a fear in some small places that they might disappear altogether. While the population in major cities has increased, the population in rural districts and small towns has stayed about the same. Not actually shrinking, many towns appear static, and are undergoing demographic changes that do not augur well for the future: an ageing population, and employment opportunities limited so that the district or town is therefore unlikely to woo back younger, talented members of the population who may have been raised there, but who have since sought education and employment opportunities elsewhere.

This has resulted in low morale in some towns. Visible objects that assert distinctive local identity may give the town a lift. As one entrepreneur told me, 'We wanted to be famous for something!' They are hardly going to ask, 'Does our town really need to exist?'

Embedded in these town celebration tactics are assumptions of towns as totally permanent entities. There is no acknowledgement of the conception that in the greater scale of time, some towns are in fact ephemeral. In New Zealand we have had numerous examples of towns that thrived as important centres and that have now almost totally disappeared. Charleston on the West Coast of the South Island was once a gold-mining town, with more people than Wellington. Further north, Denniston was a thriving coal-mining town. It is now deserted. There are legends of over forty hotels once dotted along the Hokianga Harbour, when it was an important transport route. At Eketahuna in the Wairarapa there was sufficient exasperation and concern at the diminishing population, that in 1978 one resident wrote a book about it, *Why Did They Leave Eketahuna?*[8]

In more recent years motorway bypasses have almost completely obliterated some towns; or look as if they soon will (for instance, Hikurangi and Waipu, both to the north of the North Island). Whoever said small towns should be permanent? Changing conditions — faster cars, and better roads increasing acceleration through the landscape, with less need for service stops; or perhaps changing local land use — mean that some small towns are no longer economically useful or socially necessary. Where this is so, are the identity assertions discussed here almost totally acts of wilful nostalgia? Is the drive to maintain such towns a way of maintaining against the odds what is in effect living in a museum, of no interest except to the inhabitants?

There is certainly strong feeling outside the main centres that urban people do not recognise the contribution made to the economy by rural producers, and that this lack of acknowledgement renders them invisible. Parochial pride wants outsiders to know of local achievements, and about successful local produce and resources. This information does not hit the news very often. Newspapers and television routinely deal with crime rather than with crops, with disasters rather than successful harvests. If the rest of the country is to know about success in the hinterland, then local people must proclaim it themselves. In the enterprises outlined above, this is precisely what they are doing.

The contemporary trend is for producer-marketer boards to place trademarks that exclude specific local reference. ENZA apples, for instance, are simply New Zealand apples. The label does not acknowledge the particular regions in which this fruit is so successfully grown. This forces anonymity on the growers, and on their locality. Similarly, kiwifruit when exported are simple New Zealand kiwifruit: not specifically Te Puke or Katikati or any other kiwifruit. National is carnivorous of local.

After over a century of successful export of dairy, sheep and beef products, new industries are being developed. Many are flourishing. Rural industries have never had such a diverse range of products to offer. But the marketing of their produce is often the reverse of the French *appellation contrôlé* system, where the local delicacy or product is registered, celebrated, and provides an official claim-to-fame for both grower and locality.

This is a reversal of the trend for global homogeneity of products. Fast food, beverages, clothing items, appliances are the same almost everywhere. The interest in assembling these symbols of locality in towns derives from a refusal to accept anonymity. The increasing global interdependence of economic life, with uniformity in consumer goods — we can buy the same stuff here as almost anywhere else — increases the need to assert the distinctively local. Local identity risks submersion; these objects and events try to redress this.

Tourism

Representations of place via the kinds of symbols described above take on even stronger meaning if considered in the context of world tourism. In the 1990s the world's biggest industry of all keeps accelerating. While many famous tourist destinations are glitzy, sophisticated cities, maybe small, charming, interesting places, with a bit of ingenuity, can also get a look in?

Local entrepreneurs away from the main visitors' centres are aware that sitting about waiting for something to happen or for people to come is too passive. Tourists have to be enticed. Even then, a giant roadside shearer in a fairly ordinary small town will not result in a flood of tourists filling the motels and eating at local restaurants. But the large roadside object will at least tell the tourist something about the locality. This is a form of show-and-tell; a way of making an impression, which will add to the sum of their visit. Through the invention and execution of a roadside object, everyday culture is invented; and tourists are one group that consumes it.

For most travellers, places they have visited blur in the memory, become 'that place where we saw . . .'. When these visitors take away an impression of New Zealand as 'clean, green and beautiful', they might also recall its roadside icons. Giant shearers, kiwifruit and paua shells must inevitably become symbols in the visitors' consciousness that stand for the whole. In this way these objects go far beyond representations of small localities, and become symbols for the nation. As a list they are not necessarily new icons — some have already appeared on postage stamps! — but the realisation of them in giant, physical, photogenic form expands their iconic status.

Sharing the icons

The invention of the local is also invention of the national. The sophisticated image-making industry at a national level steals local successful events and symbols, assembles these into a montage, then claims them as national. For instance the famous Fluteys and their paua house at Bluff are used in bread advertisements. Through this sort of exposure they become part of kiwi identity, not just of Bluff. The elderly couple in the quirky house, the apotheosis of paua, stand for kiwi ingenuity. In this way, kiwiana is born.

For Bluff, there is nothing to lose in sharing an icon. Indeed, the extra attention valorises and endorses the local community. As Fred and Myrtle Flutey amused themselves by gradually smothering their house with paua shells, and invited visitors in to look, via the visitors' gaze they invented themselves as tourist attractions. Fred's visitors' book attests to this, as the names listed over the years move from local to mainly overseas visitors.

These national icons drawn from very specific local sites are nothing to do with sophisticated taste, or pretensions to it. They illustrate city preconceptions and imaginings about the periphery. There is no point building a giant roadside shearer in a large city. Its only possible site is somewhere where it will command a towering presence, and not be diminished by surrounding large buildings. Besides, sited in Te Kuiti it is a reminder that people in small rural localities such as this created the nation in the first place! As they laboured to become the 'backbone of the economy', generating export earnings for the benefit of the whole nation 'on the sheep's back', it is entirely appropriate that a roadside shearer should find its place here.

For years a revolving kiwi was an icon in Auckland, with others in Palmerston North, Wellington and Christchurch. The large kiwi stood aloft on the Kiwi Bacon factory on New North Road, Kingsland, from the 1960s. When its revolving mechanism finally broke down, the kiwi sat still. On this Kingsland site it was an icon, strongly identified with a nationally familiar product. It was photographed by numerous photographers, painted by artists; and finally removed from its perch in 1989 when Huttons, the owners of Kiwi Bacon, rationalised their businesses nationwide.

The Kingsland Kiwi has now been resited on a hotel near the Auckland International Airport. On this site it is no longer an icon. It does not stand up against the sky, towering above passers-by below. We can no longer look up to it. Lost in the airport hotel signage on that stretch of road, the bird has sadly shrunk! This naïve or crass commercial effort to appropriate the bird has displaced a national identity symbol. It is no longer part of a brand, its name reiterated by everyday consumption. 'Kiwi Bacon' has passed on. The big bird (like the Farmer's Department Store Santa Claus and the neon cowboy which for years signalled Kean's jeans shop in Queen Street, Auckland) has been preserved and culturally enshrined in images, and in memory. In the case of the neon cowboy, there was even a song about him. It began something like this:

> Billy was a neon cowboy
> Stuck up on the wall

>Outside the jeans shop down on main street
>Seen by one and all.

This was another of those highly forgettable songs that had its brief moment. Sometimes perhaps it is not such a lamentable tragedy that fragments of folk history get lost over time.

Image-making

Most image-makers and culture-makers are based in cities. They have the mechanisms for making the imagery: the technologies, graphic artists, television studios, printing industries, and all the specialists whose livelihoods come from image-making industries. The authors of this stuff have their 'day gigs' in cities, and in these work environments are actively employed to construct the culture. City culture-makers curate art exhibitions so we can see what has been chosen as 'New Zealand Art'; publish selective items about New Zealand for magazines; edit large-circulation newspapers that include or exclude some groups as 'newsworthy'; and create television programmes and advertisements that will go into every home, bearing messages about who we are.

People outside cities generally earn their livings in occupations that are quite different from those of the city culture-makers. If they want to do something to make an identity statement, they may have to start without the experiences and resources that city people, earning a living in image-making, have at their disposal. Something as large as the red socks campaign, for instance, would be very hard to organise from Kumara Junction or Whangamomona, even though successful local events are held in those places.

While some towns now have a public relations person, most do not. They do not usually have the latest technology, dollars, or skills honed by daily engagement in media to expound their arguments. Hence the profile of places outside of cities is difficult to elevate for wide consumption. Yet many town entrepreneurs have been very effective in making memorable imagery about their locality.

The most useful ally in town affirmation appears to be the local newspaper. Editors of town presses work as advocates for town promotion projects. Supported by advertising paid for by local businesses, local papers happily give mileage to town festivals and special events. When the large daily papers exclude small towns, their news will appear in the local rag. This affirmation of local projects and encouragement of readership gives the paper an important role in creating an imagined community, locally, as everyone reads the same items about the same people in their local paper.

Representations of the localities and of nation ebb and flow in style, relevance and popularity over time. This relatively new collection of local identity symbols has followed the war memorials and community halls to niches in communities; to fill a small physical space and a large symbolic one. Each category of object in its own way spells out connections between the locality and the nation.

Essentially, these locality promotion enterprises are Pakeha processes. Less than two centuries after Pakeha settlement, this part of the population is still creating its own traditions and developing landmarks to solidify notions of identity. In the 1990s, as for any decade, we live in a period of unique circumstances, affected by local, national, and international events. This current crop of signs and roadside symbols reflect the moods and dreams of the times. The range of objects described here are landmarks, not just for the motorist or the tourist, but for a nation as it constructs its identity on a daily basis.

6
All we need to know, because TV tells us so

Hi, Judy! Hi, John!
Each time we switch on the television we are reminded that we are New Zealanders. We can instantly tell which are overseas programmes. They look different. Their locations are not like here. And the people's accents are an immediate give-away. Only New Zealanders have these voices!

Our television presenters try to be clones of successful presenters elsewhere: grooming, dress and personal style mimic those of presenters everywhere. At the same time, their localness and familiarity are carefully fostered by media publicity departments to nurture viewer loyalty. This makes them people we 'know'. We might not know anyone like them outside television land, but they have the familiarity of people we see every day.

The determinedly personal tone, a chronic condition following the caring-sharing syndrome that started in the 1970s, runs through television presentation. These are nice, supportive people. They want to engender a feeling of togetherness. Television One's channel identification theme ditty demonstrates this:

> . . . make a brighter day, with my neighbour,
> together is better, together is fun, together we're one.
> Together we're growing stronger,
> together we're feeling good like we should,
> here's where we belong.
> Together we see New Zealand, we got a brand new day.
> One by one, old and young, everyone — together we're one.

The emphasis in this chirpy ditty is rigorously on 'one'; a ploy to have viewers connect to whatever they may have in common with one another, and with this television channel. We could take this too seriously; it is just a simple little television promotion song, after all. But it tells us they want us to share some sort of identity across the nation (their construct of nation) as we tune into One.

Inventing New Zealand, every day

Television transmission began in New Zealand in 1960. Yay! We had been let into the global village! This was going to be so exciting. We'd be in touch with the rest of the world. We'd see places we had only imagined before. One commentator sums it up: 'The popular demand for television and its success were, indeed, indicators of a society whose members had, in a large part, always looked outwards.'[1]

Television is dead easy. Just switch it on, and away it goes. It is the most accessible medium, present in almost every New Zealand home. Its images are instant and striking. The viewer does not have to have literary skills to gather information and entertainment from it.

Television creates a culture-in-common, and provides viewers with experiences in common. Television is the most 'pervasive socialisation medium' that there is.[2] Daily casual conversation in schools and workplaces often focuses on what has been seen on TV. However limited one's daily life, one has exposure to the world — carefully selected by programmers — through the media.

While a lot of the time-fillers are trivial overseas imports to pad out the programming schedule, during the same schedule we are also exposed to endless media images that tell us who we, New Zealanders, are. In a linguistic style unique to television (where else does anyone speak like this?) it tells us 'we' are part of a group, where 'everyone' thinks such-and-such, 'kiwis' who . . . etc. These words strive for instant bonding, and play a significant role in the fabrication of our reality.

Most literature focuses on the antisocial role of the television programme. Critics suggest this mass of imported culture invading the population's living rooms day and night has led to a 'colonisation' of our culture: the bombardment we receive of American values, in particular, erodes our separate identity.[3] Television programmes leap geographic boundaries with ease: the cultural imperialism argument has us fade chameleon-like into the homogeneity that comes with the impact of so much imported culture. In this view, the imported culture becomes the cultural haystack: somewhere in it, we might find our own distinctive identity; but it will be a hard job sifting through it. There may be something in this; but we should not underestimate our abilities to recognise our own realities from those arriving from elsewhere. 'Our own realities': it is the way these are coloured that is of interest here.

Print

In the 1660s the advent of printed text made a massive impact. For the first time, large numbers of people unknown to one another could have access to the same ideas, as those ideas were expressed in standardised language. Dominant values and beliefs could be circulated to a far wider audience than ever before.

Benedict Anderson says that 'these fellow readers, to whom they were connected through print, formed, in their secular, particular, visible invisibility, the embryo of the nationally imagined community'. Literacy began the spread of notions of 'nation'. Concepts of nationalism were therefore available to those who could read. Through this process a consciousness of nation could be developed, an imagined community created, in which people would feel included and know who was excluded. This interaction between technology and human linguistic diversity laid the basis for the possibility of a sense of sharing a nation.[4]

In nineteenth century New Zealand, the first settlers brought with them the English language and the assumption that this would be the language of the colony. They believed that quite soon the indigenous Maori language would be displaced. English was used as the first language in New Zealand, with some local dialectal differences. The New Zealand accent developed, and colloquialisms emerged. The use of English in almost all spheres of life in New Zealand conceals a history of conflict and domination over Maori. The current trend of state agencies to provide both English and Maori language on letterheads and written documents is a tokenistic redress of this.

During the rise of nationalism after the development of print, newspapers had the crucial role in developing a sense of nation. The daily newspaper-reading ritual engaged in by thousands links members of modern national communities, providing 'knowledge' in common. In the twentieth century the growth of popular broadcasting media furthered the spread of ideas.

With television, as with radio, millions of people internationally could be exposed to the same material at the same time. Nationally, the idea of an identity as a shared set of values and our individual part in something larger, the national community, could be engendered. It is difficult to imagine that before the 1960s and the development of a domestic television news service there was no mechanism that could visually address New Zealanders simultaneously, and present New Zealanders to one another on a daily basis, in their own homes.

Telling it like it is?
Every time we read a paper or watch television we are reminded of who we are. All news items are identified and located by the nation in which they take place. Local news, world news: the two are presented in distinctly different ways. And the two are expected to elicit different levels of interest, as concern for what is happening nationally is presented as being far more meaningful than events in remote places.

Our urge to believe New Zealand is 'special' and different from anywhere else is played on by the media. There is some irony in this. On the one hand we are offered a view of ourselves that many may feel is manipulated. On the other hand, if we want to demonstrate our difference as a nation, how can we do this and reach a wide audience except through that same media? The establishing of local identity and solidarity is impossible without the media. The problem is then a matter of whose version of 'us' is conveyed. This insoluble conundrum calls for us to at least understand the role of the media in telling us who we are. The processes that operate and agendas for those processes require a closer look.

Some might argue that the media plays an important integrative role in society; that it maintains consensus and fosters national pride through reinforcing central values in a way that is beneficial to this society. How else can a widely flung population have a sense of connectedness; of all being part of one whole, the nation? The media provides a sense of community for three and a half million people with things in common, things that make us unique.

This rests on the assumption that we do have values in common: that although we are culturally and racially diverse, that there are threads of commonality that link us; for instance, that we support the All Blacks, that we all care passionately about winning the America's Cup; that we can relate to images of happy smiling nuclear families having a good time at the beach: this imagery is constructed and reconstructed on a daily basis on television. It is claimed we share these values as fellow nationals.

Television likes to give the impression that as a nation we are homogeneous and egalitarian. It is in their interests to do so. Yet how can any country of many diverse groups seem to have a national identity in common?

What we have via television is a simplified identity. Distinctive characteristics of various groups are simplified by stereotypes. Media labelling means we can instantly conjure up diverse groups and attribute to them physical or psychological characteristics in common: hard-working, dole bludgers, rich, intellectual, whingeing, etc. Although we may not find all of these labels acceptable, simplification of the components of who we are as a group of New Zealanders allows snap judgement of who is most valuable, who is most authentic, and who is most representative of the ideal 'New Zealander'. Television depends on our ready recognition and acceptance of these stereotypes.

The dominance of the white middle class in all spheres of television — as presenters, as spokespeople on important issues — follows a trend we inherited when television first came this way. Following imported models of how things should be done, we see strong orientation towards the white population, with few outlets for establishing association and solidarity between Maori and Pakeha. Note, for instance, that when the struggle of the Maori is shown, it is reported as 'protest'.

The 'fuss' over Maori reclaiming land is not acknowledged as valid by all Pakeha (who fall about in hysterics if the local council wants even a few metres of their back garden to add to a reserve or to build a road). Ranginui Walker is but one Maori voice pointing out that Pakeha control of national media has defined Maori as inferior or in negative terms vis-à-vis Pakeha.[5] Prime time viewing any night of the week illustrates his objections.

During most of its transmission time, television tries to show us a society that the viewer (Pakeha) can comfortably believe they belong to. It places the viewer (Pakeha) in an assumed ideal role in relation to what is shown; the viewer (Pakeha) is invited to unquestioningly occupy that position, for instance as potential consumers (Pakeha) of items advertised. In this way 'one audience', a national audience (Pakeha), is established.

What television programmers decide are dominant values receives little challenge. The prevailing lifestyle it presents becomes familiar and possibly accessible (if we can buy the products); or totally inaccessible (if we cannot buy the products). Consumerism is equated with an ideal way of life for New Zealanders. The 'unfortunate' are shown as needing to be socialised into the same values as the Pakeha dominant group, and to attain the same material goals. As Ruth Butterworth succinctly puts it: 'power structures are replicated and reinforced by television entertainment'.[6]

Prominent British media commentator Graham Murdoch maintains that this is anti-democracy: the groups which are excluded from representations are also the groups that are excluded from the consumer culture that the media portrays and that supports the media. As perceived non-consumers, they are not a target group for television programming or advertising; therefore they are marginalised from participation in the culture as defined by television.[7] Viewers are not passive, or stupid. They know this is an idealised version of what they could be, to encourage them to earn more to spend more.

The daily reminders of national identity on television are inherent in all televisual genres. National identity is a component in television channel call signs, news programming, in local documentaries, in drama, in comedy and in advertising. In all of these we can see the selection, for instance, of icons that are familiar in popular consciousness. The use of these is to convey a sense of togetherness, as viewers share recognition that does not apply anywhere else, and can only apply here. Look; there's Rangitoto: it must be Auckland! There are some South Island mountains! Birds! Nature! Standard themes are constantly reworked.

In the same way that television programmers selectively decide which representations of certain global events to show us, they also select viewing about our own culture. The material is presented as if it is neutral and impartial. Television wants us to like what they show us! But for television to remain commercial, economic considerations have to influence content. Showing positive images of New Zealand, of a country to be proud of, is a way of supporting these economic needs.

There has to be an audience! A large number of people is required to see and hear what is produced. This audience has to be 'constructed' in some way, to know that the programme is for them, so they will watch it. Television has to find itself an audience that depends on media for information and confirmation. Hence the two — television and audience — are reliant on one another.

When Australian writer Richard White claimed that representations of national identities reflect the hopes, fears and financial aspirations of the inventor, he has television culture-makers in mind as one set of inventors. He has a clear understanding of agendas which use national identity as enticement for commercial ends. He writes that all national identities are 'false as they have been artificially imposed upon a diverse landscape and population' and furthermore we need to look closely and find out 'whose creation they are and whose interests they serve'.[8]

An advantage for television in its manipulation of our notions of ourselves is that national identity is not fixed in time, but is constantly evolving. This is valuable to the medium, as it can respond to the times, or make things happen: a national event may in fact be a media creation (such as that great 'spontaneous' show of nationalism, the welcome home for the America's Cup team). In what it shows to the audience and how it frames developments as events, television constructs society. The audience is encouraged to believe it belongs to this society, to identify with the ideas and images aired. Hence the media in general and television in particular are agents in telling us who we are. In return, the audience assumes that the received media images and representations are based on fact. Media institutions portray the images they believe the audience that they have already constructed, wants.

NZ On Air

In New Zealand, television transmission was originally controlled by government, which could define content, and carry the costs. This did not include provision of sufficient funds to develop local programmes. In effect, the government issued a licence for programmers to import material, mostly from the United States and Britain. With deregulation, more local programmes are now being made; but these are by far outnumbered by imports from overseas.

When first radio, then television, arrived, the government took a paternalistic role in guiding content and protecting the public from inappropriate material: for instance, no advertising on Sundays;

no soaps in the school holidays; and concern that any afternoon transmission might not be good for citizens. In this way, the government via television appointed themselves moral guardians of the population.

With the deregulation of broadcasting the state's role has decreased. Deregulation has meant a shift from the blend of public service objectives and commercial considerations, to a wholly commercial environment, obliged to maximise audiences, options, and financial returns. As a consequence of this change, external infiltration into the New Zealand media grows stronger. New Zealand On Air (NZOA) was established to redress this. With deregulation, television stopped being driven by the state, but still has the state, in the guise of NZOA, as backseat driver, and market forces as road map. The state is still influential through the Broadcastings Standards Authority, which the government set up to establish and monitor rules of behaviour in advertising and programming.

New Zealand On Air is a government-funded agency with the mission of promoting local content. The television licence fee pays for programmes like *Heartland* and *Shortland Street*, and services such as subtitles for the deaf. Maori broadcasting is allocated 6% of the budget. NZOA's mouthpiece is Eric, a confident little goldfish who swims about and tells us that programmes are paid for with our broadcasting fee, so we 'can see more of New Zealand on air'. In the last financial year, $916,000 has been spent by NZOA to tell us that they are spending our money.

Eric assumes there is a national audience; that there are differences between us and others. And he assumes, on our behalf, that this is a good thing, and necessary as well. Yet Eric, who looks just like any other goldfish, peers happily out of his bowl and sees New Zealanders as all much the same: a single viewing audience. We all want the same thing: to have programmes made for us, and about us, the decisions for what is appropriate to fund entirely in the hands of Eric's keepers.

The guidelines of NZOA have to fit within the framework of the Broadcasting Act. NZOA policy states that its role is 'to be a catalyst for distinctive New Zealand broadcasting'.[9] The organisation has a commitment to checking that funding benefits the largest number of fee payers through programmes designed for mainstream audiences, and programmes aimed at special interest groups. In this way we are reminded of our special status as viewers. We are not just a random or amorphous group of consumers of imported programmes, but a 'special' group having our distinction showcased for us in New Zealand programmes.

The establishment of NZOA is an explicit attempt by policy-makers to ensure local content on our screens; and that the content delivered will be 'appropriate' according to the judgement of NZOA executives. From this we readily see how television works as a government-sanctioned cultural delivery system.

All across the range, funded programmes lack much in the way of intellectual content. Despite this 'maximum acceptability' and 'lowest common denominator' approach to programme making — familiar in the imported programmes we are shown — we are supposed to be proud that these programmes are about 'us'. Viewing NZOA-funded programmes is equated to a patriotic act.

NZOA sells us a state-approved version of the nation. This is one in which New Zealand identity is constructed for the popular imagination as a harmonious multicultural society. A version of the nation that moves from homogeneous to multicultural is necessary for the state to quell possible political agitation, and for New Zealanders to accept Asian and other immigrants — and to persuade those groups that they, too, are really New Zealanders.

Fee-funded local content has increased dramatically. Hours of broadcast have also been extended, so as a proportion of all programmes shown, it has been a race to keep up the amount of local content. In 1994 the proportion of local content on television was 23.2% — close to the 23.9% local content of 1988, despite the huge increase in transmission hours. The most recent local content survey results, 1993, show a 158% increase from 1988 to 1993: from 686 hours of local content in 1988, to 1769 hours of local content in 1993. 'Local content', however, is confusing: does it include 'programmes' which present a large component of imported material, but have a local frontsperson; for example, *60 Minutes*?

NZOA supports programmes that are supposed to show 'real New Zealand'. In this way it has a hand in constructing society. With this as the driving agenda, inevitably whole classes, generations, ethnic and interest groups are overlooked. The most televisual parts of the status quo are showcased in its funding decisions, as the 'real' identity of a nation.

Before we look at some NZOA funded programmes, and other viewing, we'll stop for a quick glance at the news.

Television news: 'all you need to know'

Television uses news and current events to capture audiences, and to show that programmers take their social responsibilities seriously.[10] The presenters seem as if they practise their Serious Looks, their Lightly Amused Looks, and their Matey Looks, so they can pop these on quickly when the cue card says to. Cute banter (cued banter?) is to demonstrate that, whatever the news, these are warm, good-humoured people. They want us to *like* them. Some of them insist on calling us 'kiwis', to remind us who we are. The adoption of the cute vernacular by formal presenters in formal attire is to make us feel part of a distinct collectivity that they are part of as well.

Television has made a dramatic impact on newspaper readership. It is surely no coincidence that as television broadens its offerings (more channels, more hours of transmission, more news programmes, both local and overseas), there has been a corresponding demise in metropolitan evening newspapers. For many people, television may be their only source of news. Viewers have strong ideas about what is appropriate to show on news programmes. News presentations register more complaints than any other category of programme.

TVNZ's *One Network News* at 6 p.m. each evening is the most-watched news programme. In fact, less than fifteen minutes of news are included in this commercial news hour. The rest is sport, weather and advertising. The commentator's voice intreprets, explains and exclaims, his/her narrative guiding viewer reactions, though apparently reporting with factual neutrality. The scriptwriters for some broadcasters assume we believe everything they tell us: *We know all we need to know because John tells us so.*

Potential news stories that require greater investigation over a period of time are less likely to be included so do not become part of everyday viewer experience. Apart from constraints imposed by time and budgets, there is also the problem of there being few specialists amongst journalists, who cannot have detailed understanding of all issues.

News programmes are more highly rated in New Zealand than

in any other country.[11] The highly literate, small, remote population obviously wants news. Is this because here at the far end of the earth we know we are still essentially Eurocentric, and are afraid we are missing out on things?

However, television news is like any other consumer product: it is oriented more firmly towards achieving high ratings than to producing a high-quality product. Evidence for this includes the very high salaries paid to 'presenters', and the lack of money spent on researchers. Priority is on style, rather than content. Viewer polls show that the more-educated, best-informed viewers are the least satisfied with television news programmes. Rather than upscale the level, a lowest common denominator approach is maintained to maximise viewer numbers. The cutesy, trivial, 'feel good' items often popped onto the end of news programmes demonstrate this: cat rescued from tree by firemen, dog falls out of dingy in Rangitoto Channel, and so on.

So who gets to talk?

So who does get to talk? A local research study found that 92% of sources used in television news programmes were white Europeans; of these, 80% were male. White males were far more likely to be used to represent public institutions, politics, business, or to provide expertise on a topic. Women, when shown, were more likely to be victims, for instance of a crime, or of the application of social policy. When women were official spokespeople, it was more often on supposedly women-related areas, such as health, education and welfare. In this way, stereotypes in wider society were reinforced by television.

News is inevitably inclusive of the interests of some and exclusive of the interests of others. The voices of authority are those of political and business élites: most political information is from official sources, from politicans who have lessons in how to best impress viewers and handle interviewers. In effect, they perform as actors for our entertainment, as much as to transmit information. That these voices are the ones chosen to inform us shows that the media is not independent of the state, argues New Zealand media critic Joe Atkinson.[12] These days the voice of 'public opinion' is also increasingly used. For fleeting seconds 'ordinary people' voice an opinion or demonstrate an emotion as part of a major news item.

This vox pop tactic is supposed to democratise the news item, and link the viewers to people who are for a moment presented as the literal voice of the people, when usually, like us, they are merely viewers.

Local media researcher Sue Abel insists that 'bias is not a conscious act on the part of those working in the media, who do the best they can to present a fair account of the day's news'.[13] If they want to take any other than the approach prescribed by their organisation, they will be stymied. Abel has explanations for the institutional monoculturalism of news programmes. She notes the lack of appropriate staff to handle non-Pakeha issues; and the time and budget constraints that make it hard to get to Maori news sites (often not conveniently placed in cities). In a Maori hui situation, information is not succinctly delivered to fit the sound-bite collecting style of television; nor are the most appropriate spokespeople easy for Pakeha news-hunters to identify. Often news items concerning Maori are ignored until their actions are loud and public, for instance at a public protest. Coverage of these events then suggests that this is pretty much all Maori do that is newsworthy. On the main news programmes the items are presented in a Pakeha context, with Pakeha interpreting events according to Pakeha interests.

In their daily representations of New Zealand, the groups that make the news programmes wield enormous power. Their choice of what is news becomes what is 'important'. Through this editing process, television news delivers only what 'they' deem we should see. Those excluded are denied opportunity to gain national status, so are unlikely to be perceived as very important members of New Zealand society.

National identity

Television news programmes have implications for the notion of national identity. News presenters speak to 'New Zealand' — the general public — with frequent use of 'we', 'us', 'our', these pronouns conjuring up a consensual society. Media presenters speak of 'the public interest', or refer to the 'national community'. They chirpily imply a democracy that is not present. 'The public' does not consist of a mass of equal individuals, but of groups with unequal resources and access to power. Media claims of a national identity on our behalf then needs questioning. In whose interests is this cosy identity formulated and promoted?

'We are all New Zealanders' — or 'kiwis' — 'naturalises' cultural values to suit Pakeha, and to exclude any resistant group. We are shown a Pakeha view of the world that is claimed as universal, the media using a non-culturally-specific rhetoric of nationalism which masks Pakeha control. Television appears to act as an open forum for debate, but not all voices are welcome. News, put together by a variety of selection processes, must therefore be seen less as 'information' than as a form of cultural discourse.[14]

Television news's repeated playing of its own advertising promotions provides extra clues and insights into the way television formulates and transmits national identity. The glowingly positive and marketable pictures of 'our culture' shown to the sound-overs of, for instance, 'watch your world with us' — imply we share the same world, and will share the same understanding of events as television tells them to us. This is presented as indisputable and non-negotiable. This is know-all television, that will not acknowledge the discernment of viewers.

In colonial times, technology (the rotary press and linotype) provided the means to disseminate ideas and to define society. As transport networks improved, papers could be distributed more widely. New Zealand social theorists David Novitz and Bill Wilmot explain that from the very beginning, xenophobia and conformity have been consistent themes. Conservative values running through the media since those days have included the assumption of the rights of political authority, moral values, and the desirability of assimilating the indigenous Maori population. By sticking with these values and attitudes, they could never reflect the full range of New Zealand life.[15] Radio and television inherit this evolved set of values.

Television news is not the only rippling pool in which New Zealand culture is reflected and distorted. We switch now to some popular programmes, and see what they are telling us about ourselves.

Heartland and *Shortland Street*

Heartland is made by Anson Grieve Productions, and funded in part by NZOA. It takes New Zealand viewers — most of whom are urban — to rural New Zealand, and to small communities. It selects places that are not usually included in mainstream television programmes: Waimarino, Stewart Island, Bluff, the Hokianga. Like *Country Calendar*, New Zealand's longest-running television programme, *Heartland*'s tone is determinedly celebratory; it is something of a showcase for a way of life that has achieved mythical status in New Zealand. *Heartland* shows what is happening 'out there' from a highly urbanised viewpoint, and finds 'out there' that which it seeks.

The focus of the programme is on the folk-cultural aspects of small town or country district life. The most colourful 'locals' are interviewed and their activities documented as they celebrate special events, such as a festival on Stewart Island, or a race on Hokianga Harbour. The programme stays away from political issues. Presenter Gary McCormick politely explained at the end of his programme on Hokianga, where he could not remain blind to social problems, that political analysis is not the mission of the programme.

Heartland has now delivered over three dozen programmes. All are well-padded with advertising, which indicates that the corporate advertising buyer knows New Zealanders will watch the programme. The myths are hence utilised by corporations, who realise this is a great sales site.

Whether or not the way of life shown in small town New Zealand is accurate or not, is not the issue. Of interest here is the fact that there is clearly an audience for *Heartland*'s versions of New Zealand. It is assumed most viewers will identify with or at least recognise the people portrayed as our 'fellow New Zealanders'. The rural 'character' is a familiar, worthy stereotype, one to which we can connect nostalgically as part of our own past, or that of the nation. The underlying themes include adherence to the old egalitarian myth: that while some folks might live in odd places and do unglamorous jobs, they are no less human for it. They are good blokes and good women, all doing their bit for the country, and making a valuable contribution to national character.

Gary McCormick presents as a good-natured chap who happily joins in traditional local rituals, from racing with a dead wild pig on his back at Waimarino, to joining a group of Wainuiomata housewives for a risqué lingerie party, complete with male stripper. McCormick is more than mere presenter of the programme. He can go to any town or rural district and be welcomed as the Kiwi Bloke who'll have a go. He helps keep Kiwi Blokeness alive, both by his own participation, and by hunting out kiwi blokes in each location. His role as home handyman in the Mitre 10 hardware chain advertisements further reinforces this image.

The programme cheerfully reinvents traditional mythologies. It adds to the sum of New Zealand (urban and rural) viewers' concept of what it means to be a New Zealander. The traditional way of life that has long had a place in New Zealand consciousness is acted out by real people. The programme-makers look for stories that illustrate these expectations. New rural entrepreneurship (shown on *Country Calendar*) is omitted. The emphasis is on vernacular culture, as undiluted by urban cultural values as possible.

The presentation of these lifestyles assures the urban viewer that the traditional way of life is intact, that small-town New Zealand is as wholesome and stable as ever. The myth-making overlooks accounts of small-town alcoholism, unemployment or domestic violence, or any expression of dissatisfaction. All is well. And fun. Togetherness, friendship, hard work and an assumed sense of unity subsume any differences which may be present. The makers are quite sure that viewers do not want a sociology lecture; they want entertainment.

For years most New Zealand television programmes and films were set in rural New Zealand: the quirky, vernacular place of popular mythology. *Mortimer's Patch*, *Smash Palace*, *Skin Deep*, *Vigil*, *Came a Hot Friday* — all contributed to the sense of who we are; sometimes a bit bleak, admittedly, but with rolling green hills and real (*rural*) people. This was a welcome relief from the fakery of imported celluloid entertainment.

Recently there has been a shift to greater focus on New Zealanders as an urban population. The current most popular presentation of an urban version of 'us' (paid for with our broadcasting fee, so we can see more of New Zealand on air) is *Shortland Street*. The original agenda for the programme was to encourage more younger viewers to watch New Zealand-made programmes. The popularity of this early evening soap is outstanding by international standards.

This programme has now been running for three years, and episodes regularly hit the most-watched programme ratings of each week. It is held up as an example of successful New Zealand-made television: popular, pacey, and dealing with such serious 'real' issues as benefit cuts, homosexuality, and environmental matters, while keeping the standard formulae of the soap genre: romance, infidelity, teenage escapades, gossip and rumour. The characters are carefully drawn from a range of ethnic groups and ages. As in most soaps, they are still all beautiful, inner-city sophisticated types, with many of the women actors verging on fashionable anorexia. Physical stereotypes of females and males are maintained and reinforced. House interiors are crammed with designer objects and artworks. This is not white trash culture! There are no Westies on Shortland Street.

What makes it recognisably a New Zealand programme? For a start, many of the actors are familiar from elsewhere. They become even more familiar not just through regular viewing, but by their constant presence in the popular press: their personal traumas and dramas are ready fodder for local women's magazines. There is even a *Shortland Street* fanzine. Their profiles are kept high by invitations to appear as local 'celebs' at various events, invited along to add gloss. And if you live in inner-city Auckland, or on the North Shore where the programme is filmed, you are likely to spot *Shortland Street* actors buying their groceries at the local supermarket, frequenting cafés, shopping, or going to the movies. A friend's sister/daughter/neighbour may be in, or connected with, the programme.

Those connections based on contact and familiarity in the 'community' are also present in the programme. The hospital setting functions as a small community, with 'locals' whom we know, so we are locals, too. In this way the anonymous viewer, and the culture they experience, are linked to a constructed, imagined community recognisable at the clinic. The values of the clinic reflect idealised beliefs in society out there in viewer land: that whatever our relative status (doctors, nurses, orderlies) we all have a role to play, and are all equally valuable.

In S*hortland Street* we recognise familiar language and colloquialisms. Maori words are used in casual conversation by Maori characters. The clinic is given a Maori name as well as 'Shortland St', as is common practice for most New Zealand official insitutions. Included are customs and cultural rituals that occur only here in New Zealand; familiar ways of celebrating; particular food and drink; objects in the sets familiar from local shops or magazines (or even our own homes!); art on the walls by artists we can name: all of these familiar components make this a programme about 'us'.

There are also familiar locations. Outdoor scenes are shot around Auckland, and other places that we know are mentioned. Dr Ropata left the Shortland Street clinic to work in a medical practice on the East Coast. The two Drs Thornton go on a whale-watching holiday. Two characters live on a boat, on a familiar bit of Auckland waterfront.

The focus is on the personal lives of the clinic staff. Patients are often very thin on the ward indeed (in episodes in mid 1995 almost all of the patients were also staff, or their family members. I suppose it cuts the expense of employing extra actors). For all the bed-hopping, *Shortland Street* is essentially a very moral programme, with an emphasis on cultural sensitivity: the goodies are loved, the baddies are punished. An issue is shown from various points of view as different people react to it. For instance in August 1995 two young students in the programme marry, to be eligible for a student loan. In this way 'real' issues and ways of reacting to these issues are demonstrated to the viewer. Viewers are shown that on any issue there are choices to be made. The possible choices by characters on *Shortland Street* are intimated to be similar to those available to us, the viewers, in our lives.

Throughout the programme there are often references to current issues. That this is a private clinic in itself reflects recent changes in public health care, as the state encourages more citizens to take out medical insurance to cut pressure on state-funded health services. Issues and events gaining attention in news programmes are tackled by *Shortland Street,* such as racism, 'cultural safety', the 'recovered memory' of a sexually abused character; and alternative therapies for cancer patients, not just as a healthcare option, but also to possibly increase revenue for the clinic.

Reference to everyday events and personalities outside the programme connect the fictional world with the real world the viewer inhabits: on Red Nose Day (a fund-raiser for sudden infant death syndrome) a box of red noses for sale sits on the Shortland Street reception desk; when Nick thinks he might become a star as radio talkback host The Love Meister, another character comments, 'If Marcus Lush [alternative-style newsreader on TV2's *Newsnight*] can succeed, anyone can!' This attention to daily events and characters firmly ties the programme to place and time.

There was low viewer confidence in this programme when it started. Many called it 'Shortbrain Street'. But it gradually found a niche. Its New Zealand viewers have doubled since it first went to air and it now sells well overseas (the ultimate New Zealand affirmation, for anything made here!). It still receives funding from NZOA, but this is justified on the grounds that the profits it makes subsidises other programmes.

Do these programmes fill the NZOA brief of reflecting and developing New Zealand identity and culture? Are they showing a distinctly New Zealand way of life? Should a television soap be a vehicle for the development of culture? If we understand that television reflects society back on itself, like a mirror, while at the same time it constructs society, by producing and transmitting subtle ideological messages, then can *Shortland Street* and *Heartland* be claimed as models for these processes?

We can see that in some ways *Shortland Street* develops parallel to the development of New Zealand culture. Just as culture itself is not static, neither is any aspect of 'our culture' (the topics dealt with by the writers) that is acted out on the programme: This dynamic shows how cultural identity and television transmission are complementary. Both are flexible, both are unpredictable. Cultural identity can be manipulated by television, drawing from the culture, processing it, then feeding back an altered version.

While superficially they are utterly different programmes, it is easy to see many of the same values reflected in *Shortland Street* as in *Heartland*. The emphasis in both is on a particular 'community': a group of people sharing their daily lives in a casual but cohesive fashion, creating a subculture with clear boundaries to appropriate behaviour. *Heartland* does this by revisiting safe, traditional myths, the makers always welcome because of perceived status for the locality appearing on television. For once they are not being overlooked! The only *Heartland* episode over which there was a lot of objection when it was shown was the one on Wainuiomata. Some local people felt affronted that the programme made a heroine of an ingenuous blonde housewife, and that it suggested that all anyone in Wainuiomata does is drink beer, play football, and attend rude parties. Criticism was so heated that TV1 used that criticism as teaser for a repeat showing in August 1995! You see: television *can* take criticism . . . into the arena of advertising.

Despite this one controversial episode, which drew complaint because many locals thought it was unflattering (showing that they consider the programme-makers should function as positive public relations agents), *Heartland* on the whole treats with paternalistic benevolence the interesting and eccentric characters in very small places. This basic apparent respectfulness while uncovering the quirky has gained the programme huge popularity. Simultaneously, small communities have been included where they are usually overlooked. Okay, not everyone was happy at Wainuiomata; but at least a programme was made about the place!

Gary McCormick's first small-town programme, well before *Heartland,* was *Raglan By The Sea*. That, too, received criticism from the local business people who thought they were not represented as befitted their status. But McCormick's agenda is not to seek out local big-wigs. If he did, it is likely too many towns would look exactly the same. His focus is on citizens not ordinarily accorded official status, but whose idiosyncrasies make them interesting, and who, purely by living there, are entitled to represent their places as much as any member of the local council or Rotary club.

It will be some time before *Heartland* runs out of places to film. The content of these programmes presents versions of New Zealand that are clearly desirable to viewers: sentimental notions of a way of life that other people (those people so willing to be filmed) are keeping intact on our behalf. They add to the sum of our concept of New Zealand culture.

Good on ya, Gary! You've done it again!

The traditional egalitarianism embedded in *Heartland* and *Shortland Street* is not intact in all New Zealand programmes. Are those two programmes suffering cultural lag, as they hang about with old values? Or is the fact that both programmes are so popular, evidence that the ideologies inherent within them are still believed in by viewers? We switch now to a programme that has completely reassembled the old set of mythologies, as it eagerly ushers in a new set. Is this type of programme an aberration; or the way television, and New Zealand, are heading?

Gloat television

Success!, formerly called *Made in New Zealand*, is made by Communicado and shown on Monday nights on Television One. This weekly programme, aired in 1994 and 1995, is one of the most extreme examples of television as purveyor of myths to the populace. The focus is the new environment of free enterprise. Owners and managers of new businesses, and of established businesses taking new approaches, explain their routes to success. The programme presents a New Zealand where 'anyone' can 'have a go' in business, and succeed; any success they have will be good for them, and good for us. The notions of economic recovery in the 1990s are reinforced, and positive, beaming presenters almost literally sing the praises of these dynamic companies. ('Sing': for some reason presenters in this programme vocalise their comments in sing-song accents, apparently led by an off-camera conductor recently laid off from an orchestra, and who needed a new career. Cringe-making puns punctuate the commentary. I haven't figured out why the presenters adopt this 'style'.)

This programme joyfully promotes business success, with unquestioning support for New Right policies, instituted by supposedly visionary capitalists. It implies that wealth is plentiful, accessible and there for the taking. Go for it!

The magazine-type presentation pays more attention to style than to analysis of just why the businesses shown are so successful. The sparkle-toothed presenters bob about factories and engineering works amongst the machines, stating the obvious. (Peter Vershaffelt tells us airily that the twentieth century has seen many important innovations! Gosh! Good thing he told us!) They beam their joy at the *Success!* we are witnessing. This playschool-style business news encourages viewers to believe in economic recovery, and that business success is possible for anyone (despite the fact that the Department of Labour records that well over half of small businesses established in New Zealand fail in the first year).

The overall message — that New Zealanders are winners — endorses government free-market policies. The programme celebrates and promotes the economic 'recovery', as if this is a consensus view. There is no coverage of the problems resulting from government policies. If individuals fail, then they are to blame, rather than structural problems. The positive effects of new business are emphasised, reinforcing New Right ideology.

The audience is cast as possible future *Success!* stories: potential entrepreneurs who just need a great idea, a bit of flair and Hard Work to set them on the fast track to business achievement. Meantime, between the programme's segments, they can watch the ads and anticipate these consumer items and services as their rewards: banks, insurance, wine, holidays, computers, cell phones, TV, stereos.

The programme is an effort to foster pride in the business success of others, and to assure the viewers that 'we' are doing well. The emphasis is on new business products, profits, and methods; there is no mention of any tactics that might be seen as controversial, manipulative, exploitative or underhand, as the means are justified by the ends. The ability to take advantage of legislative changes such as the Employment Contracts Act is celebrated. This Act has historically been responsible for the reduction of wages and conditions of workers in a manner unprecedented in New Zealand. However, in the programme shop-floor workers are never interviewed. This larger picture is always ignored, because business heroes are good guys. Nothing must contradict or negatively colour or make complicated their story: the playschool presenters do not like messy plots, and they want every business entrepreneur to live happily ever after in *Success!* heaven.

Absolutely no explanation of the broader conditions is provided. Redundancies, displacement of other firms, the mopping up of expertise laid off during the restructuring of Crown enterprises, have all apparently made no impact. Wage workers, their numbers and conditions are excluded. Single preferred interpretations are presented that support the party line. (One might be forgiven for suspecting this programme is National Party funded.)

We are told that the resulting wealth acquired by *Success!*ful company practices is always the result of hard work — indicating that poverty or business failure must be the result of laziness, rather than structural inequalities. That New Zealand has other impediments to success is never examined: for instance, the problems of being half a world away from markets, and one of the developed world's lowest ratio of graduates and postgraduates in a working population. Those featured on the programme are portrayed as scrupulously honest and upstanding. The proud presenter assumes a share in this success, for he or she is the messenger bringing the news.

The programme indicates that business is much like sport. Key words from New Zealand's sporting tradition keep recurring: team, competition, competitors. All of this is taking place, of course, on the brand new 'level playing field', which has been created by new government regulations.

In presenting these *Success!* stories, this programme draws on many of the traditional myths of New Zealand identity. In pioneering spirit the new entrepreneur has the kiwi do-it-yourself approach to problem-solving, and is oblivious to traditional hierarchies that might have barred access. The Protestant work ethic is still present, but with shrewder overtones. A lot of the stories are updates of legendary No. 8 wire and kiwi ingenuity. The arena is fraught with risks and dangers — company failure, bankruptcy — but the business person charged with entrepreneurial zeal charges heroically into this new economic and cultural environment fostered by the National Government.

This perky language is used to persuade viewers and entrepreneurs into the attitudes of the programme makers' New Right beliefs — a glorious public relations exercise for the businesses portrayed. Many companies phone in with requests to be included in the programme.

National identity values are revamped and projected onto a relatively new environment — business. The emphasis on individualism, on survival of the fittest — who can battle and survive the free market — and on strong characters (predominantly male/white/Pakeha) are used to promote national pride, and to invite identity with 'our' successful business people.

Success! is a prime example of how television selects what to show. It demonstrates how wealthy television production houses can amplify the voices of the most powerful in society. The poor, wage earners and underground groups cannot muster the resources to make their voices heard in a prime time programme that advocates their needs; images of them are presented instead as spectacles, for instance in street protests, where civil disorder gets prominence over the messages they are trying to convey. Those groups do not have the economic might or media power to counter or challenge the monetarist attitudes — which television itself supports, as it strives for profits.

The content of Gloat Television long abandoned any subscription to that earlier famous myth, egalitarianism. *Money* and *Holiday* are other programmes that fit the Gloat category. The content, motives and structure of each of these programmes counter the notions of equality which nurtured our colonial roots. The leap is from 'there is no real poverty in New Zealand' in the 1950s, to the fictitious 'level playing field' and 'economic recovery' that is claimed to benefit us all in the 1990s. Gloat programmes try to convert the casual viewer into believing in the new economic order; that the developing economic climate based on American-style capitalism is what the new New Zealand is about.

Success! is one of the processes by which the new myth is transmitted to a population. Through propounding the values of the dominant group, stating this as something we can all be proud of and see as a new emerging component of identity — business ingenuity and international *Success!* — a new component is constructed and imposed on the national identity of the whole.

We can see from this programme that New Zealand society is not static, but is one that is undergoing rapid change. The programme acts as a catalyst for change in national identity, nurtured by programme-makers and programmers. We must wait to see where the divisive new monetarist policies lead us. How much of the population really believes in the myth of recovery? To be convincing, that recovery will require far more beneficiaries that can at present be counted.

In material terms, the business people on this show are the *Success!*ful people in our society: those who get the greatest material rewards and status. In consumer culture the entrepreneurs are the biggest consumers. Yes, they have every right to celebrate their achievements; and of course we viewers are pleased if business really is flourishing. This could, however, be delivered in a programme that looks objectively at business, at a far broader picture than the proud claims of the owner-manager. And we'd prefer a programme where the director asks the presenters to please *shussh* the singing.

And now: a commercial break.

Weetbix heroes

Ads are the unadvertised programmes we watch in the gaps between the scheduled ones. The *Listener* or *TV Guide* does not tell us when particular ads will be shown; we have to curl up and wait for them.

Most discussions of advertising — populist, academic or theoretical — take a hostile stance, abusing the way ads interrupt programmes, and their patriarchal consumerist mentality. This hostility shows that viewers are not totally passive when planted in front of the television screen.

Advertisements average about ten minutes of every viewing hour during all hours of transmission. Long infomercials are also shown, the late night ones perhaps a useful service for insomniacs. Through repetition and saturation coverage across the networks, advertisements provide an unavoidable environment in which the programmes are placed. That environment has to be one we can relate to, or it will fail. Hence the advertising environment makes a point of showing us things with which we can connect, by utilising sentiments such as national pride and recognisable heritage values to sell products. The products to which these values are attached include, well — almost anything at all. Everything from health care and banking to beer and junk food, utilises and reflects nationalism, and addresses this to the collective mind, thus hoping to unify viewers. The viewers become not an agglomeration of diverse individuals, but a group with consumer urges in common, their other differences washed away.

For instance, in the lively Lotto ads, corporate advertisers fill the frames with joyful New Zealanders engaging in everyday activities. They play sport, relax in the sun, have fun and enjoy life, all against a distinctive New Zealand landscape — familiar because of the frequency it is shown on television. Even landmarks we have never physically visited are familiar. The sound track is sung by Annie Crummer, the words of the song reiterating the visual imagery about what it means to be a New Zealander. It seems almost incidental that the ad is inviting us to buy Lotto tickets (under the guise of playing a game: like Lotto, identity recognition is a huge inclusive team game, not a gamble with few winners).

Images of nationalism are ladled onto local products such as Lotto, and onto products sold here by multinationals as well. For the latter, foreign ownership and manufacture is camouflaged under the cultivation of local/national imagery to articulate the appropriateness, here, of consumption of the international product.

Global campaigns are readily adaptable for local markets.

Commercial definitions of nationalism are developed not just by New Zealand agencies, but also overseas, for us. At the same time, advertisements encourage us to shift our notions of personal identity from the parochial to a global consumer culture, where people drink Coke, and wear Levis and Nikes. For the viewer-consumer, there is no apparent contradiction between the two kinds of message. The local vernacular is mediated to represent our individuality and distinctiveness; for global products, shared values rather than different values are accentuated.

Ads have to compete not just with one another, but also with scheduled programmes, and against that silencing enemy, the remote control. If advertising has been elevated to an art form of consumer capitalism, to compel us to watch, then some agencies have this down to a very fine art indeed. Colenso and Saatchi and Saatchi appear to be particular specialists.

Colenso's unsubtle and sentimental Bank of New Zealand advertisement draws from a popular nostalgic myth that every New Zealand family has its summer holidays at the modest family bach. These were happy, memorable times, when intact nuclear families played Scrabble and Monopoly in the evenings. Worries and financial concerns were washed away by the tide, time and the wonderful, paternalistic BNZ. In the similarly nostalgic Mainland cheese and Toyota ads, residues of a vernacular way of life are portrayed, with much the same values as the *Heartland* series. The good-humoured rural characters in both of these stand for a way of life in which few of us participate, but which nevertheless represents the mythical national way of life.

My favourite current ad is the Weetbix ad with Hillary and Tensing pausing nonchalantly to consume Weetbix before they embark on the final stage of the ascent of Everest. We know this must be 1953. The youthful Hillary says, as he perches on the mountain ledge just below the summit, 'I knew a sherpa once who could eat ten Weetbix in one go!'

Sherpa Tensing [another child actor] peers up at the summit. 'Do you think we can do it?'

Hillary [happily intent on his Weetbix], 'I know I can eat eight!' The orchestral music swells to a grand crashing crescendo, and the choir voices soar:

Kiwi kids are Weetbix kids;
Kiwi kids are Weetbix kids!'

In this series of three advertisements based on heroic New Zealanders, the histories and achievements of Hillary, Peter Snell and Jean Batten triumphantly imply a history for Weetbix. When those heroes were making those great achievements, the product Weetbix was around, too. In fact, according to Richard Wolfe in *New Zealand! New Zealand! In Praise of Kiwiana,* Hillary really did take Weetbix to the Himalayas. New Zealand's past is firmly linked with the product. Another ad for the same product shows a family shopping in a supermarket and telling us that in good times and hard times, Weetbix is always there; placing it firmly in the up-and-down economic history of a nation. This ad is worthy, but lacks panache.

In the Peter Snell ad, Snell's mother (also played by a child) says, 'My son's a kiwi kid, surely that counts for something?' It does: he goes on to win a gold medal at the 1964 Olympic Games. And Ed Hillary, up near the summit with Tensing, says, 'In my country there is no such word as assumpuctare [impossible].' Earlier in the Hillary ad we see the sceptical English being ridiculed. Child actors play posh London Explorers' Club members reading their papers in their élitist sanctuary, while our chap is out there on the mountain. We — Hillary — Weetbix eaters — (same thing!) — can show them! And 'we' do . . .

In both these ads the competition with others is articulated as men against whole other nations. The later, softer, Jean Batten ad has far less ominous foes, simply Ms Amelia Earhart, a stormy ocean to cross in a fragile plane, and a broken fuel lead, which is readily fixed with a hairpin by the ingenious Ms Batten.

'Kiwi kids are Weetbix kids' uses national pride as a component of the desire for the product. The product is associated with famous heroes. Hence both nation and product are heroic. These advertisements select from popular history to draw attention to and enhance their product. With wit, humour and nostalgia, Sir Edmund Hillary, Peter Snell and Jean Batten act as role-models for the consumption of Weetbix.

The essential theme in each Weetbix advertisement is achievement. Ordinary New Zealand kids from average families (we get glimpses of the average families in the Snell and Batten ads) can achieve great things. The new generation (younger Weetbix eaters) are shown that we have a history of heroism, which implies positive features of the present, and positive possibilities for them. Even this generation, born long after heroes retired from their chosen arenas, can celebrate their achievements, especially in this decade, which is not a golden age of New Zealand sport.

History and nostalgia intertwine. Middle-aged people will remember listening to these major events on the wireless. The sound effects on the advertisements include radio commentary, as the sports people's achievements — and Weetbix's claim in these — are announced to the world. The heroes as public property live on in popular mythology, personifications for some of the best things about New Zealand. Weetbix takes advantage of this, by choosing only the most famous of all, who will be instantly recognised by viewers. Popular ideas of New Zealand heroes are converted into impetus for product loyalty. There is a sense that whatever else is going on, we should celebrate positive moments in our history and rise above the conflicts and injustices of the present, which might eventually go away.

Weetbix products are made in New Zealand and are familiar everyday items associated with ordinary family life. But they have now become an 'in-group' product for children, who like the idea of being a 'kiwi kid'.

No one at Sanitarium knows all the details of the origins of Weetbix. Sanitarium bought Grain Products Ltd in Australia in 1926, thus acquiring Weetbix. The product was advertised through the use of street posters. Prior to the purchase of Grain Products and their Weetbix line, Sanitarium had produced Granose Biscuits since the 1890s, though this was not a malted biscuit. Until the 1920s the main cereal breakfast product in New Zealand was rolled oats, used to make porridge. Porridge was soon overtaken by the new convenience food, Weetbix (no cooking! Just add milk!). Now it is a familiar product that consumers can recall throughout their own family domestic history. That in itself is a positive value that Sanitarium can take advantage of against outside competition.

The world's greatest travellers — but kiwis can't fly!

The Weetbix advertising campaign makes clever use of readily recognised traditional heroes. However, there may be only so many emotional symbols that can be harnessed by associations with prosaic little wheat biscuits. The 1994–5 Air New Zealand advertisements called *Birds* go much further than this in the manipulation of emotion; and at the same time try to instil in us belief in another 'tradition'.

Birds claims for itself the tenuous assertion that New Zealanders are some of the world's great travellers. The voice-over tells us: *There is one nation of people that loves to fly, and one airline that flies them. Air New Zealand — the airline of the world's greatest travellers.*

'Greatest travellers': this implies that we all zip off constantly, when in fact much of the population would be extremely hard pressed indeed to raise an airfare. Alternatively, of course, we can be claimed as great fliers: we live so far away from anywhere else that to go there involves flying a great distance! And we do go, because a lot of what we want is simply not available here . . .

Birds, like the Weetbix ad, was made by Saatchi and Saatchi, the filming taking four months, with the film crews travelling to 45 different locations. The advertisement was first screened on 12 June 1994, at 7.30 pm. The full length of the advertisement is 3 minutes 20 seconds. More often fragments, or shorter advertisements with clear visual references to this one, are shown. It gained quick attention for its at-first-glance-convincing image of single flying gannets gradually uniting to fly in koru formation (the airline's logo). The unique animation for this advertisement was done by Animation Research Ltd, Dunedin. *Birds* was released in time to compete with the award-winning British Airways operatic advertisement, featuring huge numbers of people formation marching into changing images. In something of an operatic duel, Dame Kiri Te Kanawa's voice was chosen for *Birds*. She sings 'Po kare kare ana', a traditional Maori love song, which most children learn at primary school.

A press release of 10 June 1994 from the regional sales and marketing manager of Air New Zealand stated that 'the commercial reflects New Zealand's natural cultural heritage. . . . It's a 1990s view of New Zealanders and their heritage that captures both the mood of the times and the warmth of that bond between kiwis and their national airline. . . . It will become the backbone of the airline's corporate advertising for the coming years.'

We know that in New Zealand there are unique bird species. Assorted easy-to-recognise birds are employed by the ad to lend tradition to the notion of New Zealanders' preoccupation with flight. That flying is a natural part of New Zealand life is suggested by the use of the native birds: the gannet, the heron, the kea, fantail, tui, spoonbill and saddleback — all native fliers of New Zealand. Alas, and ironically, the kiwi, New Zealand's most recognised national symbol, could not be included. The poor kiwi cannot fly.

There are 34 scenes in this celebratory bird's-eye view of the nation. Blue skies and green landscape conveying fresh, natural, unpolluted scenery are shown as Temuera Morrison tells us we are 'a nation that loves to fly'. For some (migratory?) reason these birds fly only over countryside and bush, not cities. Like aeroplanes, they have metaphorically risen above whatever unaesthetic or insoluble problems may rest below.

The birds selected demonstrate an array of characteristics. There is the gannet with its wide wingspan, powerful, beautiful, and a long-distance flier; the graceful, beautiful and rare white heron; a colourful saddleback; the highly territorial oystercatcher; the familiar tui; wood pigeons; the endangered kokako; and playful cheeky fantails. This is a roll call of fascinating and aesthetic New Zealand birds. Their very familiarity unites viewers: only this population, here, is likely to recognise these unique birds as New Zealand wildlife. (Though many people would not have seen these species in the wild, they are familiar from school books, posters, coins, postage stamps, and so on.)

The sequence juxtaposes birds and bush and emotive scenes featuring people who look like New Zealanders are supposed to look (readily recognisable because of the locations in which they are placed). These individuals show joy, sadness, reuniting, separation: all 'airport emotions'. Pakeha, Maori, Asian and Polynesian, across class and age — 'ordinary' New Zealanders — are presented in a wide range to cover viewer identification, and reference to the international carrying service of the airline.

Three generations are represented, children used as potent symbols of the family and of the future. Happy children convey a happy, peaceful, racially harmonious society. The children given centre stage are boys: 'he' is the universal pronoun; these lads can build the future of the nation. The girls will presumably watch and help, and hold the banner. Maori are integrated with other images in sentimental shots of children with 'Haere Ra' signs.

There is nothing subtle about this ad's symbolism. After all, it has to be read very quickly by viewers, to instantly produce the required warm fuzzies. Imagery includes something every single viewer can relate to. The heart-tugging emotional tones vary: there are not just happy scenes, but reunion, farewell, celebration and love, manipulating the viewer to pick at least one with which to identify. Identity and culture are actively promoted and reworked into nationalism. Watching the ad involves sharing a common symbolic experience, which simultaneously shows our separateness from anywhere else. Our national airline is promoted as totally representative of all of us; an 'us' reconstructed to fit the ad.

Air New Zealand began life in 1940 as TEAL (Tasman Empire Airways Limited). A teal is also a species of duck: the bird association was explicit right from the beginning. In 1947 it was renamed the National Airways Corporation (NAC); this was altered again in 1965 to Air New Zealand.

In 1989 the airline changed from total state control to public ownership. These days Air New Zealand is jointly owned by New Zealand and Australia. The ownership includes 65% New Zealand nationals (public listed shares), 19% Qantas (Australia), 4% Japan Airlines, and 6% foreign investors. It is an oversimplification to call this a New Zealand company.

Airports throughout New Zealand service the airline. The advertisement implies that through this national network it has an important role in unifying national culture. A rugby team flying to play in another province demonstrates this linking.

This corporation is using what it believes is the most effective means possible to convince us to support this airline. To this end, its faith is in the power of sentimental notions of nationhood. Makers of both of these ads — Air New Zealand and Weetbix — are clearly aware of its importance, power and appeal. It must make an impact; otherwise advertisers would not use this ploy. The practice demonstrates the constructed nature of national identity: it can be created by ad men, fed to us many times daily, then taken on board as part of our understanding of what constitutes acceptable and representative national imagery.

These images and motifs recur endlessly: in ads for cars, travel, food and almost any other product. Nature can be relied on to be picturesque; and 'kiwi (male) ingenuity' will probably elicit a smile from the viewer (as in the Lotto ads, where a bungy-jump from a bridge is a way to catch a trout; or the Marmite ad, where a linesman cleverly and heroically restores electric power to a township by innovatively using a Marmite jar to replace a missing power insulator).

What we see on television has a bearing on the way we see the world and the ways we act in it. To protest, 'But it's just an ad!' is to state obliviousness to the impact of received images. Our own sense of national identity is inevitably informed by experiencing consistent imagery. We are told who we are often enough; and we are shown constantly. Kindergarten children know that 'kiwi kids are Weetbix kids'. This is the mark of a successful advertising campaign, but of concern when one considers the ethical issues of stuffing commercial messages into children's heads. However, it also demonstrates how from early childhood children are socialised to learn who they are. Advertising is a potent site for national identity explication.

'Have you driven a Ford lately?' takes us on a journey through the countryside. Toyota maintains the rugged kiwi bloke mythologies. Cheese ads take us back to a nostalgic rural life. All of these are based on fictions about vernacular culture, turned into something greater: iconic statements of identity, with which we identify because we 'belong'. The place shown is separate from any other nation. Where else looks like this? Because even if we have never been there, we will instantly recognise the sweeping native bush of Fiordland, or the abundant Canterbury Plains, or the dramatic Southern Alps.

All ads present as if speaking to everyone who watches; but are really aimed only at particular groups. And all maintain consistency with the myths of affluence and happiness and consumer joy. As media analyst Michael Pickering writes, the ads promote 'mythic forms of association, belonging and cultural order'. These images become the continually rerun versions of, and memories for, New Zealand.

Sports

Sports broadcasts take up more viewing time than anything else, even ads. 'New Zealanders love rugby!' The media has steered sport into a major position in national identity formulation for over a century. It has united spectators in their belief that their nation shares a collective identity, while reflecting qualities that in this society are seen as desirable: macho prowess, individual effort, disciplined training, and a chance to prove successful against far larger countries.

'Before there was a well-defined national market in New Zealand, or even a very effective national state, rugby tied together the collection of localities and provinces into a national body,' Geoff Fourgere tells us.[16] In these terms, the game pre-dates the emergence of a New Zealand nation. At first a sport for the élite, it became the national game by the end of the nineteenth century. Newspapers quickly picked up on the game and coverage of rugby matches became the vehicle for local identification.[17]

Support for the national game links provincial teams throughout New Zealand with the rest of the country. A national community is created by such language as 'our players', 'our team', 'the whole of New Zealand'. The unity is conveyed in spite of any underlying differences. Any major win against international teams is a time to reaffirm unity and collective identity. This sense of national community is only possible via the media.

State values of identity are explicitly expressed through the support of male-orientated sports. In 1995, special legislation was hurriedly passed to enable the Warriors to play their first Auckland game against the Brisbane Broncos.[18] A ban on all tobacco sponsorship prevented the Warriors from playing on their own turf (the match was to open the Winfield Cup). The Warriors had generated phenomenal media hype leading up to this match: to win against traditional archrival Australia was roughly like winning a major war, in terms of what it might generate for national pride. The government let the match go ahead so the spin-off celebrations of the expected win could benefit and be enjoyed by the nation.

On the big day nearly 25% of government MPs attended the match, which received major media attention. The competition against the Australian team was like two nations meeting at the boundaries. The *New Zealand Herald* described the crowd as a 'sea of green and blue clothing and accessories' worn by the Warrior supporters, with the Bronco supporters 'loudly defiant in their gold and maroon battledress'. Macho cultural values of watching sport and drinking copious quantities of beer spilled into the news coverage: the same *Herald* item commented on fans with video cameras to use as 'memory aid(s) to help fill in the hazy bits in the morning'.[19]

Watching sport and drinking beer: each is valued male behaviour. The guy not playing but drinking instead is still asserting his manhood. The two are solidly linked by breweries' sponsorship of male-orientated sports. The All Blacks are sponsored by Steinlager, the Warriors and cricket by Dominion Breweries, Team New Zealand by Steinlager, and Lion Red has been supporting rugby league since 1966. Meanwhile, the women's national netball team is sponsored by Milo and Caltex: chocolate drink and service stations.

In a *Metro* magazine article shortly after the Warriors-Bronco match, writer Warwick Roger describes rugby league spectators as an example of 'white trash culture'. For Roger this is apparently the working-class area of culture, which he says relies on media constructions of national identity, including the heavy mass commercialisation of sport. He quotes C. K. Stead's comment on the link between the promotion of sport and nationalism: 'It appeals to people who think they haven't got an individual identity unless they have a collective identity.'[20] He misses the point that this process extends well beyond league fans. I am fairly confident that Mr Roger would not describe America's Cup fans as 'white trash culture'; yet their chance to participate as spectators at the live event is far less than for league watchers; and there is an even greater site (the parade!) for the stirring, by the media, of nationalistic fervour.

Rugby or league: in each case these male-orientated sports dominate sports news coverage (between them taking up over 350 hours of transmission in the first half of 1995 on Television One alone). Each sport is claimed to have a significant positive uniting role in the national psyche. Each game is treated as an exhilarating major national ritual, inviting vicarious participation. The games unite spectators in their belief that their nation shares a collective identity, when sport actually excludes great chunks of the population. Sports coverage keeps alive traditional male virtues, relegating women to the sideline: selling baked beans, perhaps, if they happen to have been wife and mother of All Blacks.

The claimed unity of sport was very publicly questioned in 1981, during the Springbok Tour protests. The protests split the population across racial, gender and social boundaries. This illus-

The giant roadside shearer at Te Kuiti commemorates international shearing champions from the area, and the contribution of sheep farmers to the local and national economy. John Lyall

Weetbix makes high achievers! Hillary and Tensing, played by child actors, show off the breakfast cereal that has taken them to the summit.
Courtesy Sanitarium

Two popular Shortland Street characters, Carmen and Guy, on the cover of the programme's very own fanzine. The series has been sold to Britain, Sri Lanka, Indonesia, the Seychelles, Fiji, Jamaica, the Bahamas and Botswana.
Courtesy TVNZ Enterprises

Footrot Flats figures on a barn in Northland. Figures from Murray Ball's cartoon can be spotted as murals on farm sheds throughout New Zealand.
Claudia Bell

What the definitive 'Southern Man' Drinks, Dresses, Talks, Drives, thinks ... John Lyall

Rugby-mad males, kiwi ingenuity, mateship: Palmerston North students who built a grandstand in their lounge to watch the World Cup (winter 1995) on a big-screen television. *Real New Zealanders!*
Courtesy G. Brown/Manawatu Evening Standard

Still stunning, even with the tide out. Mitre Peak, Milford Sound, is one of New Zealand's most readily recognised icons. Endless reproductions of its image ensure its familiarity. John Lyall

Kiwiana stamps: icons posted around the nation. John Lyall

trates an interesting contradiction: it has long been assumed that rugby integrated the males of this country, yet the events in 1981 showed how divided New Zealand really is. Rugby coverage since then again conveys national harmony, unity and homogeneity, when events in 1981 prove that this was/is not so.[21] Any public events that the media lead into celebration have to be low risk, certain of not attracting dissenters who might wreck the event on the day and undermine these cosy, cohesive interpretations of who we are. It is no surprise at all that television leaps in behind the *Black Magic* America's Cup campaign; but makes nowhere near the same effort to push support for the fleet of yachts sailing up to protest at Moruroa.

That television shows so much sport and makes endless claims of the national heroism inherent in sports achievement can be contrasted with New Zealand's relatively poor industrial productivity internationally and poorly educated, low-skilled workforce compared with other industrialised nations.[22] TV's sports coverage as a reflection of the dominant interests of the culture ignores these other aspects of New Zealand life.

Myths and fairy stories

Television entertainment and news function in much the same way as myths and fairy stories in pre-industrial society. Just as Red Riding Hood instructed small children about stranger danger, and Goldilocks taught other moral lessons, so do the new fictions, posing as something else, tell us about us: who we are, New Zealanders. These mythologies are constructed and administered to us by the new storytellers, television.

From television we can quickly learn what is normal and acceptable and what is not. Boundaries between 'us' and 'them' are conveyed on a daily basis as visual imagery. By inclusion, exclusion and illusion we come to know ourselves and others.

Television has claimed the role of cultural maintenance of the New Zealand Pakeha myth: the middle-class, happy, financially comfortable nuclear family, the good society, the sporting heroes and sports-loving culture, nostalgically linked to the land, racially harmonious, surrounded by unique flora and fauna. If we behave properly and don't make a fuss over political issues, we will all live happily ever after!

Some might argue that this is the 'stabilising myth' of Western societies.[23] But this is to miss the point that our support for the way television transmits our culture to us (because mostly it goes unchallenged) is support for pressure to conform to prescribed versions of national identity or national pride. Television presents conditions as 'natural'. In this way middle-class Pakeha values are constantly projected onto the masses by the medium, with the assumption that these are universal values, and to the benefit of us all.

Sometimes when television claims to speak for 'us', it does, by taking on a self-conscious watch-dog role on specific, isolated events. But just as often it deprives viewers of a right to opinion by transmission of the delusion that the televisual discourse is our own, as in the embracing pronoun 'we . . .' in commentaries. If the audience does not have shared values, then the media will create them.

Television does not present reality, but through its considered reconstruction it creates a sense of reality that is ideological, while it claims it shows the truth. This is not reality, but hyper-reality, reliant more on image and spectacle than on content. Many events would not take place except for the media; some events take place only on television, and bear no relation to the real world at all.

This imagined community created by television is hard to ignore. It has become an intrinsic part of modern society. Many Pakeha people have limited contact with 'other' groups, for instance ethnic groups, so rely on the media to give information on those groups outside our own experience. The shallow national identity we are sold probably benefits us, if we are middle-class Pakeha. There are token efforts to address this shallowness, by a cut-and-paste of ethnically-specific programmes at non-prime times: attempts to satisfy groups without economic clout. But for the most part, all groups are subsumed under the one ideology and the dominant set of national symbols.

7
Nostalgia and kiwiana

National stereotypes — recreating myths
Big strong men playing sport in black jerseys; the farmer and his dog at home in rugged nature; the picturesque landscape; wholesome country living: such identity imagery is instantly recognised by New Zealanders, whenever and wherever it appears.

Writers, actors and cartoonists have built careers around this sort of thing. Fred Dagg (played by actor John Clarke) eventually took off his gumboots at the back door and never put them on again. Murray Ball closed the gate on *Footrot Flats*. Both of these legend-makers know that as culture changes, caricatures become dated and are no longer appropriate. But their residues remain. As mentioned in Chapter Five, a character who looks like Fred Dagg with his gumboots has been revived as town icon at Taihape; and a scribbled cartoon or an actor dressed as this figure is instantly recognised in any context. And *Footrot Flats* cartoon books and merchandise are still about. While the originators of each have abandoned the perpetuation of these particular characters and myths, their creations have consolidated in popular culture.

Meanwhile Bogor, another cartoon Man Alone in a black singlet, is still relentlessly teasing hedgehogs, snails and pine trees. And Barry Crump has remained a very 'Good Keen Man'. Crump's character made his first impact in that novel over thirty years ago, and has survived, producing in effect two legends: first the one in the book, and now the Crump celebrating thirteen years of touting Toyotas. Perhaps he has been less anxious than Clarke or Ball to move on to other things? Maybe he simply does not want to give back the Toyota?

These 'national characters' all reiterate the favourite male myths: the inexorable rural Man Alone, ever self-reliant, and suspicious of emotional attachments as symbolised by women. The blokes depict the culture as quintessentially male. In *Footrot Flats* the corruptive influence of Cheeky Hobson is a persistent threat to the mateship of Wal and Dog. Wal's Aunt Dolly is the domestic tamer, trying to organise the chaos of Footrot Flats. In Barry Crump's books the women are domestic monsters who get in the way of mateship. Fred Dagg occasionally refers to the 'Mrs', mother of his seven sons, all called Trevor Dagg. But she remains offstage, presumably inside making pikelets, tea and roast dinners for Fred and the seven young Trevors. In these fictions the dilemma is of mateship versus mating. The precarious masculine world of male culture is under constant threat from the women who only want to comfort and domesticate. Their 'civilising influence' is something these blokes want to escape. Bogor does not appear to know any women. He relies entirely on hedgehogs, snails and pine trees for friendship, though he appears to quite like his chainsaw, too.

Through these incarnations, the masculinity of New Zealand myths is sustained into the present. Evidently these fictive folk heroes continue to strike a chord. The continuing popularity of Crump has had him wind up as one of the 'Famous New Zealanders' on the 1995 postage stamp issue. About 90,000 people cast votes, and Barry Crump was selected in the category 'fine arts and literature'. Mr Crump was pleased at the honour: 'I represent the back country bloke; they work bloody hard to keep this country going.'

The Southern Man roadside billboards advertising Speights Beer draw from the same keep-this-country-going bloke-and-the-elements anti-woman tradition — or if not anti-woman, with clear ideas about all a woman is good for. The Speights posters feature a rugged outdoor type (male!) in swanndri, gumboots and stockman's hat, out with his dog, mustering. The backdrop of the high country suggests that this is his land.

This frontiersman is a 'real kiwi bloke'. Words on the pub posters tell 'How to be a Southern Man: all you ever need to know about Drinking, Dressing, Talking, Driving and thinking Southern Man style'. (Note: 'thinking' does not start with a capital 't'.) Potential Speights Beer drinkers are told to 'never let a woman drive unless he has had a few'; and 'one for the road means two for the road'.

A Speights-drinking Southern Man 'only likes animals he can ride, muster or whistle at'; 'respects women who drink Speights out of a jug'; and 'only visits the North Island to watch the Otago rugby team'. The product is promoted to drinkers who presumably enjoy these sentiments.

In this incarnation, the real kiwi joker is a sturdy figure indeed, a down-market Marlborough (cigarette) man, with character tough enough to pit against the environment in which he works. Presumably men who do not fit this image are not worth drinking with, and are not Man enough to drink Speights. There is no counter type, no Northern Man.

The persistence of the same bloke stereotype to stand for ultimate masculinity is difficult to ignore. And it is hard to imagine any other male stereotype catching on. The well-groomed male characters portrayed in *Shortland Street* would have to be dismissed as wimps because they hang about urban designer interiors worrying about their Relationships. They are not Men's Men, so are unlikely candidates to represent New Zealand masculinity.

The good-humoured characters Dagg, Crumpy et al have helped maintain the stereotypes. By keeping it comic, any attack by feminists can be dismissed as lack of a sense of humour. Their creators make a living — in some cases an excellent one — from their work portraying the mythical New Zealand rugged country bloke. The traditional bloke characteristics are readily recognised, not because they are necessarily based on real people whom we know, but because this 'type' has now been around for a very long time. The accessible national joke is drawn from the dominant thread that runs through the recounting of national history, with farmers for generations epitomising the self-reliant, ingenious Man Alone.

Homestead and grounds; house and garden

Romanticised versions of the rural way of life have remained as a central theme in national myth-making.[1] In the 1990s we are seeing a growing industry of attempts to capitalise on such traditional Pakeha myths. New Zealand 'colonial' has evolved into a distinctive consumer style, a set of fictive references drawing from an international fashion for a generalised 'colonial' country style (as in Mediterranean Style; Japanese Style; Country Style). In New Zealand the emphasis is on objects made from kauri and rimu, and a generalised mock-rural ambience.

If one has a penchant for such things, one can fill one's home with colonial-style items. There are numerous 'country-style' furniture stores brimming with brand new reproduction brass beds, kauri chests, kitchen dressers and chiffoniers. Retail outlets selling these nostalgia objects draw from a very generalised concept of 'country' and 'past', happily mixing reproductions of artefacts from American colonial times (Amish quilts and Sante Fe sleigh beds) and 'olde' England (candlesticks and tableware) with New Zealand kauri furniture. At Early Settler, a large store in Ponsonby Road, Auckland, specialising in this sort of thing, the furniture has both a familiar and a foreign look: familiar styles for tables, dressers and Scotch chests but made mainly from teak, mahogany and rubberwood; oh, and from something called 'English tawa'. The aim seems to be to offer a vast selection of 'colonial' furniture, but that term is used very loosely indeed. But the crowning items are those made in genuine native timbers, especially kauri or rimu: timbers that are available only in New Zealand. Decorative accessories to arrange with this furniture include wicker baskets, dried flowers (English style), embroidered sheets and cotton throws.

Early Settler is located in the very trendy and popular Ponsonby café district — that part of New Zealand's largest city that prides itself on being very street-smart chic. Early Settler, SPQR (a very fashionable café) and Videomagic (for video hireage) condense a span of time into just three adjacent shops. The late twentieth century is terrific: we can choose between a prissy Victorian four-poster bed; or a video of beautiful actors using one.

Advertising — for similar furniture sold in another store — promises they are the 'antiques of the future'. There is no reminder that these are inexpensive reproductions of antiques of the past, to create an ambience of the past, to suit the taste of those who either prefer antiques, but cannot afford them; or prefer these objects, because they are newer.

The new interior we can create with this furniture illustrates how we can take a vague idea about New Zealand colonial history, assemble artefacts to represent it, and come up with a domestic environment that reconstructs this mythical vision of the past. 'The past' conjured by being embodied in new consumer goods such as mock-colonial kauri rocking chairs and kitchen tables is reproduced on a daily basis. Intrinsic to ownership and display of these objects is reiteration of the popular myths. To fill one's home with such objects is to some extent to attempt a relocation across time: to claim an historic association with place, which avoids attempts to resolve what a 'New Zealand' style might look like, if put together from artefacts of contemporary design.

Fabricated 'traditional country' style transmutes historic fictions into contemporary consumables. The secure, homely look of the imagined past is reinvented for the post-modern interior. Domestic objects of the past, prettified, exaggeratedly display those virtues lacking in more obviously mass-produced modern goods. The 'hand made' and 'hand crafted' are recast not as clumsy and inconvenient, but as rustic and charmingly quaint.

These artefacts which are stylistically associated with country living suggest, in one's home, a particular family history. In the present era the traditional family 'home' is a real estate commodity as much as (or more than?) a repository for family sentiment across generations. People's mobility through occupation, locality, residence and country has shoved aside attachment to the particular house, particular locality, or particular geographic area. While most of our ancestors arriving in New Zealand did not come from the gentry, the current gentrification of some homes suggests a past that includes a gentility and class status that are in fact romantic fictions. Indeed, real estate advertisements and 'open home' magazine articles in New Zealand publications imply added value when they state, 'much loved English home barely touched by the passage of time'; 'reflects the emotions and character of yesteryear'; or 'step back in time and experience the grace and splendour of yesteryear, with beautifully landscaped English gardens'.

And so the colonial past is packaged as 'style'. The established country homestead look drew wry comment from Jean Baudrilliard in *Cool Memories*: 'They had taken out such a good insurance policy that when their house in the country burned down, they were able to build another one older than the first.' [2]

This country-style merchandise utilises the past as picturesque template for those for whom aesthetic values must be prescribed. For the manufacturers and retailers, 'country' is another look, marketable because it in uncontroversial. Every furnishing item in the house can be reproduced to fit this look, making it easy to recreate rooms in stores. For consumers, the process may be seen as a exercise in sentiment for the way things were not.

The choosing and buying of these items is a rejection of contemporary design, which is a more difficult choice for many consumers to make, given its inherently individualistic statements. Besides, new design carries with it no apparent domestic or national history. The cosiness factor of old-time furnishings, patchwork quilts and ceramic candlesticks recalls households — whoops, homesteads — in living or imagined memory: a grandmother's or great-aunt's kitchen, perhaps, remembered as always welcoming, comfortable and cosy, and not troubled by anything nasty happening in the world.

Along with the nostalgia furnishings there has been a recent huge wave of nostalgia gardening. Christine Dann explains that by the 1850s, six hundred years after the first cottage gardens were created in England, cottage gardening was flourishing 19,000 kilometres away from its country of origin, in New Zealand.[3] Suitable climate and soil conditions here, along with the cultural tradition of 'do it yourself' have made gardening both a popular pastime and a serious industry. New Zealanders spent $195.45 million on their domestic gardens in 1994. In 1995 they can shop for plants and other garden supplies from over 350 sales outlets. The current fashion for old-fashioned gardens has provided new interest in lavender, old roses and box hedges. Lovingly planted around the old villa — or the new townhouse — these plants recall (hypothetical) childhood and granny's (hypothetical) garden, while indicating a newly claimed gentility and leisurely elegance in the late twentieth century. Bird baths, sundials, fountains and other garden accessories embellish the artificial nature. Cute bird nesting-boxes and ornamental garden taps painted 'heritage green' (with sweet little English birds as decoration) draw romantically from a far longer garden tradition than our own. These items connect as much to Peter Rabbit as to Sissinghurst. Doesn't matter: they are cute; and, more importantly, they look *English*.

Part of the success of these items has been because of the need for 'prescription' gardening; a desire for a distinct style to follow, to accommodate a generation of home-makers perhaps not as skilled at gardening as their parents. Their motive might be less the pleasure and therapy of gardening, and more the desire for an attractive property, with good resale value. While the most popular purchases at garden centres in the 1990s are 'instant colour, instant garden' items, the traditional cottage garden look is promoted by and popular in gardening magazines and television programmes. Many of the decorative accessories fit the gift sales section of garden centres, which are an expanding part of the industry (and do very well: they are open seven days, and have parking outside!).

These items on sale for nostalgia house-and-gardens are intriguing. We are reaching the year 2000, leaving colonial times further and further behind. Yet there has been a huge revival in popularity of items that grandma tossed out when she wanted her house and section to look more 'modern'. Out went the 'ugly old furniture' when formica arrived; in went the concrete as a driveway to accommodate the family's new car. Out went the bread-making gear and bottling equipment as bread and canned food became readily available commercially. Visit any craft shop and see objects that attempt to appeal primarily for being 'hand made'. New-old teddy bears (just like those we had as children), reproduction old-fashioned wooden toys, gismos and coochicoos in calico, floral prints and gingham: here, also, we see traditional objects manufactured and manipulated into commodified nostalgia and myth. Packaging on some new lines of toiletries suggest the home-made simple potions of great-grandma, presented to look as if she made them yesterday. Sweet little pots of jam with floral fabric lid covers tied with ribbons fit the same genre. Through the new objects a gentle, genteel hyper-coloniality is sustained to replace lost colonial relationships. The aesthetic trappings of imperialism convey another time, with Victoria the Queen reigning over nostalgic New Zealand; not Elizabeth II. The items connect the consumer to positive romantic notions of the past, a safe and pretty place with which to link from the (disturbed?) present.

Okay: not everyone setting up house in New Zealand wants to surround themselves with mock colonialia (or is it coloniabilia?). And many of us, please, do not want replica items from granny's sideboard or dresser for Christmas, thanks all the same. But that does not mean we can divorce ourselves from the pervasiveness of this stuff. Neo-colonial style has crept into popularity and visibility. It is hard to walk into any city shopping centre without seeing reference to it.

Shops and shopping

Reference to the style is also present in the contemporary architecture of some New Zealand shopping centres. In the hunt for a style that states something about who we are, this seems to have caught on.

English writer Fred Davis suggests that the fashion for nostalgia partakes of one of the great dialectic processes of Western civilisation: 'the ceaseless tension of change versus stability, innovation versus re-affirmation, new versus old. . . .. Its role in this dialectic is that of a brake from the headlong plunge into the future'.[4] New colonial villages, such as those at Albany, Kumeu and Levin can be read as efforts to evoke just such stability, and re-affirmation. In keeping with the traditional tone of the 'village' concept, the architects of these shopping centres have included generous references to New Zealand's Victorian domestic architecture. Each building, while clearly new, has gables, finials, wooden lace, and turned wooden balustrades incorporated into the design, to recall the colonial wooden villa.

Havelock North claims the 'village' label to distinguish it from nearby urban Hastings. Flower-boxes and hanging baskets adorn the streets. A commissioned sculpture of a village blacksmith (on the site of the original smithy) contributes to the ambience. The new shopping complex in the village, with its smart colonial-style buildings, adds further support to the 'village' concept, with balustrade verandahs linking the cottagey shops.

These centres are aimed at everyday local consumers, with the expected local businesses: pharmacies, hot bread shops, stationers and appliance outlets. The goal seems to be to enhance the local; to imply through fabricated rustic charm a traditional sense of local 'community' values to compete with glitzier shopping options elsewhere. The similarity of the architecture chosen for these buildings, whatever the town, conveys that the 'New Zealand' style is colonial.

The design of these shopping centres suggests a clinging on to 'heritage'. Heritage representations are plucked from the economic and political climate of their time. The mythical charm of the past displaces conflict and tensions of the present. Besides, the building styles are familiar. Contemporary architecture itself may seem uncertain to people commissioning designs for a shopping mall, which has to be acceptable to local shoppers. These designs based on safe, pretty buildings of the past avoid the risk of something architecturally controversial in the present. Their advocates perhaps do not see this architectural reactionism as an expression of belief that the present in their locality has little to offer, and the height of local progress and prowess was achieved a long time ago. Has it really all been downhill since then? At the same time, local reverence for the past, the respect for heroic ancestors discussed in Chapter Three, quells criticism.[5] It is a pity that there appear to be limitations for connecting the present to the past in a critical and creative way. Meanwhile, these new little villages articulate an identity that earns the term 'quaint'.

The style they are trying to preserve has resonances of old buildings found all over New Zealand: the ubiquitous domestic villa. Currently this is a popular style undergoing new appreciation, and spawning small industries in renovation materials: for instance, new wooden lace off old patterns, new ceiling mouldings, stained glass decorations, and reproduction kauri fittings.

At Stratford in Taranaki quite a different project of nostalgic image-making is underway. Blessed, or possibly cursed, with a name with instant associations, this small rural town (population about 5,500) is trying to fashion itself into New Zealand's Shakespeare Centre.

Stratford was named in 1877, its site chosen for the development of a town on the banks of the Patea River. At the Taranaki Waste Land Meeting on 3 December 1877 the town was named Stratford-on-Patea. Streets of the new town were to be named after characters in Shakespeare's plays. Lysander Street, Prospero Place, Hamlet Street, Lear Street; they are all there, in Stratford.

The Stratford Mainstreet Society in 1995 is still working with this theme for the town. The aim is not to try to recreate Stratford-upon-Avon, but to make their town distinctive from all other New Zealand towns. It already has the name, the street names, the relationship with the river and the strong interest in being known as the Shakespeare Centre for New Zealand. It is therefore deemed appropriate that the streetscape planning and other town development should encourage the implementation of 'Elizabethan' elements and design. This is to be combined with gardens of plants depicted in Shakespeare's works. Landscaping is to include knot gardens, cottage gardens, herb gardens and trees aligned to the Elizabethan era. Cobbled and flagstone paving are being laid to further enhance the environment, and building owners are encouraged to extend the theme by creating mock-Elizabethan façades. Dovecotes are planned for Prospero Place and elsewhere, to add charm. The planners are keen that 'the concept will not be without humour with the inclusion of "vagrants" in stocks and pillories on the Northern roundabout and "gibbets" suspended from the prominent poles and structures during festivals'.

Best wishes to the organisers of this little Elizabethan theme town in Taranaki. Their project is ambitious, and taking an enormous amount of work. The intriguing issue is the sense of obligation to recreate a history that never did exist in New Zealand (Shakespeare: born 1564, died 1616. Stratford-on-Patea: founded 1877). The simple historic accident of naming the town over a century ago has resulted in this scheme in the present.[6]

Out of the catalogue of looks that constitute 'New Zealand colonial', the rural myth seems to be getting the most outings. The values implied by popular mythologies of traditional country living are recycled to create an ambience. These values spill over, supposedly, to inhabit the quality of the goods on sale, even where the merchandise is totally unrelated to the theme myths. A wander around any central city boutique district, and the window shopper can spot displays of fashion garments suitable for casual urban wear with posters of 'real men' in mythical rural settings as backdrop (lounging against picturesque old barns; leading their horses over the landscape). A store of expensive designer garments on Broadway, Newmarket, one of Auckland's more up-market shopping Meccas, even has hay bales dotted about its otherwise extremely contemporary elegant space. New Zealand is not known for its Saville Row apparel, but for its swanndris. Hay bales in a Broadway boutique invite association with the latter, rather than the former, whatever garments are on display.

A far more detailed orchestration of random objects of rural decor can be seen in a popular supermarket chain.

Have you been to a Big Fresh supermarket? For those of you who do not have access to this urban wonder, let me tell you about my local Big Fresh.

As soon as customers get to the doors at any Big Fresh it is obvious that this is more than a supermarket. Shoppers are in for a cultural experience. As one uplifts one's trolley, the sound of chooks clucking can be heard. This recorded sound is an attempt to convey a farm yard ambience.

After selecting from the huge range of fresh fruit and vegetables, one moves on to the meat section. The sound is of cows mooing. Are they mourning their lost loved ones, whose remains are now neatly cut and plastic packaged steaks and stews in the refrigerated display? Or are they reassuring us that they accept their fate, and moo encouragement for us to buy?

Against farmyard sound effects one can simply chug on and fill one's trolley; or pause to gaze at the mezzanine displays. Models of farm people and animals which look as if they have escaped from Old MacDonald's Farm are arranged on wide ledges around the perimeters of the stores. Yokel farmers laze about on verandah swings, or slump over barbed wire fences, amid casually strewn, vaguely rural, colonial bric-à-brac. Their mural backdrop is of sun-lit fields, forever green and gold. The wall of refrigerators sits beneath a mural of a pastoral landscape.

Signage in the store continues the mock-rural ambience. Numbers and letters are printed in text matching wool bale brands, on rough hardboard. At the checkout the signs are arranged amongst old saddles and miscellany from ancient stables.

The theming of the supermarket is obviously to convey to us the farm-freshness of the products, recalling visions of the wholesome and abundant country farmhouse kitchen. Indeed, many grocery lines bear labels featuring these same themes (made famous for a moment when once on her television show Dame Edna Everage said she only bought food items that had pictures of country cottages on the packets. Despite her flamboyant super-stardom, there is a nook or cranny in her heart that longs for a simpler life).

Country Crock, for instance, is a yellow substance to spread on bread. Its name and packaging present heavy-handed visions of rustic bliss. Countrysoft, a blend of butter and margarine, combines the marvels of the new (low cholesterol, spreadable, scientifically formulated, manufactured in an hygienic urban factory, modern) with the 'goodness' and *tradition* of the old: pure, natural, from the country, part of the New Zealand heritage. The same nostalgic messages are present on many other grocery items: Farmbake Cookies (made in urban factories), Orchard Harvest carpet spray, and Country Breeze air freshener.[7]

At the Big Fresh supermarket the concerted arrangement of decor recalls mythical times when everything was extremely cosy in the farmhouse. The presentations are accessible to the shopper's imagination: everyone can identify with New Zealand's pastoral heritage. The displays are material representations of a mythical way of life. Big Fresh's play with country style commodifies the consumable component of nostalgia, by adding these values to the inherent value of the groceries for sale in the supermarket.

Big Fresh is a chain of ten supermarkets in mainly North Island cities (four in Auckland, and one each in Whangarei, Hamilton, Napier, Wellington, Christchurch and Dunedin). The first Auckland Big Fresh opened in 1989. The chain is owned by Dairy Farm International Ltd, a major multinational, part British-owned and based in Hong Kong. A company spokesman told me that the country décor theme was central to the original concept when the stores were designed. The same theme is used in their Australian stores.

'Oh, so this is not necessarily *New Zealand* country style being referred to?' I asked.

'Oh, yes,' he assured me. 'In New Zealand we use New Zealand items, in Australia we use Australian ones. It is quite authentic.'

Nostalgia: selective cultural archaeology

The processes described perpetuate the mythologies, commodifying the abstraction 'way of life' into objects to generate financial and social returns. Compared with the 'existential' nostalgia of, for instance, Wakefield's day (arising from notions of alienation under industrial capitalism tied to Utopian ideals of a Pacific paradise), contemporary nostalgia is not only sentimental, it has another dimension. In an age when virtually anything can be bought and sold, nostalgia itself becomes a commodity, a commercially seductive component of many consumer goods.

In mass culture (urban culture!) the distinction of new from old, and the insistent hanging on to that distinction, might be dismissed as trivial and of little social significance in a small country. Nevertheless, the very pervasiveness of this style of imagery enforces a version on a daily basis of who we are. Through its constant presence we receive daily reiteration of shallow mythologies that give us a collective past, as Pakeha living in New Zealand. Individuals need to make no great effort to dig up local or national history: this populist version surrounds us, eliminating any need for closer investigation. Through these representations we superficially 'know' our past, and know who we are, distinct from any people anywhere else.

As mass communication supplants folk wisdom, folksiness is re-evaluated, recalled and commodified as quaint, charming, nostalgic and saleable. Nostalgia is exploited as the seductive component of consumer products. The current commercial interpretations of the 'great way of life' tack onto other received ideas from the past, contributing to ideas of national identity for both local people and outsiders.

Nostalgia and utopia; so what's new? European settlers arriving as pioneers were in some measure responding to visions of a pre-industrial golden age in Britain. They knew how great the past was, because it was celebrated in the songs, art and folk legends of popular sentimental collective memory. Dean MacCannell reminds us that 'every society necessarily has another society inside itself and beside itself: its past epochs and eras and its less developed and more developed neighbours; and a previous state, a "Golden Age" which retrospectively always appears to have been more orderly or normal'. He reflects that the lack of local traditions stimulates an appetite for relics of pre-industrial life, an appetite that accounts for the hugeness of the international heritage industry.[8] The local written histories referred to earlier are further tangible demonstration of this drive to convey a positive past matching popular mythologies. The demonstration of worthiness in the past is assurance of worthiness now, despite the anxieties presented by current uncertain conditions. Any unpleasantness in the past is obliterated, or recast in positive terms, and charm and goodness are ladled onto what may in fact have been very ordinary.

The sense of present times being in crisis and unpredictable is a normal phenomenon in society. Hence a culture may draw heavily from nostalgia: an accessible option when the possibility of gaining common control of the future has been steadily abandoned. British cultural commentator Raymond Williams explains how the revival of nostalgia as a response to political disillusionment is 'simple escapism, and excluded from practical thinking'.[9] For Williams, contemporary nostalgia-based utopianism is a drive to reaffirm feelings and relationships that have been displaced by the present order, or threatened by it. His view seems to fit what is happening in New Zealand, when we look at the ways national identity is reconstructed on a daily basis.

American writer David Lowenthal suggests nostalgia does not

denote so much despair of the present and future, as 'longings for times that are safely, rather than sadly, beyond recall'. That those days are out-of-reach makes nostalgia a safe fantasy. This is not a yearning for a past that was; rather, for an integration and completeness lacking in any present. 'History reveals and nostalgia celebrates an ordered clarity contrasting with the chaos and imprecision of our own times,' he explains.[10] The collected relics in (for instance) local museums, versions of which are also displayed in homes and shops as décor chic, actually construct those mythical times, and embody their supposed virtues.

All of this might make one misty-eyed. But these sentiments ignore history. No one ever experienced 'the present' as we now view 'the past'. In popular imagination history seems to be a different thing from the more flexible, manipulable 'past'. In fact, history is often perceived as rather boring, because it is based on pedantic fact. A revised 'past' is far more attractive because it is more open to subjective impressionism, rosily untainted by reference to pre-literacy, or class issues, or religious and moral practices repugnant in the later twentieth century. The view of pre-modern society as a moral unity is a generalised, romantic interpretation of the past against which to play out the social and moral inadequacies of the present.

It is unsurprising that whole societies are prone to nostalgic visions of the past (time unspecified). If the present is difficult or deficient, and the future uncertain, then of course the past is going to look more attractive. That artefacts of the past are physically available provides a material basis for the construction of nostalgia. Family photographs, personal and communal possessions, local landmarks and national icons link us to the past, and are carefully preserved, proclaiming a 'better' time. Collective nostalgia restores, however temporarily, a sense of socio-historic continuity in the face of possible discontinuity. On those days when we wonder 'what will become of us?' or 'what is happening to New Zealand?' nostalgia is a conservative way of avoiding tackling the hard things. Selective nostalgic memories are our way of reinventing the past, and of having it invented for us, for instance through the current crop of television commercials. Let's face it: how many New Zealanders really owned a bach? And a lot of New Zealanders would never have had fresh-baked 'cookies' in a cosy farmhouse kitchen (especially since they were always called 'biscuits' in those olden days).

The advantage of using nostalgia in the construction of national identity ideas and values is that it is totally free of social analysis or any conflict. If it looks as if some of our ancestors had a pretty tough time of it, we can skip any analysis with facile sympathy: 'poor things!'

Their times — our concept of the past — are imbued with special, positive qualities that contrast with perceptions of the present. These qualities become significant for the way they are juxtaposed upon particular features of our present lives, maintaining and affirming present identity. 'You have it easy! Food! We didn't have food! Crust of bread and dripping between eight of us; and we was lucky!' Hardships of the past are transported into jokes, or anecdotes that convey the heroism of sheer survival.

Commercial nostalgia aimed at tourists

In the reconstruction of colonial identity in local museums and town promotion projects described earlier, nostalgia about local history takes on a commercial value; or a potentially commercial value. Local entrepreneurs can see that local identity, or local history, could be a commercially viable product. The centennial war memorial hall up the road might be shabby but still useful. But it is no longer the focal point of most communities. New energy is going into building something that still has specific reference to the locality, but with emphasis on the commercial potential of local historic events and idiosyncrasies.

For instance, at Gore concerted efforts are going into reconstructing the once-famous Hokonui still. During prohibition, the thirsty citizens of Gore acquired their illegal liquor from moonshiners who hid their stills in the nearby Hokonui Hills. Today, as a town development enterprise, a new still is being built to represent the old. It is hoped that this will prove to be a popular year-round tourist attraction for the town, providing some local employment while conserving a local legend as a material artefact. South of Dunedin and with a population of around 9,300, Gore does not get much attention in the national press. But with insistent entre-preneurism it might. And through preserving a local legend it is also preserving national myths (about prohibition, illegal alcohol manufacture and gold-mining).

In a similar way, the superb collection of kauri and gum artefacts at the Otamatea Kauri and Pioneer Museum at Matakohe conserves another strand of national history. The museum is a popular attraction on the tour bus route heading north through the Waipoua Forest. The giant kauri trees there attract thousands of visitors each year, who come to marvel at the sheer size of these ancient giants (*Agathis australis*). As the road through the forest is sealed kilometre by kilometre each year, this trip becomes more popular with tourists, with a parallel increase in visitor numbers to the museum.

We know that this is a 'local' institution; but it possesses a collection of national treasures, which, if placed alongside everything else on display in a national museum, would not enjoy the status they achieve in a small specialist museum. At Matakohe this museum does not present merely a component of national history; it suggests the total history of the immediate area. In this site-specific context the artefacts of local social history, the remnants of the timber-milling industry, and the present iconic status of the remaining giant kauris in the forest, together create a retrospective heroism for the historic loggers. While the remaining kauri trees are now protected, the felling of much of the forest at an earlier time is safely valorised.

The museum employs nearly a dozen people, the café next door a few more. It functions as a important landmark for the district, its one public claim to fame, bringing people into Matakohe who would otherwise probably not notice this little country district or learn anything about its unique history.

At Katikati simply proclaiming the past might do the same thing: gain attention while commemorating history. Through the organising group's commitment to the ongoing public murals project, people in this town are exhibiting nostalgic ideas about their town. The images are then optimistically commodified into souvenirs. This public relations exercise encourages new businesses and leads to population growth, as Katikati is seen as a very 'go ahead' little town.

The nature tourism operator also draws from nature mythologies. The (predominantly urban international) tourist is taken back to the way things were: to primeval forests, ancient fiords, waterfalls and lakes where the purity of the water symbolises the purity of nature itself. Experiences of 'untouched' nature appear to have high status on tourism itineraries. The flowery language of tourist brochures proclaiming the grandeur of nature reinforce the positive sentiments of the beauty, bounty and adventure of nature.

While these projects and processes are in themselves nostalgic, they are also expected to generate income and become local employers. This is possible because visitors want to buy nostalgia items and will pay for nostalgia experiences. From interviews with entrepreneurs trying to promote towns and cities, it is evident that nostalgia is an important feature in the construction of identity and in the maintenance of that identity for both local people and outsiders.

Kiwiana: instant nostalgia

Evocation of an instant sense of New Zealand is also achieved by so-called kiwiana. Since *New Zealand! New Zealand! In Praise of Kiwiana* was published in 1989, the icons of kiwiana seem to have achieved even greater prominence.[11] Tack a Buzzy Bee onto almost anything at all, and there you go! The Buzzy Bee, a popular toy for post-war baby-boomers, reached a peak of popularity in the early 1950s, when around 40,000 of these toys were sold each year. The original brightly coloured pull-along clack-clack toy is now a collector's item. Imitations come in various colours, with striped wings, have four wheels not two, and run silently. For the generation that first chewed on these and kicked them about as toddlers, they have become a standard symbol for New Zealand. Prince William was given one when he visited New Zealand as a toddler. He played with it on a rug spread on the lawn outside Government House, with his parents happily beaming. This news photograph was flashed around the world. One can also buy little Buzzy Bees as ear-rings, brooches and decoration on merchandise in souvenir shops. The toy was featured as part of the kiwiana set of postage stamps, released in 1994 (in the same set as gumboots, swanndris, jandals, fish and chips, pavlova, hokey-pokey ice-cream, and kiwifruit).

The famous Edmonds Baking Powder label with a golden rising sun could be part of this set. The *Edmonds* 'Sure To Rise' *Cookery Book* is the all-time best-selling New Zealand publication. It resonates with memories of the fragrance and taste of fresh, fluffy home-baked scones, and the rather less impressive ones turned out at school cookery classes. Those were the days before the baby-boomer generation grew into adults who were seduced into using wholemeal, and who are now probably more likely to buy focaccia than bake scones. The first version of the recipe book was published in 1907, the de luxe in 1955. The two books have had a total of over 3.4 million sales, almost outnumbering the total present population. The baking powder itself is the only one available in New Zealand shops, long out-living a succession of competitors.

Perhaps the 'Sure to Rise' icon was left off the postage stamps series because it is, after all, an advertisement. But when a large Sure To Rise poster makes it into a High Street fashion boutique, we have an interesting demonstration of the relationship between kiwiana, nostalgia for vernacular cultural icons, and commerce. In Paris, Texas, a shop in High Street, Auckland, a mural of an old Rinso advertisement also has a place, along with an old-fashioned wringer washing machine and wooden washboard. Elsewhere in the store, wall racks display leather boots against a backdrop of a Kiwi nugget poster.

The 'museumification' of some shops, supermarkets and restaurants is a fashion which helps keep kiwiana and other images of social history present to the viewer's gaze, something to consume along with the coffee, food and other items for purchase. A traveller's café at Huntly is decorated with large photographs of an historic mining disaster; and a bar in the Waikato makes much of its location in a farming district, by 'theming' all décor around 'cows', starting with a large roadside concrete cow and calf near the car park. At the Bushman's Centre on the West Coast of the South Island the theme is traditional rural occupations, in a vigorously vernacular restaurant, with corrugated iron walls, matai tables, and animal-skin-covered seating (possum burgers, anyone?). As New Zealand cultural commentator Nigel Clark observes, '. . . the museum itself is no longer simply an inventory of objects simulating an external world, it is becoming a point of reference for the simulacra which now constitute the world beyond its walls . . . an imaginative resurrection of that which is disappearing. All those traditional mediums and idioms of the museum: the glass cabinet, the decontextualised fragment, the artefact on a pedestal, the series of related objects, the recreated scene or context . . . find a healthy afterlife (elsewhere).'[12] The very healthy state of the current fashion for nostalgia suggests this a secure afterlife indeed.

Nostalgia and myths

Jean Baudrillard comments that 'when the real is no longer what it used to be nostalgia assumes its full meaning. There is a proliferation of myths of origin and signs of reality; of second-hand truth, objectivity and authenticity.'[13] So where's the problem? This stuff looks innocent enough, it is not too challenging to go along with it; surely it doesn't hurt anyone, and it is a way of conveying Pakeha identity, both in the present day and in the past.

Some commentators suggest that nostalgia may be read as a failure of the collective consciousness to deal with modernising processes in contemporary society. They have found little evidence that these problems are likely to constitute an historic crisis resulting in the overthrow of current systems as we know them. Groups that want to resist appear to lose themselves in nostalgia or disassociation (as in 'not my problem!', the new alternative to 'she'll be right!'), rather than expend energy in organised resistance to change at the socio-political level. Nostalgia is a more accessible process than resistance, for those decrying social change.

Are the threats coming from globalisation provoking this preoccupation with nostalgic versions of our culture? Observer Roland Robertson suggests that the homogenising requirements of the modern nation state (given ethnic and cultural diversity) could well be the impetus to nostalgia as a feature of contemporary life. Globalisation, he insists, has been the 'primary root of the rise of wilful nostalgia. Indeed, wilful nostalgia as a form of cultural politics has . . . been an aspect of globalisation'.[14] He adds to this a case for an emphasis on national-societal identity, an individual nation asserting difference against the rushing tide of global processes that encourage sameness.

Nostalgia obviously has an enormous and highly functional role in the perpetuation of national mythologies. Perhaps it works as a convenient safety-valve, as it allows time to be assimilated? Individuals can relax and get used to the idea of societal change before having to actively participate. As an unconstructive, conservative response to contemporary society, it provides a way of accommodating dominant belief systems without challenge.

Is the past simply the easiest, safest resource for the collection of uncontroversial identifications? Is this selective cultural archaeology truly the best we can do? Perhaps the employment of nostalgia as guiding paradigm serves to replace our fragmented origins with a generic past, to construct a more confident ownership of our collective history. Subscribing to fictional roots turns a blind eye to the falseness of the collectively invented Pakeha origins, a fake history-in-common which constructs a much more unified history for Pakeha. There are enough of the genuine artefacts around with actual family historical associations to contextualise the bought-in colonial artefacts and reproductions.

It seems as if it is too hard to forge an identity that includes many diverse groups. Indeed, many Pakeha are finding it difficult to accept that new migrant groups really may have a permanent place here. Resorting to cultural nostalgia is a way of excluding newcomers, and re-asserting Pakeha primacy. The new exotic groups do not share this heritage. By reproducing Pakeha emblems of heritage and kiwiana, we keep reminding them of this.

The disabling effect of this sentimental nostalgia is that orientations to the future are left to others: business people take care of business, politicians take care of politics; and many of the rest of us float, or flounder, along in the wake of decisions made on our behalf. Is it this lack of everyday pro-activity, amid more acclaimed remnants of the past than obvious orientations towards the future, that gives the impression to many visitors that New Zealand is a 'quaint little country'?

8
But we are all New Zealanders!

A recent story of fleeting fame was about a bunch of ordinary kiwi blokes in Palmerston North. They just wanted to watch the rugby World Cup with their mates. So they hired a big-screen television set for the duration of the games. Then they decided they'd like a grandstand. They'd need some timber, so they took the ute over to Eketahuna to get some. They piled it on the tray, and drove on back to Palmerston North. Then, in the great tradition of matey co-operation, and with 'typical kiwi ingenuity', they built a wooden mini-grandstand in their lounge. It faced the large television set. Wearing team colours and rugby supporter gear — scarves, hats, badges — they drank their tinnies and cheered the All Blacks on; and ended up, grandstand and all, photographed for the *Manawatu Evening Standard* and reproduced in the *New Zealand Herald*.[1] This item gained worldwide attention via Reuters. It showed the world the values New Zealanders tell themselves they should have.

The media likes a story such as this. There are no baddies, and it is apolitical. It talks directly about national identity values in terms of these nice young ordinary blokes who want to male-bond while they watch rugby. A later article about the attention these blokes had received internationally said that in 'true, modest kiwi bloke fashion the fame was not getting to the guys' — showing that these rugby-loving handymen are models for the sort of character a kiwi bloke should be. Even the use of the words 'kiwi' and 'bloke' strive to shore up the matey vernacular, which is not nowadays heavily used in everyday speech.

Were readers overseas interested in this article? We can only assume that news items such as this continue to support the long-established image of New Zealanders: that our identity is inextricably tied with the All Blacks, and our main communal celebrations are rituals that involve blokes and sport. Blokes watching footie have a well-established place in the national culture. A popular myth is revitalised, yet again. This little item, like material in the previous chapters, demonstrates some of the mechanisms that promote, for both national and international observers, expressions of identity.

The same essential packages of mythologies and symbols can be wheeled out whenever required: blokes playing sport, the farmer character at home in rugged nature, the inevitable picturesque landscape. Identity imagery is so readily recognised, that it reads instantly as 'New Zealand', whenever and wherever it appears.

We can see deployment of these standardised notions of New Zealand attached to numerous products, services, and official documents. The familiar imagery is omnipresent. It is attached to everything from political party campaigns to advertisements for motor vehicles, banks and breakfast cereal. This process of recycling and restating must be worth doing for companies to use it. When any company or organisation promotes itself with the use of these images, the inherent claim is that they, the company, are part of the collective fictive 'us'. If these familiar images are shown, we will immediately know that whatever they are attached to is about 'us', so are likely to take a closer look. Anything about ourselves must be interesting! The use of symbols and mythologies which change over time (*Black Magic!* Red socks!) shows that what constitutes identity is flexible and can be manipulated.

National good

As political parties compete for power, manifestos promise to support the 'national good'. Voters are the judges of this: they choose, essentially, the party which they see as best enhancing national identity. No political party can run counter to this expectation in the electorate, though election promises are not legally binding, and support for one set of interests over another can be labelled 'for the national good' — such as economic reform. Clearly, 'identity' is not a given or an absolute, but a set of values that can be manipulated and modified for particular purposes at particular times.[2]

When opposing political parties base their claims on the same goal — achievement of the national good — where we disagree we challenge on the basis of their vested 'special interests'. As competing factions insist that their own interests and those of the nation are the same thing, we suspect their agendas. What are they really up to? Experience of politics and politicians has taught us to be suspicious.

We are less questioning when national identity imagery is claimed on our behalf without such obvious competition. There are other things to think about each day than what the BNZ hopes to gain by showing us that advertisement for their services that features a sentimental story about a quiet little seaside bach. Nor are most of us much bothered about why 'they' fly the national flag behind the Weetbix packet in the Edmund Hillary and Jean Batten ads. There is no counter-argument articulated in these displays (no claims about *their* bach from other banks; no other cereal company trying to tug the flag away). For the short moment that the image is present, there is not time to construct an argument against it. The image is simply and vaguely assimilated; and then the next, and the next. Every advertisement cumulatively reinforces the same simplistic national identity. Even between competing products, there is no conflict in their shared collective imagery of identity. They all construct the same New Zealand.

'For the national good': this concept is used as justification for particular sets of values, expediently flexible. Every powerful group justifies itself by claiming to represent the national interest, and in identifying itself with national identity. This must appear to work for the good of all, but in New Zealand the dominant group is Pakeha. They hold the nation's purse strings, and they dominate the social, political and cultural landscape. 'For the national good' underpins enormous quantities of Pakeha myth-making.

'National identity': the very idea assumes a unity, over-riding differences related to gender, ethnicity, class or religion. The term encourages individuals (the public) to identify with interests which have been presented to them as their own. 'National identity' as an all-embracing concept works like a national club open to everyone. If people haven't joined it is seen as their fault for not making the necessary adaptations to 'fit'. The idea of a national collectivity persists, despite our inability to create a society in which the myth of harmonious co-existing groups translates into the national reality of equality between different identities.

National identity as an 'assumption' of values in common enables the most powerful groups to maintain power. Those groups — the state and big business — act out their representation of, or concern for, national interests, as a way of hanging on to their own status and privilege. An apparent altruism is implied, or at least a set of interests in common with 'everyone' else. This is a deft little trick which ensures profits and power. Everyone is (apparently) happy, because any oppositional voices have limited access to a platform. Besides, most individuals are too preoccupied with survival to even notice; or too helpless to do anything about it.

The collective imagining of an identity in common does not prevent individuals from having other social identities. However these are often publicly undermined in favour of the qualities of the dominant group. In fact, the possibility of assorted other social identities probably supports the minimal collective identity shared by the plurality of groups — the more diverse the population, the greater the need to have 'something in common'. For instance, we often see letters to newspapers arguing that 'we are all New Zealanders' when some issue has been tossed up that emphasises plurality. This deliberately, blindly sidesteps the lesser opportunities of some citizens. National identity is easy to affirm as a blanket to conceal differences, when those differences are inconvenient.

The issue of national identity and the state comes up most often in New Zealand in discussions about international relationships for security and trade. In the 1990s there is strong encouragement by government and big business for New Zealanders to support our becoming 'part of Asia'. In redefining ourselves in this way, it is suggested we increase resources and interests towards Asia, to form mutually advantageous relationships. This would run alongside the shift of traditional economic and political ties from Europe to Asia, as new trade markets are sought. (In 1995, 40% of all exports went to Asian markets, compared with just 17% in 1970.) In 1994 New Zealand reduced Pacific Aid and increased aid to some Asian states. This was a symbol of the growing relationship with Asia, where new conservative New Zealand government policies sit very comfortably.

This has had a mixed response in New Zealand, including concern for national identity. Indeed, one prominent Auckland secondary school has a group of parents agitating for 'Pakeha cultural safety' in their school, as resistance to the influx of Asian students. These students, it is thought, undermine the school's cultural traditions and compete for awards and honours that 'should' go to local students. A *Listener* poll in October 1994 showed that more than half of those polled wanted fewer Asian immigrants.[3] Racist reactions in some suburbs has been masked by concern expressed at pressure on limited resources to integrate non-English-speaking children into mainstream classes at local schools. It seems that most New Zealanders want tourists from Asia, and Asian students here for education (they were welcome for short stays). By 1990 there were more Asian tourists to New Zealand than from anywhere else. They spend more than other tourists. In short: their money is welcome! But changes to New Zealand culture, through a greater number of permanent residents who are Asian, are apparently less welcome.

Politicians' insistence on calling this country 'part of Asia' demonstrates that official identity is arbitrary and manipulable. Where expedient, regional orientation may be a component of national identity.[4] While policies on external affairs might make these claims, these are run alongside attempts at building a sense of national community. Any new formal affiliation will be claimed as in the public interest, or for the public good, while underplaying the sectional interests they represent.

Over 80% of New Zealand's population is still of European origin. The state still clearly most strongly represents the interests of these white New Zealanders. At the same time, the cultural make-up of New Zealand's population is changing, with a slowly increasing portrayal of New Zealand as multicultural by the image-makers. This does not for a moment mean a redistribution of power amongst diverse cultures. Rather, it can best be read as overt recognition and encouragement of a broader range of consumer groups. New movements, conditions and factors arrive, emerge or evolve: for instance, the green movement, the 'Asian Invasion', the privatisation of medicine and the deregulation of education. As new conditions arise, the commercial potential of each in relation to national identity is calculated by those with most to gain. It is their mission to foster the growing new groups for their own interests.

This book has explored some of the influences that encourage us to share an identity. The examples included demonstrate how identity is constructed for us. But we need to know that not everyone fully submits. Individuals accept and assimilate the notions to various degrees. Our concepts of 'nation' — who we are, in an international context — do not subordinate our other sources of self, such as gender, ethnicity or religion. At the same time, though, we learn to recognise features of nation claimed to represent 'us all'.

'But we are all New Zealanders!'

National identity instils in individuals the desire to believe in a 'real New Zealand'. By the constant subtle reiteration of this concept, and rejection of any criticsm, the message is reinforced. The existing scheme of things is held as unchallengeable. The same values are distributed and perpetuated daily, over and again, for instance through the family, the education system, and the media. The ideas of national identity are fostered and recognised roughly in common across diverse groups. These ideas most closely match the values of the groups with most to gain. Ideological values become read as 'common sense', and actual social contradictions are masked. Social inequalities fade into the background as 'natural' or 'unfortunate'.

Through these manipulations some individuals claim superiority over others. In this institutionalised nurturing of prejudice and discrimination, generalisations and stereotypes are also part of common sense. Notions of 'us' and 'them' are encouraged, setting barriers between the people who claim to be part of the same thing, under the rubric of 'nation'.

Critics of the processes described in the earlier chapters — the creation and absorption of recognisable representations of nation that favour a particular group over others — argue that the need for coherent national identity comes from the need to support the status quo. National identity unites people in a sentimental way, including those who gain little in the current economic climate. Dissatisfaction is diverted, distracted by the opportunity to 'share' national pride in major public events. Hence the disadvantaged can go on participating in an inequitable economy, under the acceptance of the 'national interest'. The children of the disadvantaged may indeed believe 'kiwi kids are Weetbix kids', with bacon and eggs (or any other alternative) long off the menu; or indeed never on it.

Graeme Turner, an Australian writer on nationalism, argues that 'mythical inventions [carry] regressive consequences for the nation that believes in them'. In New Zealand, we can see the exclusion of women from the national character, the marginalisation of Maori, and representations of the country that focus on just one class group. There are large disparities between 'the licensed batteries of national imagery and the "realities" of national cultural experience', these the consequence of long-standing discrimination, oppression and imperialism.[5]

The assertion of national identity can be read as a social control mechanism to maintain order and quell resistance that could logically occur as a result of the large gap between rich and poor. A false image of nation is encouraged by the élite to members and non-members alike. These visions perpetuate the injustices of social life.

In capitalist societies such as New Zealand, it is the job of the state to create and maintain conditions in which profit-making is possible. While the state claims to act in the 'public interest' (but which public?) it also reproduces social inequalities, disenfranchising some groups. The concept of national identity is a handy one: by insisting we are all 'one', any notions such as class consciousness, or priority of other problematic identities, is suppressed. Encouraging a belief in an identity in common — one New Zealand — is a form of social control.

Projects and ploys to incite mass recognition of national values held in common (or apparently in common; or more-or-less in common) is a useful process for the management of diverse people. Processes that assert national identity on their behalf submerge other identities, such as race, gender, class. These can be conveniently marginalised if those groups 'choose' (1990s buzz word!) not to shelter under the national identity umbrella. The denial of those identities is well-rehearsed in that tired statement, 'But we are all New Zealanders!' This oppressive sentence either naïvely overlooks, or deliberately refuses to acknowledge, diversity and difference for any groups not fitting that version of identity being presented as 'national'.

Paternalistic authority is exercised in all spheres of society, even over such apparently personal matters as values, myths, ideals and morality. This form of social cohesiveness is reinforced constantly; for instance in television news programmes, where an attitude towards any news personality or event is always made clear.

If this is all a con-job, why are we so easily conned? Simply because most of us don't wander about each day counting the national identity claims expressed on our behalf. Besides, they are not always easy to count. This is a *Drowning by Numbers* game — it's hard to spot them all.

Change

Ideas about who we are alter with the fluctuations of time: with changes in national and international events and relations, and in political ideology. We can readily observe these changes over generations. Older people who were part of the War generation, then experienced the Depression, developed attitudes and values that formed their notion of New Zealand, a notion that today's younger generation could hardly be expected to identify with.

When my daughter was living in the south of France her elderly grandmother kept sending her postcards of Hamilton, where she (the grandmother) lived.

'I like to do my bit for New Zealand, and especially for Hamilton,' she explained. 'You must always put your own country first.'

The naughty grand-daughter wrote on a postcard of Paris, 'Thank you for the cards of Hamilton, Grandma. It looks so glamorous. I can't wait for the next one.'

'You see!' said the grandmother happily. 'I knew she'd love to see pictures of Hamilton!'

Meanwhile my daughter, in her carefree twenties and enjoying living in France, hoped she could extend her visa, wished she had an EEC passport, and expressed her observations of northern hemisphere differences with some wonder. On a moonlit walk with her boyfriend, she did not recognise the stars, always of interest since camping holidays as a child. 'I don't know the names of their stars,' she wrote. 'There is no Southern Cross here!'

Her own country was far away, and, for the moment anyway, far less *fun*.

'But Grandma, New Zealand is a bit boring,' she said on a birthday phone call.

'Well, yes,' said the also well-travelled grandmother. 'But you must be loyal. I hope you are telling everyone nice things about New Zealand. And don't forget to tell them all about Hamilton, will you!'

Official and popular ideas about the nation are continually created and recreated. For instance, in World Wars I and II it was in the 'national interest' to foster patriotism (national pride) in one's country. With this attitude, New Zealand troops could risk their lives for their country, and families could bear loss as duty, heroism and patriotism. These assumed values were questioned during the Vietnam War by a generation watching war played out on television in their sitting rooms, who were suspicious of the political authority (American) that allowed such a war to happen; and who had learned to query anything that impinged on the rights of the individual.

1980s, 1990s
The 1980s and 1990s have seen new messages about identity; messages opposite in meaning to those attached to our national identity up to the mid 1980s. The care promised by the welfare state, 'from the cradle to grave', is over. This belief survived historical political responses to Depressions, wars and changing governments. But social solutions are no longer seen as important as economic ones for the overall well-being of society.

The old approaches to social need were established as part of our national psyche: they spoke of collective responsibility, paid for by taxes, that would take care of all New Zealanders. New Zealanders were protected from 'economic reality' by the welfare and education systems. These approaches fed the egalitarian myth; a myth which had the ability to blind us to actual inequalities, institutionalised and based on race and gender.

By the mid 1980s political and economic forces were mounting an assault on almost every aspect of our society. State Owned Enterprises were being sold, and health, education and welfare systems redesigned. A wave of ideological change displaced government responsibility for social objectives in a restructured, re-rationalised economy. Changes in policy direction that were taking place involved a systematic and fundamental alteration of the basic ideology on which New Zealand society had operated for so long. New Right policies, strongly driven by the Business Round Table and government economic advisers, have led to a complete restructuring of society. 'User pays' (or goes without!) and the corporatisation of state-owned monopolies — these were alien concepts in New Zealand. Low-income groups are increasingly excluded from many aspects of New Zealand social life. Where will it all end?

The effect of all this on national identity has been profound. The population has moved from a certainty about our identity as a welfare state with an egalitarian ethos of collective responsibility, to a new and insecure situation couched in new language: 'level playing field' (battlefield?), 'window of opportunity', and so on. Inevitably, there has been growing uncertainty about destiny and identity.

In this new version of New Zealand the rhetoric of politicians and business interests tries to persuade us to a new collective sense of ourselves, and to control of representations of identity via the media. Now, beyond what we ever experienced before, we are bombarded with messages that restate who we are; that try to make cosy and intimate a jolly, cheerful vernacular culture (for instance, the endless schmaltzy and patronising references to us as 'kiwis' on television news programmes). National identity formulation is once again seen as another tool in the arsenal the state uses to perform its role, fostering a system that advantages some groups over others.

The egalitarian myth was able to persist for a long time because class differences were less rigid here than in England. There were enough props in place to keep a rough equilibrium in place, and so to feed that myth. It has now been shoved aside, and new myths are being built by those who have the most to gain from the new edifice; it is essentially being built by them, for them and in their interests. This is how national identity formulation comes about. Those quite happy with the way things are evolving are those with the most to gain.

The collective imagination

From our school history classes we know about Wakefield's interest in transporting to New Zealand the English home county social structure, a project he formulated while in Newgate Prison. Wakefield knew the power of the imagination, and that there was the potential to help it along a bit: 'most people can be induced to exercise their reason only by some enticement addressed to their imagination,' he suggested.[6] He began his own programme of image-making.

His vision matched a nineteenth-century nostalgia for a way of life already under threat by the industrialisation of England. Nostalgia was one of the underlying premises for the proposed construction of the new colony. This was simultaneously a forward-looking and pro-active decision for immigrants to better themselves, while drawing their vision of the colony from idealised versions of the past. Emigrating to New Zealand could be seen as an act of considered and hopeful nostalgia.

Settlers in the early days of colonisation wrote of hardships and unpredictable circumstances they had overcome as newcomers, from a position in which they were now members of the new society. They had evolved from 'new arrivals' to those who 'belonged' to the new colony. Sinclair writes that the term 'New Zealand native' referred to New Zealand-born Pakeha, as well as Maori, from as early as 1886, when the majority of Pakeha living in New Zealand were born here.[7] As they developed land, settled into occupations, and raised families, their commitment to this country was established. Their own sense of belonging here to New Zealand was reiterated as they observed the next waves of newcomers.

When New Zealand historians[8] track nationalism back to late last century, they show that the 'success' of the colony through its early productivity affirmed its distinction as 'the best place in the world'. Those enjoying this success transmitted this pride on to the next generation; and so it continued, as a central motif in the Pakeha belief system. My generation of post-war baby-boomers, brought up in a period of peace and economic optimism, were told over and again how lucky we were to be born here and not anywhere else. Our parents and teachers went along with the myths they had inherited, and passed them on to us. We knew that other countries had a few good things too: America had drive-in movies, Australia had koala bears, and England had interesting old castles and Mars Bars. But we had the 'great way of life', and I understood that we were internationally very, very famous for this.

From these messages and stories we forged our identity values. In terms of performance on the world capitalist stage, we knew we had nothing to live down and plenty to live up to. If we followed the same ethic of 'hard work', the next generation would maintain New Zealand's success as both a nation with a healthy export industry, and as a 'great place to bring up children'.

For while it may be almost impossible to sum up what constitutes Pakeha culture, or articulate the essence of this, for Pakeha themselves there is obviously strong awareness of their own cultural distinctiveness. This anthropological-sociological notion is stated in such phrases as 'people like us', 'real New Zealanders' or 'kiwis'.

In New Zealand the juxtaposition of Pakeha against Maori, or against Australians, or against Asian or other immigrant groups, is a way of affirming boundaries and differences.

The sense of belonging is constantly evoked by various means: the use of language (English, and distinctive colloquialisms); the shared knowledge of history or ecology; solidarity in secular interests such as sport; and joking.

'What is the only thing wrong with Australia?'
'It's above water!'
'What's the difference between Australia and yoghurt?'
'Yoghurt has a live culture.'

It does not seem to matter that these jokes are reversible. A standard joke in Australia is:

'What do you think of New Zealand?'
'I never do.'

And we once had a Prime Minister called Rob Muldoon who suggested that the exodus of New Zealanders to Australia was not a bad thing. He kindly pointed out that it 'raises the IQs of both countries'.

The jokes are another example of ways of showing that we know who 'belongs' here. People's attachment to a country, and articulation of that commitment, reinforces mythologies of place. The constant process of self-validation works to protect national, and therefore personal, identity.

New Zealanders want to see themselves as 'different' (from anyone else); and they readily identify themselves as 'belonging' here (because they belong nowhere else). Many national values appear to rest on a nostalgic concept of the 'great way of life' here (in selective memory, at no determinate time). Cradle-to-grave welfare provision, suburbs of state houses and farm subsidies are remembered as symbols of those times. 'User pays' had not been invented. 'They' had not changed the superannuation scheme. Small companies had not been assimilated into larger ones; milk was four pence a pint; rural districts included a named local dairy factory to process dairy products; there were post offices seemingly everywhere; and there was always somewhere to park the car. Events changed all of this; and the remembered past was enhanced.

Memory, like identity, is not fixed, but yet another subjective construction of reality. It is often drawn from as a source of consolation and pleasure. Mythologies of how wonderful this country was (in selective memory) create an idealised vision of New Zealand.

And now . . . ?

This book has offered a discussion of some of the ways we tell ourselves, every day, who we are. In this analysis, 'New Zealand' starts to look like a brand name, as familiar as Watties or L and P.

While the examples I have given draw from the past for their content, they are all recycled constantly in the present. These myths have their basis in the nineteenth century; it seems we have hardly evolved from colonial values. The constant reworking of the same ideas about who we are gives these outdated representations no chance to fade away. Sure, they get a bit of spit and polish: slick new television ads through the use of computer graphics give the fine art of fakery a digital authority. But the content is consistent: a romanticised past that never was, and a mythical present that avoids dealing with issues that are too hard.

Given the tired look of so much national imagery, are there new ways in which we could re-imagine our collective identities?

As we near the year 2000, is there any chance of a place for new images that show hybridity rather than Pakeha purity? Or are we stuck with this predictable and oppressive consensuality, which insists on a single set of images, a single national character, and a single version of history?

How many perfect photographs of Mitre Peak do we need? Will we continue to trot out the resilient landscape, the macho bloke, the nostalgic fantasies, as representations? With increased attention to tourism, are we in fact likely to see more, rather than less, of this stuff? Is the national imagination unable to come up with anything else?

The idea of nation supposedly engenders a sense of community across a large number of people. But the representations and symbols of national identity counter this sense of 'one big happy family' by omitting so many sectors.

Who really honestly believes this imagery is accurate? As larger numbers of New Zealanders grow increasingly disillusioned with their society, the myths become transparent. There must be potential for more progressive and inclusive representations.

I grew up understanding that other countries were wildly admiring, but also a bit envious, of us, because we had all the best things. We didn't have kangaroos, or a great desert, or the Eiffel Tower; we were convinced that what we had here was better than these. This fantasy New Zealand now has far more sophisticated modes of transmission and a glossy new look; but the content is long overdue for revision.

Endnotes

CHAPTER 1
Where am I? Invention and myth-making

1. Graham, Jeanine, 1981, 'Settler Society', in W. Oliver and B. Williams (eds), *The Oxford History of New Zealand*. Wellington, Oxford University Press, p 115.
2. Discussed by Miles Fairburn in chapter one of *The Ideal Society and Its Enemies* (1989, Auckland, Auckland University Press).
3. Ibid, p 33.
4. For instance, by M. Fairburn (op cit); Jock Phillips, 1987, *A Man's Country?*, Auckland, Penguin; and Keith Sinclair, 1986, *A Destiny Apart*, Wellington, Allen & Unwin/Port Nicholson.
5. So *those* must have been 'the good old days'! A recent (1995) World Bank measure ranks New Zealand twenty-ninth (equal with Ireland) for national standard of living.
6. Hirschberg, Matthew, 'Land, Lifestyle and the New Zealand National Self-Image', paper presented at Western Social Sciences Association Conference in New Mexico, April 1995.
7. Wolfe, Richard, 'Zealandia — Mother of the Nation?', *New Zealand Geographic*, 23, July–September, 1994.
8. Anderson, Benedict, 1983, *Imagined Communities: Reflections on the Origins and Spread of Nationalism*, London, Verso.
9. Ibid.
10. Hirschberg, M., op cit.
11. Thank you to my students in the Stage III sociology paper 82.304 in 1995, who wrote a far wider range of comments than can be included here.
12. Despite this, New Zealanders turn out in larger numbers to vote in national elections than do Americans.
13. Bedggood, David, 1980, *Rich and Poor in New Zealand: A Critique of Class, Politics and Ideology*, Wellington, Allen & Unwin.
14. Considine, Bob, 1989, 'Inequality and the Egalitarian Myth', in David Novitz and Bill Willmot (eds), *Culture and Identity in New Zealand*, Wellington, GP Books.
15. Chairman of the Auckland Chamber of Commerce, quoted in the *New Zealand Herald*, 22 May 1995.
16. *New Zealand Herald*, 22 May 1995.
17. Bell, Avril, 'The Construction of National Identity in the Television Advertising of the New Zealand 1990 Commission', paper presented at the National Media Conference, Melbourne, 22–25 September 1990.
18. Mitchell, Austin, 1972, *The Half-Gallon, Quarter-Acre, Pavlova Paradise*, Christchurch, Whitcombe and Tombs.
19. Fairburn, M., op cit, p 23.
20. Friedman, Jonathon, 1990, 'Being in the World: Globalisation and Localisation', in Mike Featherstone (ed), *Global Culture: Nationalism, Globalisation and Modernity*, London, Sage.
21. Robertson, Roland, 1990, 'Mapping the Global Condition: Globalisation as the Central Concept', ibid.
22. Crump, Barry, 1960, *A Good Keen Man*, Wellington, A.H. and A.W. Reed.
23. Graham, Susan, 1962, *This Land I Love*, Wellington, A.H. and A.W. Reed, p 11.
24. Mitchell, A., op cit.
25. McLauchlan, Gordon, 1976, *The Passionless People*, Auckland, Cassell.
26. Mitchell, A., op cit, p 9.
27. McLauchlan, G., op cit, p 1.
28. 'Pakeha', in Michael King (ed), 1991, *Pakeha: The Quest for Identity*, Auckland, Penguin. Michael King

describes this term as 'one that simply denotes — as its origin intended it to — people and influences from Europe' (p 8). His authors in this collection of articles used the term 'in preference to European to distinguish between those things that are currently European, and those that originate in Europe, but have undergone change as a result of the juxtaposition of history, geography and culture in New Zealand. In other words, they see "Pakeha" as an indigenous expression to describe New Zealand people and things that are not Maori.'

29. Awatere, Donna, 1984, *Maori Sovereignty*, Auckland, Broadsheet.
30. King, Michael, 1988, *Being Pakeha*, Auckland, Hodder and Stoughton.
31. Phillips, J., op cit.
32. Orange, Claudia, 1987, *The Treaty of Waitangi*, Wellington, Allen & Unwin/Port Nicholson with Historical Publications Branch, Department of Internal Affairs.
33. Yensen, Helen, Kevin Hague and Tim McCreanor (eds), 1989, *Honouring the Treaty*, Auckland, Penguin.
34. Spoonley, Paul, 1995, 'Constructing Ourselves: The Post-colonial Politics of Pakeha', in Margaret Wilson and Anna Yeatman (eds), *Justice and Identity: Antipodean Practices*, Wellington, Bridget Williams.
35. King, Michael (ed), 1991, op cit.

CHAPTER 2
Clean, green and beautiful — the nature myth

1. Game, Ann, 1991, *Undoing the Social: Towards a Deconstructive Sociology*, Milton Keynes, Open University Press, p 169.
2. Pound, Francis, 1983, *Frames on the Land*, Auckland, Collins, p 19.
3. Ibid, p 20.
4. Eisen, Jonathan and Katherine Joyce Smith, 1991, *Strangers in Paradise*, Auckland, Vintage, p 45.
5. Ibid.
6. Main, William and John B. Turner, 1993, *New Zealand Photography from the 1840s to the Present*, Auckland, Photoforum, p 24.
7. Mitchell, W. J. T., 1994, *Landscape and Power*, Chicago, University of Chicago Press, p 15.
8. Hirschberg, Matthew, 'Land, Lifestyle and the New Zealand National Self-Image', paper presented at Western Social Sciences Association Conference in New Mexico, April 1995, p 9.
9. Fairburn, Miles, 1989, *The Ideal Society and Its Enemies*, Auckland, Auckland University Press, p 29.
10. Sinclair, Keith, 1986, *A Destiny Apart*, Wellington, Allen & Unwin/Port Nicholson, p 6.
11. Phillips, Jock, 1987, *A Man's Country?*, Auckland, Penguin.
12. Wolfe, Richard, 1991, *Kiwi — More Than A Bird*. Auckland, Random Century, p 18.
13. Hirschberg, M., op cit, pp 14–15.
14. Ibid, p 7.
15. *North and South* magazine has been running the series 'My Home Town' as a popular monthly feature since April 1986.
16. Park, Geoff, 1987, 'Understanding and Conserving the Natural Landscape', in Jock Phillips (ed), *Te Whenua Te Iwi*, Wellington, Allen & Unwin/Port Nicholson with the Stout Research Centre, p 97.
17. MacCannell, Dean, 1992, *Empty Meeting Grounds: The Tourist Papers*, London, Routledge, p 11.
18. Wilson, Alexander, 1992, *The Culture of Nature: North American Landscape from Disney to the Exon Valde*. Cambridge, Blackwell.
19. Quoted by a local newspaper reporter in the *West Coast Times*, 12 November 1992.
20. MacCannell, D., op cit, p 306.
21. Ryel, R. and T. Grasse, 1991, 'Marketing for Eco-Tourism: Attracting the Elusive Eco-Tourist', in *Nature Tourism*, California, Island Press, p 164
22. MacCannell, D., op cit, p 115.
23. Barthes, Roland, 1973, *Mythologies*, London, Verso, p 143.
24. Szabo, Michael, 1993, 'New Zealand's Poisoned Paradise', New Scientist, July.

CHAPTER 3
'My grandmother had one of those!' At the museum

1. Blatti, J. (ed) 1989, *Past Meets Present: Essays About Historic Interpretation and Public Awareness*, Washington D.C., Smithsonian Institute Press, p 61.
2. Game, Ann, 1991, *Undoing the Social: Towards a Deconstructive Sociology*, Milton Keynes, Open University Press, p 165.
3. Barthes, Roland, 1973, *Mythologies*, London, Verso, p 143.
4. Phillips, Jock, 1987, *A Man's Country?*, Auckland, Penguin.
5. Ibid.
6. Sinclair, Keith, 1986, *A Destiny Apart*, Wellington, Allen & Unwin/Port Nicholson.
7. Game, A., op cit, p 164.
8. Higham, George, 1990, *Early Manukau: Secrets of Yesterday*, Papakura, self-published.
9. Chapman, Sam, 1973, *Sam Chapman's Coromandel in the Golden Days*, Coromandel, self-published.
10. Moore, Lucy B., 1989, *Waves of Change in South Warkworth*, Warkworth, Warkworth and District Museum.
11. Wade, Jean, 1979, *Song of Two Waters: An Early History of Waiatarua*, Waiatarua, self-published.
12. Phillips, J, op cit, p ix.
13. Cohen, Anthony P., 1985, *The Symbolic Construction of Community*, London, Tavistock, p 99.
14. Robertson, Roland, 1990, 'After Nostalgia? Wilful Nostalgia and the Phases of Globalisation', in Bryan S. Turner (ed), *Theories of Modernity and Post-modernity*, London, Sage, p 50.
15. MacCannell, Dean, 1992, *Empty Meeting Grounds: The Tourist Papers*, London, Routledge, pp 82–84.
16. Ryan, Mary, 1989, 'The American Parade: Representations of the Nineteenth Century Social Order', in Lynn Hunt (ed), *The New Cultural History: Essays*, Berkeley, University of California Press, p 132.
17. Noted in full by Keith W. Thomson in *Art Galleries and Museums in New Zealand*, Auckland, Reed, 1982: 'a museum is a non-profit-making, permanent institution, in the services of society and its development, and open to the public, which acquires, conserves, researches, communicates and exhibits for purposes of study, education and enjoyment material evidence of man and his environment'.
18. Hobsbawn, Eric and Terence Ranger, 1983, *The Invention of Tradition*, Cambridge, Cambridge University Press.
19. Blatti, J., op cit, p 5.
20. Lowenthal, David, 1985, *The Past is a Foreign Country*, Cambridge, Cambridge University Press.

CHAPTER 4
One million dollars worth of hokey-pokey ice-cream Expo 88

1. Craik, Jennifer, 1992, 'Expo 88: Fashions of Sight and Politics of Site', in Tony Bennett et al (eds), *Celebrating the Nation*, Sydney, Allen & Unwin, p 143.
2. Bower, Hilary (ed), 1990, *The Pavilion of New Zealand*, Auckland, Dow.
3. Ibid.
4. MacCannell, Dean, 1992, *Empty Meeting Grounds: The Tourist Papers*, London, Routledge.
5. Bennett, Tony, 1992, 'The Shaping of Things to Come', in Tony Bennett et al (eds), *Celebrating the Nation*, Sydney, Allen & Unwin, pp 123–141.
6. Eco, Umberto, c. 1986, *Travels in Hyper-reality* (translated by William Weaver), San Diego, Harcourt Brace Jovanavich, p 296.
7. *National Business Review*, 4 October 1991.
8. *Export News*, 23 May 1991, p 12.
9. Greenhalgh, Paul, 1988, *Ephemeral Vistas*, Manchester, Manchester University Press, p 1.
10. Spoonley, Paul, 1995, 'Constructing Ourselves: The Post-Colonial Politics of Pakeha', in Margaret Wilson and

Anna Yeatman (eds), *Justice and Identity: Antipodean Practices*, Wellington, Bridget Williams.
11. Bower, H., op cit, p 4.
12. Craik, J., op cit, p 142.
13. Fry, Tony and Anne-Marie Willis, 1988, 'Expo '88: Backwoods into the Future', Cultural Studies, 2 (1), January, cited by Tony Bennett, op cit, p 132.
14. Boissevain, Jeremy (ed), 1992, *Revitalising European Rituals*, London, Routledge.

CHAPTER 5
Have you seen the giant roadside shearer at Te Kuiti?

1. Bell, Claudia and John Lyall, 1995, *Putting Our Town on the Map*, Auckland, Harper Collins.
2. Maclean, Chris and Jock Phillips, 1990, *The Sorrow and the Pride: New Zealand War Memorials*, Wellington, GP Books, p 10.
3. Ibid.
4. *New Zealand Herald*, 24 October 1995.
5. This phenomenon in towns across Europe is discussed by Francisco Cruces and Angel de Rada in 'Public Celebrations in a Spanish Valley', in Jeremy Boissevain (ed), 1992, *Revitalising European Rituals*, London, Routledge.
6. *New Zealand Events Update* is the official monthly newsletter for the New Zealand events industry.
7. 'Shears Sign Flirts with Folly — Locals', *New Zealand Herald*, 12 September 1995, sec 1, p 14. Another Masterton critic dismissed the proposed sign as 'blatantly phallic' with 'strong overtones of virility worship' ('Golden Shears Sign Gets Nod', *Evening Post*, 13 September 1995).
8. Glendinning, Danna, 1978, *Why Did They Leave Eketahuna?* A report on a study of outward migration conducted by the Wairarapa Education and Rural Services Committee, Masterton, Wairarapa EARS Committee.

CHAPTER 6
All we need to know, because TV tells us so

1. Butterworth, Ruth, 1989, 'The Media', in D. Novitz and B. Willmot (eds), *Culture and Identity*, Wellington, GP Books, p 152.
2. Ibid, p 157.
3. This is discussed in detail by Geoff Lealand in *A Foreign Egg in Our Nest? American Popular Culture in New Zealand*, Wellington, Victoria University Press, 1990.
4. Anderson, Benedict, 1983, *Imagined Communities: Reflections on the Origins and Spread of Nationalism*, London, Verso, pp 40–46.
5. Walker, Ranginui, 1989, 'Maori Identity', in D. Novitz and B. Willmot (eds), op cit, p 43.
6. Butterworth, R., op cit, p 156.
7. Murdoch, Graham, Keynote address at the Broadcasting Conference, University of Auckland, Auckland, 7–10 June 1994.
8. White, Richard, 1992, *Inventing Australia*, Sydney, Allen and Unwin, pp vii–viii.
9. NZ On Air. *Iriirangi te Motu* (statement of intent 1995/96).
10. Fiske, John, 1987, *Television Culture*, London, Methuen, p 281.
11. Atkinson, Joe, 1994, 'The State, the Media and Thin Democracy', in Andrew Sharp (ed), *Leap Into the Dark*, Auckland, Auckland University Press.
12. Atkinson, Joe, 1994, 'Structures of Television News', in Phillipa Bollard (ed), for the New Zealand Broadcasting Standards Authority, *Power and Responsibility: Broadcasters Striking a Balance*, Wellington, New Zealand Broadcasting Standards Authority.
13. Abel, Sue, 1992, 'Television News and Monoculturalism: A Case Study of Waitangi Day 1990', unpublished MA thesis, University of Auckland, p 28.
14. Dahlgren, Peter and Colin Sparks, 1991, *Journalism and Popular Culture*, London, Sage.
15. Butterworth, R., op cit, pp 143–146.
16. Fougere, Geoff, 1989, in D. Novitz and B. Willmot (eds), op cit, p 113.

17. Phillips, Jock, 1987, *A Man's Country?*, Auckland, Penguin.
18. *New Zealand Herald*, 10 March 1995.
19. *New Zealand Herald*, 11 March 1995.
20. Roger, Warwick, 'Vulgar and Proud of It', Metro, April 1995, p 97.
21. Perry, Nick, 1994, *Dominion of Signs*, Auckland University Press, p 19.
22. See Butterworth p. 60
23. Pickering, Michael, 1990, 'Mass Communications and the Quest for Cultural Identity', *Sites*, 21, Spring, pp 44–63.

CHAPTER 7
Nostalgia and kiwiana

1. Bell, Claudia, 1993, 'Rural Way of Life in New Zealand: Myths to Live By', unpublished PhD thesis, University of Auckland.
2. Baudrilliard, Jean, 1990, *Cool Memories* (translated by Chris Turner), London, Verso, p 199.
3. Dann, Christine and Tony Wyber, 1990, *Cottage Gardening in New Zealand*, Wellington, Allen & Unwin/Port Nicholson.
4. Davis, Fred, 1979, *Yearning for Yesterday: A Sociology of Nostalgia*, London, The Free Press, p 116.
5. I have discussed this process in more detail in 'Brushing Up the Past: Commodifying Local Histories', *Sites*, 30, 1994, pp 131–152.
6. Stratford in Ontario, Canada, (population 27,000) also celebrates its association with Stratford-upon-Avon, and established a Stratford Shakespearean Festival in 1953. Previously called Little Thames, around 1840 the town was renamed after Stratford-upon-Avon. The name has been the sole impetus for this festival.
7. I would like it to be generally known that I did not have a research grant to make these grocery purchases.
8. MacCannell, Dean, 1992, *Empty Meeting Grounds: The Tourist Papers*, London, Routledge.
9. Williams, Raymond, 1973, *The Country and the City*, London, Pallidan, p 123.
10. Lowenthal, David, 1985, *The Past is a Foreign Country*, Cambridge, Cambridge University Press, p 4.
11. Wolfe, Richard and Stephen Barnett, 1989, *New Zealand! New Zealand! In Praise of Kiwiana!* Auckland, Hodder and Stoughton.
12. Clark, Nigel, 'On the Intractable Object of the Museum: From the Hetero-tropic to the Hyper-*Museul*', paper presented at the Post-colonial Formations Conference, Griffith University, Brisbane, 7–10 July 1993.
13. Baudrilliard, J., op cit.
14. Robertson, Roland, 1990, 'After Nostalgia? Wilful Nostalgia and the Phases of Globalisation', in Bryan S. Turner (ed), *Theories of Modernity and Post-modernity*, London; Sage.

CHAPTER 8
But we are all New Zealanders!

1. The rugby fans were photographed by Graeme Brown of the *Standard* on 27 May 1995. Brown insists that, contrary to rumours about beer-swilling students, when he visited, these lads were drinking only tea, coffee and juice.
2. Mulgan, Richard, 1994, *Politics in New Zealand*, Auckland University Press.
3. *New Zealand Listener*/Heylen monitor, New Zealand Listener, 15–21 October 1994.
4. O'Neill, Terry, 1995, *The New Zealand State and National Identity Formation*, unpublished MA thesis, University of Auckland.
5. Turner, Graeme, 1994, *Making it National – Nationalism and Australian Popular Culture*, Sydney, Allen & Unwin, p 5.
6. Harrop, Angus John, 1928, *The Amazing Career of Edward Gibbon Wakefield*, London, Allen & Unwin.
7. Sinclair, Keith, 1986, *A Destiny Apart*, Wellington, Allen & Unwin/Port Nicholson.
8. For instance, M. Fairburn, 1989, *The Ideal Society and Its Enemies*, Auckland, Auckland University Press; Jock Phillips, 1987, *A Man's Country?*, Auckland, Penguin; and Keith Sinclair, 1986, *A Destiny Apart*, Wellington, Allen & Unwin/Port Nicholson.

Bibliography

Abel, Sue, 1992, 'Television News and Monoculturalism: A Case Study of Waitangi Day 1990', unpublished MA thesis, University of Auckland.

Anderson, Benedict, 1983, *Imagined Communities: Reflections on the Origins and Spread of Nationalism*, London, Verso.

Atkinson, Joe, 1994, 'Structures of Television News', in Phillipa Bollard (ed), for the New Zealand Broadcasting Standards Authority, *Power and Responsibility: Broadcasters Striking a Balance*, Wellington, New Zealand Broadcasting Standards Authority.

Atkinson, Joe, 1994, 'The State, the Media and Thin Democracy', in Andrew Sharp (ed), *Leap Into the Dark*, Auckland, Auckland University Press.

Awatere, Donna, 1984, *Maori Sovereignty*, Auckland, Broadsheet.

Barthes, Roland, 1973, *Mythologies*, London, Verso.

Baudrilliard, Jean, 1990, *Cool Memories* (translated by Chris Turner), London, Verso.

Bedggood, David, 1980, *Rich and Poor in New Zealand: A Critique of Class, Politics and Ideology*, Wellington, Allen & Unwin.

Bell, Avril, 'The Construction of National Identity in the Television Advertising of the New Zealand 1990 Commission', paper presented at the National Media Conference, Melbourne, 22–25 September 1990.

Bell, Claudia, 'Brushing Up the Past: Commodifying Local Histories', *Sites*, 30, 1994, pp 131–152.

Bell, Claudia, 1993, 'Rural Way of Life in New Zealand: Myths to Live By', unpublished PhD thesis, University of Auckland.

Bell, Claudia and John Lyall, 1995, *Putting Our Town on the Map*, Auckland, Harper Collins.

Bennett, Tony, 1992, 'The Shaping of Things to Come', in Tony Bennett et al (eds), *Celebrating the Nation*, Sydney, Allen & Unwin.

Blatti, J. (ed), 1989, *Past Meets Present: Essays About Historic Interpretation and Public Awareness*, Washington D.C., Smithsonian Institute Press.

Boissevain, Jeremy (ed), 1992, *Revitalising European Rituals*, London, Routledge.

Bower, Hilary (ed), 1990, *The Pavilion of New Zealand*, Auckland, Dow.
Butterworth, Ruth, 1989, 'The Media', in David Novitz and Bill Willmot (eds), *Culture and Identity in New Zealand*, Wellington, GP Books.
Chapman, Sam, 1973, *Sam Chapman's Coromandel in the Golden Days*, Coromandel, self-published.
Clark, Nigel, 'On the Intractable Object of the Museum: From the Heterotropic to the Hyper-*Museul*', paper presented at the Postcolonial Formations Conference, Griffith University, Brisbane, 7–10 July 1993.
Cohen, Anthony P., 1985, *The Symbolic Construction of Community*, London, Tavistock.
Considine, Bob, 1989, 'Inequality and the Egalitarian Myth', in David Novitz and Bill Willmot (eds), *Culture and Identity in New Zealand*, Wellington, GP Books.
Craik, Jennifer, 1992, 'Expo 88: Fashions of Sight and Politics of Site', in Tony Bennett et al (eds), *Celebrating the Nation*, Sydney, Allen & Unwin.
Cruces, Francisco and Angel de Rada in 'Public Celebrations in a Spanish Valley', in Jeremy Boissevain (ed), 1992, *Revitalising European Rituals*, London, Routledge.
Crump, Barry, 1960, *A Good Keen Man*, Wellington, A.H. and A.W. Reed.
Dahlgren, Peter and Colin Sparks, 1991, *Journalism and Popular Culture*, London, Sage.
Dann, Christine and Tony Wyber, 1990, *Cottage Gardening in New Zealand*, Wellington, Allen & Unwin/Port Nicholson.
Davis, Fred, 1979, *Yearning for Yesterday: A Sociology of Nostalgia*, London, The Free Press.
Eco, Umberto, c. 1986, *Travels in Hyper-reality* (translated by William Weaver), San Diego, Harcourt Brace Jovanavich.
Eisen, Jonathan and Katherine Joyce Smith, 1991, *Strangers in Paradise*, Auckland, Vintage.
Fairburn, Miles, 1989, *The Ideal Society and Its Enemies*, Auckland, Auckland University Press.
Fiske, John, 1987, *Television Culture*, London, Methuen.
Fougere, Geoff, 1989, in D. Novitz and B. Willmot (eds), *Culture and Identity*, Wellington, GP Books.
Friedman, Jonathon, 1990, 'Being in the World: Globalisation and Localisation', in Mike Featherstone (ed), *Global Culture: Nationalism, Globalisation and Modernity*, London, Sage.
Game, Ann, 1991, *Undoing the Social: Towards a Deconstructive Sociology*, Milton Keynes, Open University Press.

Glendinning, Danna, 1978, *Why Did They Leave Eketahuna?* A report on a study of outward migration conducted by the Wairarapa Education and Rural Services Committee, Masterton, Wairarapa EARS Committee.

Graham, Jeanine, 1981, 'Settler Society', in W. Oliver and B. Williams (eds), *The Oxford History of New Zealand*, Wellington, Oxford University Press.

Graham, Susan, 1962, *This Land I Love*, Wellington, A.H. and A.W. Reed.

Greenhalgh, Paul, 1988, *Ephemeral Vistas*, Manchester, Manchester University Press.

Harrop, Angus John, 1928, *The Amazing Career of Edward Gibbon Wakefield*, London, Allen & Unwin.

Higham, George, 1990, *Early Manukau: Secrets of Yesterday*, Papakura, self-published.

Hirschberg, Matthew, 'Land, Lifestyle and the New Zealand National Self-Image', paper presented at Western Social Sciences Association Conference in New Mexico, April 1995.

Hobsbawn, Eric and Terence Ranger, 1983, *The Invention of Tradition*, Cambridge, Cambridge University Press.

King, Michael, 1988, *Being Pakeha*, Auckland, Hodder and Stoughton.

King, Michael, 'Pakeha', in Michael King (ed), 1991, *Pakeha: The Quest for Identity*, Auckland, Penguin.

Lealand, Geoff, 1990, in *A Foreign Egg in Our Nest? American Popular Culture in New Zealand*, Wellington, Victoria University Press.

Lowenthal, David, 1985, *The Past is a Foreign Country*, Cambridge, Cambridge University Press.

MacCannell, Dean, 1992, *Empty Meeting Grounds: The Tourist Papers*, London, Routledge.

McLauchlan, Gordon, 1976, *The Passionless People*, Auckland, Cassell.

Maclean Chris and Jock Phillips, 1990, *The Sorrow and the Pride: New Zealand War Memorials*, Wellington, GP Books.

Main, William and John B. Turner, 1993, *New Zealand Photography from the 1840s to the Present*, Auckland, Photoforum.

Mitchell, Austin, 1972, *The Half-Gallon, Quarter-Acre, Pavlova Paradise*, Christchurch, Whitcombe and Tombs.

Mitchell, W. J. T., 1994, *Landscape and Power*, Chicago, University of Chicago Press.

Moore, Lucy B., 1989, *Waves of Change in South Warkworth*, Warkworth, Warkworth and District Museum.

Mulgan, Richard, 1994, *Politics in New Zealand*, Auckland, Auckland University Press.

Murdoch, Graham, Keynote address at the Broadcasting Conference, University of Auckland, Auckland, 7–10 June 1994.

O'Neill, Terry, 1995, 'The New Zealand State and National Identity Formulation', unpublished MA thesis, University of Auckland.

Orange, Claudia, 1987, *The Treaty of Waitangi*, Wellington, Allen & Unwin/Port Nicholson with Historical Publications Branch, Department of Internal Affairs.

Park, Geoff, 1987, 'Understanding and Conserving the Natural Landscape', in Jock Phillips (ed), *Te Whenua Te Iwi*, Wellington, Allen & Unwin/Port Nicholson with the Stout Research Centre.

Perry, Nick, 1994, *Dominion of Signs*, Auckland, Auckland University Press.

Phillips, Jock, 1987, *A Man's Country?*, Auckland, Penguin.

Pickering, Michael, 1990, 'Mass Communications and the Quest for Cultural Identity', *Sites*, 21, Spring, pp 44–63.

Pound, Francis, 1983, *Frames on the Land*, Auckland, Collins.

Robertson, Roland, 1990, 'After Nostalgia? Wilful Nostalgia and the Phases of Globalisation', in Bryan S. Turner (ed), *Theories of Modernity and Post-modernity*, London, Sage.

Robertson, Roland, 1990, 'Mapping the Global Condition: Globalisation as the Central Concept', in Mike Featherstone (ed), *Global Culture: Nationalism, Globalisation and Modernity*, London, Sage.

Ryan, Mary, 1989, 'The American Parade: Representations of the Nineteenth Century Social Order', in Lynn Hunt (ed), *The New Cultural History: Essays*, Berkeley, University of California Press.

Ryel, R. and T. Grasse, 1991, 'Marketing for Eco-tourism: Attracting the Elusive Eco-Tourist', in *Native Tourism*, California, Island Press.

Sinclair, Keith, 1986, *A Destiny Apart*, Wellington, Allen & Unwin/Port Nicholson.

Spoonley, Paul, 1995, 'Constructing Ourselves: The Post-colonial Politics of Pakeha', in Margaret Wilson and Anna Yeatman (eds), *Justice and Identity: Antipodean Practices*, Wellington, Bridget Williams.

Szabo, Michael, 1993, 'New Zealand's Poisoned Paradise', New Scientist, July.

Thomson, Keith W., 1982, *Art Galleries and Museums in New Zealand*, Auckland, Reed.

Turner, Graeme, 1994, *Making it National — Nationalism and Australian Popular Culture*, Sydney, Allen & Unwin.

Wade, Jean, 1979, *Song of Two Waters: An Early History of Waiatarua*, Waiatarua, self-published.

Walker, Ranginui, 1989, 'Maori Identity', in D. Novitz and B. Willmot

(eds), *Culture and Identity*, Wellington, GP Books.
White, Richard, 1992, *Inventing Australia*, Sydney, Allen and Unwin.
Wilson, Alexander, 1992 , *The Culture of Nature: North American Landscape from Disney to the Exon Valde*. Cambridge, Blackwell.
Williams, Raymond, 1973, *The Country and the City*, London, Pallidan.
Wolfe, Richard, 1991, *Kiwi — More Than A Bird*, Auckland, Random Century.
Wolfe, Richard, 1994, 'Zealandia — Mother of the Nation?', *New Zealand Geographic*, 23, July–September.
Wolfe, Richard and Stephen Barnett, 1989, *New Zealand! New Zealand! In Praise of Kiwiana!* Auckland, Hodder and Stoughton.
Yensen, Helen, Kevin Hague and Tim McCreanor (eds), 1989, *Honouring the Treaty*, Auckland, Penguin.

Index

accent, 22
advertising, 114–15, 126–7, 150–8. *See also* media; television
agriculture, 65, 111, 115–16, 119–20, 122–3
Agricultural Heritage Museum, Hamilton, 55, 65
Air New Zealand *Birds* (TV ad), 155–8
Alexandra Blossom Festival, 119
All Blacks, 89, 131, 183
America's Cup, 13–7, 89, 93, 131, 161
art, 30–1, 110–14
'Asian invasion', 7, 186–7
Auckland Warriors, 89, 159–60
Awatere, Donna, 26

Barthes, Roland, 60
Big Fresh Supermarket, 172–4
Bogor, 163–4
Britain, relationship to, 6–7, 18–19, 21–2
bungy jumping, 43, 45
Burton Brothers, photographers, 31–2
Bushmen's Centre, Pukerau, 44
Buzzy Bee, 179

colonial style (reproduction): furniture, 165–9; gardens, 168–9; shopping centres, 169–72
colonisation and settlers (European), 3–6, 34–6; and pioneer myth, 35–6, 192–3. *See also* museums; nostalgia
commerce, 5, 16, 18, 19–21, 96–7, 107–8, 114–16, 120–4, 147–50; and nature, 40–5, 50–2
Cook, Captain James, 3, 92, 97, 113
Country Calendar, 141, 142
Crump, Barry, 24, 163, 164

Dagg, Fred, 93, 109, 110, 163, 164
Department of Conservation, 51, 52

Eco, Umberto, 96
eco-tourism, 45–6
egalitiarian: e. myth, 12, 23, 146, 192; e. access to nature 29–30, 48
expos, 83–102; and ethnicity, 92–4; and technology, 96, 100

family issues, 25, 58–60

Fairburn, Miles, 4, 35
fern (as symbol), 38
festivals and events, 109, 111, 117–20
flora and fauna, 37–8, 155–6
food, 90, 117–18. *See also* festivals and events
Footrot Flats, 163–4
Fox Glacier, 42

gender issues, 22–3, 59, 76–7, 112, 138–9, 141, 156–7, 159–61

Heartland (TV series), 117, 135, 140–2, 145, 146
heroes, 92–3, 153–4
history, as commodity, 64–6, 71–6, 165–79
Hokitika Wild Foods Festival, 44, 117
Howick Historic Village, 67

icons, 17, 19–20, 49–50, 108–10, 114–17, 124–6, 179–80

Kaikoura whale watching, 41; w. history, 55
Katikati murals, 61, 111–13, 178
King, Michael, 26, 27
kiwi, 17, 28, 37, 156
Kiwi Bacon revolving bird (icon), 125
kiwiana, 114–15, 179–81

language, 22, 130, 141
Lemon and Paeroa, 21, 114–15
literacy, 130
literature, 21–2, 24
local histories, 76–8
local identity, 55–7, 103–28, 131; and commerce, 115–6, 120–4. *See also* television

McLauchlan, Gordon, 24, 25
manhood, 14, 18, 141–2, 159–61, 163–5, 183–4
maps, 3, 110
Maori: relations with Pakeha, 9, 13–14, 26–7, 29–30; as commodity, 62, 65–6, 92, 94–5, 112–13, 114; language, 130; and media, 132, 135, 139; M. Land March (1975), 26. *See also* multi-

culturalism; race relations
Marlborough Food and Wine Festival, 120–1
Masterton, 121
media, 16, 102, 117, 119, 126–7, 128–62
Mitchell, Austin, 19, 24, 25
Mitre Peak, 30, 49, 195
Morrinsville, 111
Motat (Museum of Transport and Technology), 66, 73
Muir and Moodie, photographers, 32
murals, 110–14
museums, 55–82; live m., 66–7, 69; and local identity, 55–6; and Maori, 62, 65–6, 68; and national identity, 80–2
multiculturalism, 7–8, 136, 156–7, 186–9

nation (as theoretical concept), 8, 9, 81, 130
'national good', 20, 89, 184–5
national identit208y, 185–93
national image, 131; as commodity, 102
national pride, 18–19
nature, 11–12, 28–54; as commodity, 40–5, 50–2, 72, 91
New Zealand Centennial (1940), 106
New Zealand on Air, 134–7, 145
nostalgia: commericalisation of, 177–9; and furniture, gardens, 168, 169; and history, 58–60, 68–73, 112–13; and kiwiana, 179–81; and mythology, 79, 80, 181–2; and national identity, 177; and nature, 39–40; and shopping centres, 170; and Utopia, 175; and Wakefield, 192

Orange, Claudia, 26
Otamatea Pioneer Museum, Matakohe, 55–62, 69, 72, 74, 178

paua house, Bluff, 124–5
Paeroa. *See* Lemon and Paeroa
Phillips, Jock, 26, 60
Pokeno, 107–9
pollution, 52–3
print media, 130–1. *See also* media

Queensland, 67

race relations, 94–5, 138, 186–8, 194–5. *See also* Maori; multiculturalism
radio, 130–1
Rangiriri Battlesite Heritage Centre, 65–6
Riverton mural, 113–14
roadside objects, 114–7; and commerce, 116
Ross Historic Village, 60, 62–4, 75

rugby, rugby league, 157–61, 164, 183

self-identity, 10–13, 21, 24, 46–9
Shantytown, 62–4, 66, 69
Shortland Street, 20, 135, 140, 142–6, 165
signs, 107–14. *See also* murals
Sinclair, Keith, 35, 64, 193
Southern Man (Speights), 164–5
Spoonley, Paul, 98
sport, 13–18; 158–62, 183–4; and big business, 16, 160
stereotypes, 121–4, 143, 161–2, 163, 183–4
Stratford, 171–2
sublime landscape, 30–2, 42
Success! (TV programme), 147–50

Taihape, 109–10
Taranaki, 4, 55, 114, 121
Tasman, Abel, 3
Te Kuiti, 103, 114, 115, 116, 125
Te Puke, 116, 119–20
television, 13, 15–17, 128–62; and local stories, 115, 117, 118; and national and local identity, 131–4, 139–40, 140–2, 146; and news, 137–40; and sport, 158–62; and values, 132–3, 138–9, 147–51, 158, 161–2. *See also* advertising; New Zealand on Air; individual programme entries
Tolaga Bay Festival, 117, 118
tourism: and commercial nostalgia, 177–9; and Expo, 83–7; and history, 63–76; and identity, 46–9; and indigenous culture, 94–5; and nature, 40–6, 49–54; and small towns, 123–4; and the sublime, 31–3
Treaty of Waitangi, 9, 29–30, 69. *See also* Maori

United States and national self-image, 11

Waimate, 110
Wakefield, Edward Gibbon, 34, 174, 192
war memorials, 103–7; and civic buildings, 106; and community halls, 105
wars, 18, 103–7, 190–1; First World War, 104–5; New Zealand Wars, 9, 104; Second World War, 104–5
Warriors, 159–60
Watties, 19, 20
Weetbix, 89, 150–4, 185
Whataroa herons, 41
Wolfe, Richard, 37–8

Zealandia 6